adventure into creativity and activism. The two were unafraid to speak out and travel into the revolutionary zones of Cuba and Algiers as well as the unrest in Paris in May 1968. Before the days of functional handheld recording it would be quite an undertaking to seek music outside the academy, into the field, to document a planet rife with change, emotional and political, giving voice and value to the sound-worlds of the disenfranchised. As children they had seen the spectacle of hate. Growing up together their work focused on the dignity of peace and activism - through sounds, expressions, art, breath, friendship, joy and love.

On February 5, 2019 Luc would have been ninety years old. His life, work and spirit remain timeless and extraordinary informing developments in experimental music in the USA at the Columbia-Princeton Electronic Music Center and the San Francisco Tape Music Center, as founded by Pauline Oliveros, and in England with The BBC Radiophonic Workshop, as founded by Daphne Oram and Delia Derbyshire. Much of psychedelic, avant-garde and experimental rock, free improvisation, jazz and contemporary classical music has bestowed continued adulation to Luc Ferrari furthering his inspirations and intrigues into new futures of radical music exploration.

This catalogue raisonné defines, chronologically, the works of Luc Ferrari, as compiled from the archives of both Luc and Brunhild. It presents all known extant work of Luc Ferrari as an artist, author, poet, philosopher, documentarian, filmmaker, and composer — through all his famous cycles, including: *Presque Rien*, *Société*, *Réflexions sur l'écriture*, *Spontané*, *Exploitation des concepts*, *Les Réalisables*, as well as *Visage*, *Tautologos*, and *Conte sentimental*, amongst lesser known scores, *Hörspiel*, theatre works and productions.

This volume also includes interviews with Ferrari through different periods of his life and correspondence which reveal his early aspirations for filmmaking, and later in a manifesto style letter outlining the importance of democracy to sustain culture.

Commentaries and epiphanies about his creations are from the notebooks of Luc examining his own work in both real time and in retrospect, sometimes both, and always with his delightful – and insightful – charm, wit, intellect and indelible *joie de vivre*.

An Artist's Life
By Jim O'Rourke

By chance, when asked to write these words. I was in the middle of re-reading Charles Ives's *Essays Before a Sonata*. It didn't strike me just as coincidental, but fortuitous. Nothing tells you more about an artist's work as when they speak about anything *besides* their own work. It could be food, films, bee-keeping, water fleas, anything *except* the matter at hand. This is where most interviews with the artist often miss the point, by missing the point. These detours tell you more about someone's aesthetic, their values, or their standards as the things that inspire passion in them, inflame their peculiarities, or the things that raise their ire.

For an artist such as Luc Ferrari, their work was at once a playground to indulge in those questions, and a place where the answers that arose—became the next question pursued. When examining individual works in singularity, which is encouraged by the tradition of the "opus," it distracts one from seeing the big picture, an artist's *life* work, which is not just the works themselves, but *everything*—both public and private. It is then we are offered a glimpse into that private life when they speak of anyone, but themselves.

This is one of the most interesting aspects of Ives's *Essays*. Almost 100 years earlier Ives, much like Ferrari, struck a figure, both with his sense of humour and freedom from the gravity of convention, but also in his Catholic tastes for things that would seem extemporaneous to a 'musical' analysis of the works.

This hits close to home, and projects back to the days I was 'officially' studying, composing and crunching numbers in classes on Schenkerian analysis, counterpoint (pick your flavour). We were occasionally allowed to choose the work to analyse, and I took note how many times a professor would ignore a suggestion saying "*That* doesn't really apply to this class," coupled with a slight air of dismissiveness, as if a waft of something unpleasant, or more likely, unsettling, had passed their noses, "It's not really analyzable."

It didn't really bother me, however did awake in me the notion that, possibly, all this toil wasn't *the way* to music. The way was within the shoes we each walked in. This is no incredible insight, but the distinction was being made for us.

Already being enamoured by the work of Luc Ferrari at this time, it occurred to me that I wouldn't have even thought of bringing up works by him, or the work of Pierre Henry, or the many others whom we considered. Of course these were not the kind of works that dealt with pitch relationships or inverse this and retrograde that, but the idea that they didn't, struck a chord in me.

I found it easier to come to terms with the music of Luc Ferrari, and for that matter Ives as well, when I looked at their work in the context of film, and to a certain degree literature. I felt a stronger resonance between the formal concerns of Michael Snow's films and Ferrari's *Presque Rien* than I did with any other piece of music. Re-reading Ferrari's works in this way allowed me to see the distinct quality of his work which filled me with such intense admiration. It helped me climb back out of the hole from which I'd fallen, in search of that "perfect abstraction" of sound—the removal of anything concrete that could possibly emit the sounds in my ears. For many, this pursuit led classmates down different paths, still not twenty years old, and attempting to 'destroy what came before! It was the same story, different characters: 'Serialism destroys the tyranny of Harmony!'

In my own case it was electronic and tape music, which fulfilled my wish to avoid instruments (or, more precisely, instrumentalists) if I could, as well as reach for some sort of misguided 'abstract nirvana' where I sought to hear a sound completely unrelated to anything, even my ear. This is what first attracted me to the writings, what there was of [translated] in English at the time, and of Pierre Schaeffer, and the works that came out of the INA-GRM in France. I loved it, just LOVED it, but there was something about Luc Ferrari's work that kept me straying the path....

What that *it* was was something I didn't really understand until that slow, creeping feeling, finally became clearer during those classes. Of course I had been putting the horse behind the cart. Ferrari treated sounds not as sounds, but as what you could call variously as—carriers, luggage, crates, binoculars, photographs — take your pick. The sound of a car door slamming was not a sound. It was the sound of a car door slamming, and once you accepted this, you had to ask: Whose car? What kind of car? Where is this car? What colour is the car? How old is the car? Is she slamming the car door on someone's hand? (It did sound a little muted...) Why in the world would he think she wouldn't be mad when he said he had to go to Denver for work instead of going on the trip to Aspen they had been planning for a year? She's lucky he didn't break his fingers, because all told, if he had to work, he had to work, and he can't get much done with a broken hand, or even much skiing.

Out of one rabbit hole and into the other. Now everything had an implication, everything had a cause and effect, or the lack of it could turn your head and change where you stood. These sounds had lives of their own and you had to respect them. There was no going back to that magical abstract land for which I had been searching, and despite writing that, I did still search. (You can't fault someone for trying...) Once Luc Ferrari had shown me the way, it became not a tool like the one taught in classes, but an obligation, a standard to maintain, a way of life. And it became clear to me, not by reading his explanations of his music or his theories, but instead seeing his music through the lens of life.

This is the magic door Luc Ferrari has opened for us, maybe in the same way I experienced or in countless other ways. Whether by the strength of his character, or the depth of his art, we are offered different paths to learn about him, and through him—ourselves. And with this book, we all have the chance to open that door.

A Portrait of the Composer as a Young Man —

By Brunhild Ferrari

When I first met Luc he was an underwater hero, he told me that he had just fought a giant octopus. It was at the Aachen carnival, and our mutual friend Gérard Patris had brought him along to meet my father, who was also a composer. My French was poor back then, but conversation flowed — we talked about music, of course, about art, and about all our favourite books. Luc liked Jean Genet, Arthur Rimbaud, *The Songs of Maldoror* by Le Comte de Lautréamont, Alfred Jarry, and Antonin Artaud. At the time he was reading *The Horseman on the Roof* by Jean Giono. An image has stayed with me ever since, something about rice pudding.

Luc talked about the books on his bedside table: he had grown up with François Rabelais, illustrated by Gustave Doré, with *The Illiad*, *The Odyssey* — the protagonist's sensuous adventures fascinated him. There was also Apuleius's *Golden Ass*, which inspired the structure of Luc's radio piece *Jetz* (1981). He owned a 1948 edition of Joyce's *Ulysses* and read it again and again, as his annotated copy of it reveals. He also enjoyed fantasy literature, including H.P. Lovecraft, from whom he borrowed some magic formulae for his composition *Tête et queue du dragon (Head and Tail of the Dragon,* 1959–60*).*

When I arrived in Paris, Rue du Cardinal Lemoine, in the 5th arrondissement, the first book he gave me to read was *Jacques the Fatalist and His Master* by Denis Diderot. I was bowled over by it, but I also remember having to make some of it up as I went along, because my French wasn't quite up to tackling Diderot. Then he took me to his favourite book stalls on the banks of the Seine. That's where he had discovered the works of the Surrealists, which enthralled him, and also where he found so many music scores that are still piled up high in our cupboards — including a piano piece by Béla Bartòk which he played at the Conservatory, causing him to be expelled. That same year, partly under pressure from my family, we decided to get married.

That was in 1959, right in the middle of preparations for the concerts and experimental film projections at the Festival de la Recherche. Luc was in charge of organising the festival, and so that morning, right after our civil ceremony, he left for "La Recherche", and didn't return until evening with Pierre Schaeffer and his whole team.

The more I read through his writings, the more I realise what a complex man he was. Every time I come across his scores, notebooks, compositions or texts, and all the things he expressed through his life, it

Childhood photograph of Luc Ferrari, 1933 courtesy of Brunhild Ferrari

feels as though I am being introduced to him all over again from a new perspective. And there are so many images associated with his words, thoughts and intentions. Whether in film or music, actual or evoked, those images are his language. The images are just like sounds, they are a sort of narration. His music is inhabited by images, it harbours them, or gives them a mission, they can become links or exist alone autonomously. In his musical compositions, images counteract or counterbalance abstraction, and they embody the concept Luc called "anecdotal". He was concerned with images as early as the 1950s, or even earlier. His texts are full of images, they don't need illustrations.

The image, the sound of the image, the words, the noise of the word — they all expressed his emotions through the senses. His pain when faced with a world that can hurt you, but also his joy and his love of life, his despair as well as his humour, all of these emotions at once overlapped and complemented each other. He constantly transgressed the borders and limitations imposed by methods, by categories, or by the schools of thought he never subscribed to, and so he was bound to "move away from all that".

Hence the diversity and range that characterise his work, covering instrumental music, Musique Concrète and electroacoustic music, mixed music, so-called "anecdotal" music, hörspiele — those radiophonic compositions which he helped introduce in France — as well as music theatre; he also wrote and directed shows, he wrote other kinds of texts, text-scores, he did music and theatre improvisations, he created installations and directed films. Luc was active across a wide range of disciplines or rather creative spectrums and he deliberately broke with what is understood as "genre". Even though he sometimes looked towards certain "trends", it was only to turn them on their heads and then discard them almost instantly.

For example, *Presque Rien n°1 (Almost Nothing N°1, 1967–70)* had come to him out of nowhere, one night when he had placed his microphones on the window ledge facing a small fishing harbour. Some would call this Minimalism, but for him, it was more like a sequence shot, just one take, with minimum intervention.

Like a photograph you take without intending to keep it or show it to anyone. It's just a moment of reality. The real was another crucial element that came into play in his work. His approach at the time could be likened to that of the Pop painters or to Hyperrealism. It certainly is totally different from the rigid and prescriptive approach that was then rampant in France and in other European movements. This may explain why the piece had a particular impact in the USA — it was a new concept and freed music from the excessive complexity which had by then become hackneyed.

I will not go into the *Presque Rien* pieces that came later. Nonetheless I will mention those which, while remaining faithful to the principle of minimal intervention, contain a very clear social dimension. Luc observed not only nature but also society, with all its accidents and mishaps, its sadness and joy. Indeed he cared deeply about people's lives and their distress, as is very clear in *Presque Rien ou Le Désir de Vivre (Almost Nothing or The Desire to Live, 1972–73)*: in these two films shot for German television, he introduces the farmers of the Causse Méjean, in the Lozère region, describing their hardship and their struggle for survival; similarly, he shows how the inhabitants of the Larzac Plateau fight against the Army's attempt to occupy their land.

His concern with social issues is particularly visible, and not without humour, in the many *réalisables* ["enactables"] he created between 1964 and 1972. They are all driven by the same question: "Doesn't art, when it remains on a solely aesthetic plane, run the risk of masking reality, sometimes ending up as just a waste of energy?"

In the various performances of *Journal Intime (Private Journal,* 1980–82*)*, Laurence Février, Lisette Malidor and Elise Caron took it in turn to play the part of the composer; when they denounced the cruelty, and yes the stupidity, of the military, of Christian dogmatism, or of any kind of power, and when they claimed the right to have a voice and to be sensuous, Luc was in fact voicing his own opinions. I think it would be puritanical to view this as immodest or inappropriate. For he spoke of what concerns us all: ourselves, other people, the sense of intimacy that inhabits us. So why should he have to conceal his own intimacies?

That theatre piece analyses and charts the composition of *Histoire du plaisir et de la désolation (A History of Pleasure and Desolation,* 1979–82*)*. The themes for his symphony were drawn from the notebooks he was writing over that period. In them, Luc speaks of the pain that never left him, and which was partly due to his hand dystonia, or writer's cramp. This neurological condition had already taken hold by 1965, when he revealed his "great secret" in a letter to Pierre Schaeffer. Writing out instrumental scores was agony for him; that excruciating pain is also perceptible when you look at the outlines or the incredibly precise and meticulous calculation sheets he wrote for the electroacoustic pieces he cheekily liked to call "S & M" (*Sons Mémorisés,* or memorised, i.e. recorded, sounds). This is why my handwriting appears on his scores from the time we moved in together.

That pain is also evoked, in a poetic mode, in the title of his "Realist Fiction", *Musique dans les Spasmes (Stereo Spasms,* 1988). Wherever he could, Luc liked to collect fragments. He often talked to me about Joyce's "epiphanies". We used to "play" the radio, switching it on or off as soon as we'd had a lucky find, be it words or sounds. He was curious, without being indiscreet, and always keen to snatch fragments of life, or words in flight, eager to appropriate them and work them into his compositions. In his writings, his sincerity and earnestness can be disconcerting, particularly when the humour isn't immediately apparent. All of the events, or non events, recounted in the lengthy beginning of *Stereo Spasms*, all the conversations, the encounters with the "music world", I witnessed it all. And he did begin writing that piece in the way he describes: "What shall I do now? I don't feel like doing anything."

Was he lazy, as Stockhausen sometimes chided him? No, Luc was not lazy, but he was available. His ear was always open to others, happy to share his common sense with those who asked. Until one day he left us, an elegant young man of 76. He had said it — he didn't want to become an "old composer".

Brunhild and Luc, 1974

Autobiographie n°1[1]
Autobiography n°1
By Luc Ferrari

I wonder why I felt the need to write autobiographies, as if, by pondering over the past, even a false past, or distorted by memory, one could explain anything about the fleeting present. I am, as my name indicates, of Italian descent, via Corsica however. My ancestors arrived at the time of the Napoleonic conquests, most of the Ferraris deserted one after another, not out of political conviction, but because they didn't like the army.

My great-grandfather was a stonemason who cut millstones in a small mountain village. My maternal grandfather (also a Corsican) played the cornet in a customs officers' barracks in Marseilles. That's where my musical talents come from. My grandfather was also a hairdresser, but it was him who sounded reveille every morning. Tired of having to get up so early, he opened a small café which soon went bankrupt, because he was too fond of buying a round or two, and the customers took advantage. I was born in Lyon on March 18th, 1934.

I created a number of orchestral and electroacoustic pieces. Then, gradually, pieces that moved away from the academic notions of a "work", of aesthetics, or music (academicism is always stronger, its power is guaranteed by the force of inertia of its irremovable institutions, which is why one should never miss an opportunity to attack and damage it). I have travelled, not very far but a lot, recording things from life. When you've always had an instrument in hand, you are so receptive to events that you end up anticipating them. I would rather, if it isn't too late, cut the previous sentence which I find, if not wrong, at least pretentious. It may even be wrong.

This led me to create a piece titled *Hétérozygote*. And since then, I've taken *Heterozygoticism* to extremes, so much so that, all around me, I kept finding examples of that state which is obviously indescribable. So I realised that everything was becoming increasingly heterogeneous, and that a terrible and deadly struggle was being played out. On the one hand, life, advancing irredeemably and violently towards heterogeneity; and on the other hand, the monogenic structures in place, trying to resist the flood and to hang on to power thanks to solid and unassailable temples.

Brunhild Ferrari photographed by Luc Ferrari

Early Poems (1951–58)

Against the broken wheels
against nights spat out by eternity
against lost limbs
and cries
you need sounds to feel like kisses

Against glass shards that scratch and cut
against aborted clouds
against sleepy shadow of the tree
and open wounds
you need kisses shaped like seashells
What I want is
a needle that pierces through tongues

October 1951

The road probes the shadow of trees
and I look for the road
But the clouds obscure
the sun and children push the clouds
So the road leaks away
my feet dashed like kites
Children play at pulling the sun's hair
And the road follows in my footprints
Children are laughing with their hands
Why laugh when you can fly says the sun
Children follow their hands and fly

22 November 1951

As if the sky, its large cutlass, were a great tiled floor, its grain darkening speck by speck. Each tile turns from white to black.

And moves forward.

Or, swift and scattered, the tiles just morph, from pentagon to panther to tree bark to fountain to pebble (each holding on to its drop or passing it around). And so the drop goes round in a big circle, completed with each gift:

The sky revolves around its pin head. Splits into whirling glitter, mourning, a funeral dress, sparkles of joy in its wake, every shimmering thread.

The seams are showing, it's inside out,

Sewn by a finger, each finger a thread

Five sky seams.

When you see it, it whistles, the sound rises, you could even say:

"That one gave me everything"

But then the end comes, no one ever saw the sun go down.

The window goes dark, there's a whole life on the inside. And how can we know if right now there's something behind it.

Maybe it just becomes opaque.

The day has emptied its spoon and has worked hard for something unwavering, solid.

And how can we know if it's really there, or telling lies, if it is capable of even more?

Yes, that's it.

The night is saving itself. It wishes to surprise us.

It knows to keep us waiting, in silence, maybe it is waiting for us to die, so we can think: our death is more than the night.

You snatch at it but it slips out of your hands, slowly tearing its five seams, just when you're about to catch a glimpse of it, it turns away.

It is the only one these days who gets buried in white.

October 1957

19

On the cargo ship taking me to the United States [2]

You should see the dining room when the waves are swelling, especially on the first days, when objects are moving freely. The armchairs lurching creaking from one end of the room to the other and congregating in a corner. The plates flying about, the waiters falling over headlong and landing with their faces in a big bowl of peas. Only the captain remains impervious to the chaos. My coffee splashes up into my face. Jolting back, I topple off my armchair, it tumbles away and hits another table, a plate falls off and smashes, a bottle is knocked over, I've landed on the mustard jar and the waiter trips over my legs, sending his tray flying up towards a passenger, who ducks just in time.
Then the captain, unruffled, turns round calmly and, with pipe in hand, says to me:
"You didn't scald yourself, did you?"

14 December 1954

Luc Ferrari, 1954, photograph by Brunhild Ferrari

Diary of a Studious Winter

I am a quartz in the light
My facets each an oriented trap
I am forever mobile and exist
only in the rotation
that gives me weight.
I think I am the earth around the sun
I surprise myself, coming from every universe
The sun bombards me, fearful bags of marbles
trickling down my definite angles.
And I, the spider, Nature's Gesture
The universe around me wields its star-filled guts
Inextricable web of the spider
And the earth
stays frozen in a spatial rhythm.
Rotating, I obscure my own light
And I, the many-faceted quartz
Abandon myself to it, the voyage
Now the light watches me, contracts me
scatters me
and opens me up to the Movement
Our gestures are volcanic
We are the earth's effervescent crater
My mind is a lake
In the morning my eye wakes and gravitates
Twitching in the orbit, the scales of a small fish, its tail
erupting into glittering sparkles
I scratch off the scales, the bone reveals I am Charlemagne
With a fish I bash the flowers
I tear the stones apart
I scrape the earth with my thorns
I scratch the skin of the air, and I flow in its veins
My fish explodes
My moons are full of wood
I burn, I burn.

1957-58

The Rhythm is in the Sending

The distance between dispatch and delivery.

The dispatch is the antecedent of rhythm.

Rhythm is the journey, the duration of a journey within the weight of the object; its different parameters are the distance covered and the intensity of the dispatch.

Rhythm is composed of

1° intensity of the dispatch: the dynamic
2° weight of the object sent the colour
3° distance covered the frequency
4° the journey time, the duration

I - the dispatch is the antecedent, the intensity, the blood
II - the weight is the density, its depth, its expression
III - the distance is its height, its speed, its perspicacity, gesture, journey, time
IV - the time is life, the interval between birth and death.

The Object is the inanimate body before it has been projected into life.
The satellite Body dances, according to its weight, and the reflex/instinct that guides it (choice/conscience) covers the distance.

The duration is mimed and depends on the quality of the breath, on the spring of one jump within the other jump. A rhythmic jolt ruled by some internal algebra.

And the rhythm within this jump is the friction of those internal jolts with the parable of the great conductor.

1957

22

Spiral

Is the algebraic friction between small jumps and great leaps, also between jolts and organic convulsions.

The great convulsion spurts out
The medium convulsion sustains
And the small convulsion provides infrastructure and connections, the departure point and conclusion, all at once.

The First is general trajectory, the totality that acts through memory

The Second is a neurological contraction which acts through small steps backwards, it's the mirror effect, i.e. perception.

The Third is in an instant, without memory, i.e. sensation.

The Antecedent of rhythm comes before birth, the duration of the retrograde dispatch.
The impetus for birth being a position of the mirror.
You start at the moment of arrival, you cover the trajectory back to front and you arrive at the dispatch point, the birth impetus.

January 1958

Elements From a Confused Journey
By Luc Ferrari

This is a journey compiling all my compositions and creations. In that sense, it's a biographical document that lists, in chronological order, concert pieces and film music as well as one-off events or ephemeral actions that were created for specific circumstances.

Some of my works stray, in varying degrees, from my purely musical preoccupations; some are at crossover points between various branches of what might be one and the same tree. The challenge being to try and express through different means some fleeting ideas, sensations and intuitions; to observe the everyday in all its forms and realities, be they social, psychological or sentimental. This can be achieved through texts, instrumental scores, electroacoustic compositions, reportage, films, and various performances.

This sign (‡) indicates works that would be difficult or impossible to perform, not recommended or left dormant.

Portrait of Luc Ferrari by Daniel Leterrier, 1965

Compositions + Creations

Suite pour piano

Suite for Piano

Suite for Piano [4] is the first in my catalogue, the first in my life as a composer. How does a young person identify a piece as being their first — it is an improbable, incongruous statement? This is opus number one. My first painting. There were many scores before this one, some of which were completed, but did not seem accomplished, perhaps due to the fact they were too close to the obvious influences of my mentors. Those influences remain perceptible to me in *Suite for Piano*, but more diffusely, so the path towards my own identity emerged through all the traces.

World Premiere [hereafter: WP] University of Miami, 1954, Luc Ferrari (piano)
CD Auvidis Montagne, MO 782110 - 1997
Editions Salabert

1952
— 7 minutes 4 seconds

Antisonate pour piano [5]

Antisonata for Piano

The title itself is rebellious. It clearly expresses a refusal to follow a classic form. The score doesn't eschew certain conventions, with three distinct movements (fast, slow and fast); it expresses something savage and non-conformist. In the first and third movements, violence prevails in the extremely nuanced formulation of the themes and through the use of a torn melodic line articulated in a high-low unison. This was already a revolt against the serial technique, which forbade the use of octaves and, note too the second movement's use of intervals — reminiscent of the tonal system. Was this a radical gesture, or a way of claiming an affiliation with a postmodern aesthetic?

WP Institut d'art, Paris, 1955, Luc Ferrari (piano)
CD Auvidis Montagne,
MO 782110 - 1997

1953
— 10 minutes

Sonatine Elyb pour piano [6]

Elyb Sonatina for Piano

Don't count on me to shed any light on this mysterious title. I'll just say that this score is quite rigorously serial, even though highbrow critics earnestly analysing the work may find it exceedingly casual. I often speak of seriality, apologies for doing so, it happens to have been the major debate of the 1950s, when I was twenty. Electronics became the main discussion in the 1960s, and then Minimalism in the 1970s, etc. I took part in all those debates, endured them, and came out alive.

WP Darmstadt, 1956, Luc Ferrari (piano)

1

Quatuor

Quartet

This score is one of the first adventures in my life as a composer. *Quatuor* [7] goes back a very long time, so I don't quite remember what the subject was or if there had been one. Rather than a concept as such, I think it was an attempt to experiment with serial techniques, which at that time represented the avant-garde, and with which young composers strongly identified. Oddly enough, this piece was never performed unlike my other works of that period. However, looking at the score, you can see that it was amended and annotated in preparation for a concert. I forget why it didn't happen. Nearly fifty years on, this is the premiere. I am curious to hear it.

Violin, viola, cello, piano. WP Festival Les Musiques, Sainte-Catherine's Church, Marseilles, 12 May 2001, by the soloists of the Ars Nova Ensemble

1953–54

♩ = 176

Rapide

Suite hétéroclite pour piano [8]

Heterogeneous Suite for Piano

I was on a ship bound for America; but it was a cargo ship—the cheapest option. I had decided to go to meet Edgard Varèse. It was winter and the storms came and went punctuating the days, so the journey was to last about three weeks, via Cuba and Florida. I would compose short piano pieces in a lazy leisurely way. Some were calm, some agitated, others had a swaying pulse.

There in the middle of the ocean, for the first time, I perceived a near-conscious correlation between a reality in motion, outside of me and an inner commotion.

For piano. WP Maison des Lettres, Paris, 1956, Luc Ferrari (piano)
CD Auvidis Montagne, MO 782110 - 1997
Editions Salabert

1955
— 6 minutes 45 seconds

Lapidarium pour piano [9]

Lapidarium for Piano

I was absolutely fascinated by the Surrealists, and soon after reading about them, I tried my hand at automatic writing. Simultaneously, I carried out an experiment with a psychoanalyst — just like a therapy session, although instead of talking, I would write a page of music "without thinking".

Lapidarium can be considered a sort of improvisational writing, except that improvisation happens in real time, whereas writing is a slow process. This piece therefore escapes the traditional reading of grids one might use to analyse the form. The successive states are constantly renewed without ever being repeated, and a number of thematic moods emerge and develop spirally through repetition. The piece may appear rather violent due to the great difficulty I had in composing it; one might say it was a form of "self-harm". When the form and the objects are thrown around they occasionally collide.

For piano
WP Maison des Lettres, Paris, 1956, Luc Ferrari (piano)
Editions Salabert

1955
— 6 minutes

Huit petites faces

Eight Small Facets

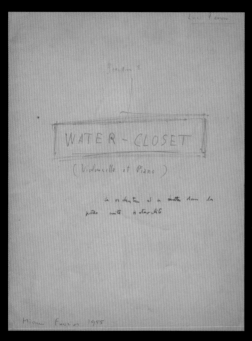

Huit petites faces score [10] courtesy of Editions Salabert

For chamber orchestra (two flutes, oboe, English horn, clarinet, bassoon, xylophone, piano, four violins I, three violins II, two violas, three celli)

1955
— 20 minutes

Tête à terre

A One to One with the Earth

TETE A TERRE

Question : Que faisait-il à la nuit, dans le champ des têtes, avec son bâton, et seulement éclairé de la petite flamme qui près de chaque tête veillait ?

Réponse : JE SUIS LE CHIEN QUI BOITE ET MARCHE OU VOUS AVEZ LA TETE ; MA LANGUE EST UN SER-PENT

For piano and voice
Poem by Roman Weingarten

MA TETE EST UN MIRACLE.

1956
— 10 minutes

(lorsque vous serez enterrés davantage, peut-être saurez-vous enfin marcher)

Luc Ferrari in Paris photographed by Brunhild Ferrari
Tête à terre by Romain Weigarten, Poemes, Christian Bourgois

Visage I

Face I

Visage[11] is the first series at the beginning of my life as a composer wherein I honestly expressed myself. Of course this is not a series in the serial sense of the term, but rather a group of compositions that have something to do with images or with Realism, as the word is mentioned, there is indeed something serial in this score.

For piano. WP Darmstadt, 1957, Luc Ferrari (piano)
CD Auvidis Montagne, MO 782110 - 1997

1956
— 5 minutes 32 seconds

Composition pp 1—9 of 12, courtesy Association PRESQUE RIEN

Visage II

Face II

Visage represented a physical reality to me. In *Visage I*, I explored the accumulation of cycles, whereas in *Visage II*, I devised a physical confrontation between two sexual bodies. I was interested in translating body movements into notes, rhythms and instruments. This was a new idea at the time but I found it useful to introduce an incongruous concept into the organisation of sounds. The audience didn't necessarily need to be aware of this, but this crucial image had to arouse my imagination.

The result is a kind of Pointillism and to accentuate the image of the body, dots had to be scattered through space. This is why the musicians had to be disseminated across the room, and the conductor had to be alone, or almost alone, on stage. That sort of thing wasn't done at the time, and deemed inappropriate. This is why this score has not been performed to this day, though it is by no means un-performable.

Two trumpets, trombone, tuba, piano, six percussionists
WP: Die Reihe, Vienna, 1961
CD Mode, mode 228 — 2011

1956
— 14 minutes

Visage II cover of original score courtesy Editions Salabert

VISAGE

2

(La Raison logique)

Troisième Version

PERCUSSION À PHYSIQUE

) deux Idées de Mur)

+

3 Avril 1956

Visage III —

La Prose du Transsibérien de Blaise Cendrars

Face III – Prose from Trans-Siberia by Blaise Cendrars

The narrator reads the prose of Blaise Cendrars, describing a sixteen year old poet's journey from Moscow through Mongolia during the Russian Revolution in 1905.

Violin, cello, clarinet, percussion and narrator
RTF recording, 1962

1957–58
— 35 minutes

Page one of score, courtesy Maison ONA Editions

VISAGE

3

La prose du Transsiberien et de la petite Jehanne de France

de

BLAISE CENDRARS

(écrit une octave au dessous)

{ Xylophone ou Marimba   X }
{ 4 Tom-toms de aigu au grave   Toms }
{ 2 Congas   Cg. }
{   Bongoes   Bg. }
{   Cymbale   Cymb. }
  Clarinette en ut ou sib   cl.

  Violon   V.

  Violoncelle   Vc.

20 février – 1 Mai 1958

Visage IV — Profils

Face IV – Profiles

For ten instruments (Two flutes, trumpet, trombone, bass trombone, string double bass, piano, three percussionists)
WP Musik der Zeit, Cologne, 6 May 1959, by the Cologne Radio Symphony Orchestra, dir. Michael Gielen
Paris Biennale Prize, 1962

1957–58
— 12 minutes

Page one of score, courtesy Maison ONA Editions

PROFILS

pour

VENTS CORDES et PERCUSSIONS

1 piccolo ou 1 grande flute en do	picc ou fl.
1 piccolo ou 1 grande flute en do	
1 Trompette en do	Trp.
1 Trombone Tenor	T.
1 Trombone Basse	Tr. B.
1 Contre-basse à Cordes	C. B.

Piano — P.

Percussion I
1 cymbale suspendue (grande)	baguettes caisse-claire	cym.
2 Woods-Block	baguettes xylo. très dures	W. B.
1 Temple-Block	baguettes xylo. mi-dures	T. B.
2 Caisses-claire		C. C.

Percussion II
1 cymbale suspendue (petite)	mailloches timbales	cym.
Timbales à pedale	baguetes xylo. mi-dures	Timb.
4 Toms	petites mailloches feutre	Toms :

Percussion III
2 Woods-Block	baguettes xylo. très dures	
1 Temple-Block	petites mailloches feutre	
1 Tam-Tam	grosses mailloches grosse-caisse	TT
1 Grosse-Caisse	baguete metal pour triangle	G. C.
	baton de bois ou pointu pour grincer	
Tambour de basque	sur le tam-tam.	t. de b.

Tous les instruments sonnent comme ils sont écrits.

Luc Ferrari

Capricorne

Capricorn

This was made for a film I never saw, and never even knew the title of. When Luc played it the first time, it was this little melody on piano and he sang 'cheek to cheek, *ça veut dire joue contre joue…*' There were no more words. I haven't found anything more, but keep searching...
– Brunhild Ferrari

Musique concrète, piano and voice
CD boxset INA-GRM - 2009
Composition Association PRESQUE RIEN

1958
— 1 minute 28 seconds

Chute libre

Free Fall

Luc Ferrari and Gérard Patris, 1958

Radio essay with Gérard Patris
CD boxset INA-GRM - 2009
Composition Association PRESQUE RIEN

1958
— 18 minutes 34 seconds

Standing, from left
to right: unidentified,
André Boucourechliev,
Bruno Maderna, Henri
Pousseur, Marina
Scriabine, Luc Ferrari,
Pierre Schaeffer.
Kneeling: Mauricio
Kagel, Earle
Brown, Luciano
Berio, Karlheinz
Stockhausen.
Lying down: John
Cage, Brussels
World's Fair, 1958

Etude aux accidents [13]

Study with Accidents

Musique concrète —INA-GRM
VP International Exhibition, Brussels, 1958
P BAM, LD 070 —1960
CD EMF, EMF CD 037 —2003
Maison ONA Editions

1958
— 2 minutes 14 seconds

Etude Floue

Blurred Study

Musique concrète — INA-GRM
CD boxset INA-GRM - 2009

1958
— 2 minutes 40 seconds

Etude aux sons tendus

Study for Stretched Sounds

The sound effects in this study are obtained from various objects which are alternately stretched and released in front of the microphone. They appear as rhythmic structures, sometimes dense, sometimes loose, whose dynamic origin is perceptible. Therefore, the sound momentum is constantly broken, creating a surprise not originally intended, but which becomes part of the organisation. *The Etude aux sons tendus* is one of my first forays into musique concrète; consequently, I now find clumsy. My main motivation when composing the piece was to investigate the rhythmic possibilities offered by the magnetic tape — cutting up, superimposing sounds, or exploiting natural movements of objects used. Stretched sounds don't constitute a criterion for analysis, but a causality applied by hand to the material itself, or a manipulatory causality exerted on the recorded sound. The idea was to use sounds like you would use an elastic band, and to build the study with samples of sounds in a state of maximum tension. The stretching reduces them to silence or, on the contrary, contracts them like a muscle tensing up ready for a jump that will not happen. Surprise, in itself, eliminates some accidents from the general process. This work was performed in 1967 at the Musée d'Art Moderne de Paris, with a choreography by Pauline Oca. Of all her choreographies, this one is the most deliberately mimetic of the music. She endeavoured to use her body as one would use an elastic object, like the string of an instrument, with the difference that she can still "play" her body even when it is totally slackened.

Musique concrète —INA-GRM
WP International Exhibition, Brussels, 1958
LP BAM, LD 070 — 1960
CD EMF, EMF CD 037 — 2003
Maison ONA Editions

1958
— 2 minutes 48 seconds

Program

Suite in the Form of a Mushroom	James Cunningham
A Piece for Tape Recorder	Vladimir Ussachevsky
Untitled	Tooru Takemitsu
Omaggio a Joyce	Luciano Berio
Tribulation, 1958	David Talcott
Song of the Second Moon	B. Raymakers

Intermission

Artikulation	Gyorgy Ligeti
350 Dash Two	Gordon Longfellow
Continuo	Bruno Maderna
Etude aux Sons Tendus	Luc Ferrari
Dialogue for Man and Machine	Henk Badings

The Vortex demonstrations are sponsored by the Audio-Visual Research Foundation with the cooperation of the Morrison Planetarium. The Foundation is organized to explore the esthetic possibilities of technological developments in auditory and visual media. Our first project, Vortex, stems directly from this approach.

Technically, Vortex utilizes all known systems of projection, along with one of the most highly developed sound playback systems extant. Yet, it is a live creation of sound and image, being performed for a specific audience. Vortex is based on a mutual complement of aural and visual elements, in which they reveal unspoken meanings about one another which exist in neither alone.

Having presented successful Vortex series in San Francisco and Brussels, the Foundation hopes to give demonstrations in Tokyo and Moscow in 1959.

Credits

Technical consultants	George Bunton and Alvin Gundred
Publicity	Gary Barrett
Announcer	Charles Levy
Special Visual Effects	Hy Hirsh and James Whitney
Technical Assistance	Junius Adams, Robert Greensfelder and David Porrazzo
Visual Coordinator	Jordan Belson
Audio Coordinator	Henry Jacobs

This complimentary program donated by High Fidelity Unlimited of Menlo Park (soon to open in San Francisco) specializing in quality high fidelity components and Ampex home music systems.

Etude aux sons tendus concert programme Vortex V, 1960 (above)

The team of the GRM in studio: Ivo Malec, François Bayle, Luc Ferrari, Bernard Parmegiani, Edgardo Canton. (Photo by Laszlo Ruszka / INA via Getty Images)

Passage pour mimes

Passage for Mimes

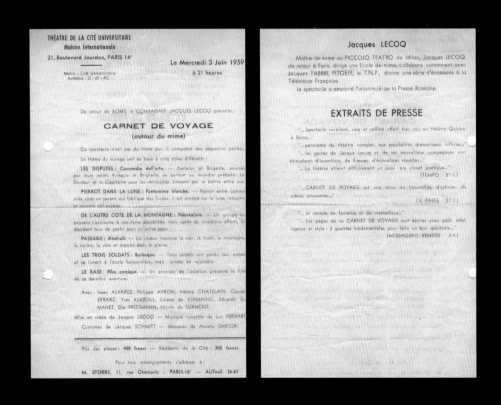

1959 Gaveau Guimet (right) and 1959 Carnet de voyage (above) original programmes

LE GROUPE DE RECHERCHES MUSICALES

de la Radiodiffusion–Télévision Française

présente

CINQ MANIFESTATIONS

de

MUSIQUE EXPÉRIMENTALE

★

1ᵉʳ et 30 Juin - *Concerts* - Salle Gaveau, 45, Rue La Boétie, à 21 heures
MUSIQUE CONCRÈTE - ELECTRONIQUE - EXOTIQUE
Bério, Boucourechliev, Ferrari, Ligeti, Mâche, Maderna, Mayuzumi, Philippot, Pousseur, Sauguet
Schaeffer, Varèse, Xenakis

16 et 26 Juin - *Expériences Musicales* - Salle Guimet, Place d'Iéna, à 21 heures
"LES IDÉES ET L'OBJET"
"L'IMAGINATION ET L'INSTRUMENT"
projections sonores commentées par Pierre Schaeffer

23 Juin   - *Image et Mouvement* - Salle Guimet, Place d'Iéna, à 21 heures
Films de : Alexeïeff, Bourguignon, Brissot, Fulchignoni, Grémillon, Hirsch, Lalou, Le Corbusier
Max de Haas, Patris, Sarrut, Schwab et Gout, etc...
avec les musiques de : Ferrari, Henry, Mâche, Philippot, Schaeffer, Varèse, Xenakis
et la compagnie de Mime Jacques Lecoq

avec la participation des studios :

Fonologia di Milano - Apelac de Bruxelles - Westdeutscher Rundfunk de Cologne

LOCATION : R.T.F. 18, rue François-1ᵉʳ, - ELY. 57-50
SALLE GAVEAU, 45, rue de la Boétie - BAL. 29-14
Chez DURAND, 4, place de la Madeleine, dans les Agences et par téléphone à S.V.P.
Prix des places : 400 - 500 - 600 - 800 - 1.000   -   Tarifs réduits : J.M.F. - A.M.J. - Etudiants
organisation de concert : M. DANDELOT

Visage V

Face V

Composed prior to joining the Groupe de Recherches Musicales of the R.T.F. (French Radio and Television). It represents an attempt to conquer various degress of an imaginary and already concrete range. The first degree is the exploration of an interval located in the low register of the instruments. The second degree is that of the unforeseeable events (accidents) causing a disturbance in the continuity. The third degree is that of the superimposed rhythms, or the irregular iterations. In the fourth degree, the dynamic profiles (variations of intensity) are superimposed producing slowly evolving sound screens. The fifth degree represents a play of musical objects; transpositions of visual objects (various rhombuses, spirals, crosses and angles). The sixth degree is that of the play with heights, dispersion and bringing together notes with variations of duration. The seventh degree is a fast dance going slowly to high instruments (progressive disappearance of the low instruments). The eighth degree completes the work by melodic structures that evolve near the high frequencies.

Musique concrète
WP Expériences musicales, Paris, 1959
LP Philips, 6536 003 — 1970

1958–59
— 10 minutes 33 seconds

Score courtesy Maison ONA Editions

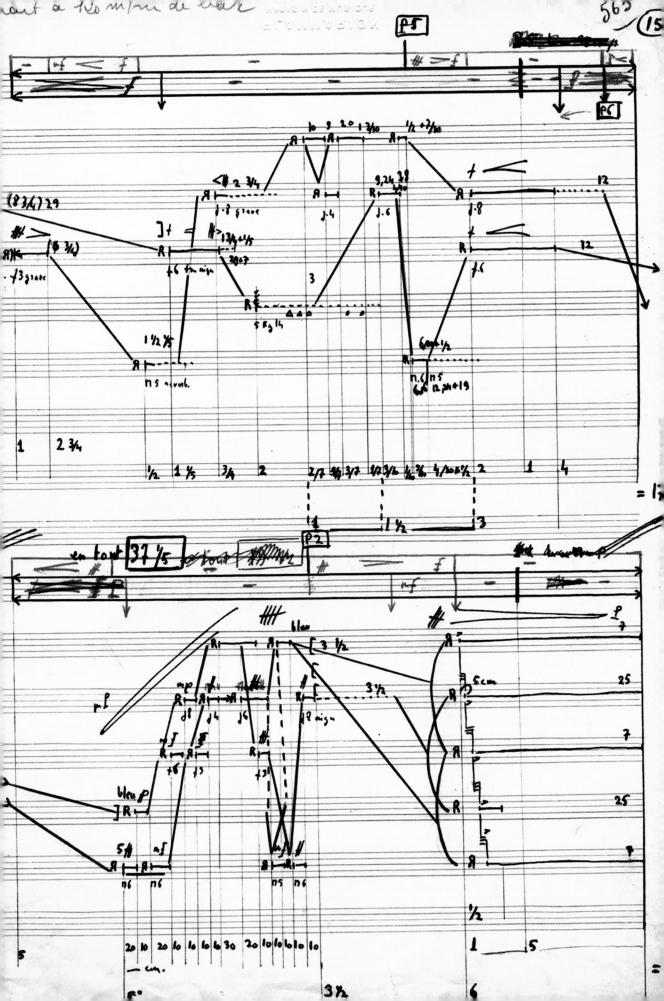

Les Etapes De La Vision
The Stages of Vision

I. The OBJECT is potentially endowed with a degree of consciousness whose aim is to
   project its own image.

   The Object wants to be seen as proof that it is Alive.

II. THE JOURNEY isn't a path, but a permanent state of availability, like a radiance, an
    extension of itself reaching out to those who will perceive it.

   The Object is not limited to its perceptible shape, but extends into space until the

   point of encounter. It seeks out the connection, and from this interpenetration it
   derives life itself, and strength to renew its own radiance and perpetuate its outline
   delineating
   its shape.

   The Object's image thus describes a circle around it. This is the Object's gravitation.
   The object wants to penetrate.

III. THE INNER EYE is the centre of the confrontation.
    The Object penetrates an element different from itself.
    Through this encounter it will be transformed
    so that the object and man are no longer apart
    so that the Genesis of Vision is free from man-object distinctions
    so that the Exchange takes place
    The Inner Eye is the core.

   On the one hand, the object generates man
   on the other, man generates the object
   the object becomes my arms and my legs
   My body becomes the tree
   the exchange happens within the space of a bounce.
   Only the Inner remains

IV. THE RETURN

   Driven, like the object, by a clear desire to be seen and to penetrate
   Man spreads himself across the matter that becomes the fruit of his meditation.
   Of Juxtaposition.

From the stomach where neither man nor the object are distinguishable, from there, the Return is accomplished. It is as if the Object were exhaled, heavy with Man, as man himself was heavy with the Object.

And thus the object is not quite itself any more, rather it is more than itself
because it has been seen
because it has undergone the exchange
because the exchange returns to the object

spreading itself across it like a giant magnifying glass

In this manner one generates radiance in the other

In Matter
from the External to the Inner
and vice-versa
in the Matter that is delineated
and whose outline reaches its paradoxical form
And vice-versa
thus are gradually juxtaposed the stages of Vision, which are the gravitation of man and of the object
within Matter
and vice-versa
from the Internal to the Incommunicable which is the centre of all objects-men
and the Incommunicable
where there is no place any more, nor path nor comprehension

But
Recognition

Les Étapes De La Production
The Stages of Production

Attempting to only deal with matter directly is as alarming as it is exciting, in the sense that intentions get translated into gestures which, through the nervous system, will become sound objects.

One needs to tame a microphone like one tames a chimney brush (the kind that looks like a hedgehog), or maybe use a hedgehog to tame the microphone. The opposite has been seen, for example a tortoise mesmerised by a microphone.

One may sometimes wonder whether the microphone is insane, as it tells very strange unexpected tales; it picks up a mote in its brother's eye and tells the story of a beam. One has to treat the microphone with utmost courtesy, whereas the piano can be played with nails, a file, a mallet or even with pliers and a hammer, as in the case for a so-called "prepared piano".

Incidentally, the piano's sturdiness should been noted here, as should its willingness to release an unforeseen soul, or at least a soul nobody had yet thought of extracting from it. Meanwhile, the microphone, with its precise, not to say obsessive, personality, captures such souls faithfully, in every detail, sometimes even exaggerating them.

I speak of the piano because it is the instrument with which any budding composer begins. It is the most convenient and familiar instrument, the most classical too, even if you don't use it the way a respectable young lady would. (We may be tempted to smile at the thought of one such delightful person, fifty years from now, practising her John Cage as we would practise our Czerny).

I mentioned that the microphone obsessively magnifies things; indeed, the slightest hesitation or imprecision, even in a hammer blow, is amplified tenfold by the microphone. The "string wrenching" must be executed perfectly, or it becomes intolerable. We pride ourselves on being able to single out the perfect string-wrenching from a thousand. The lucky winner is congratulated by the group.

I also mentioned a tortoise; it "played" a piece of paper. At one point, I thought it was playing Debussy. On further investigation, I realised the music was coming from the studio next door. Maybe the tortoise wasn't playing anything at all and maybe Debussy was in fact playing a piece of paper. In our world, how can you tell a piece by Debussy from a piece by a tortoise, since we analyse them both in roughly the same way?

The point is, we must understand that sound bodies don't at all produce the sounds we expect of them. Besides the microphone captures the most unpredictable sounds. We're often getting lost, and we start over and over until we get an interesting sound object, and then we pretend we were subconsciously striving for it all along. I'm exaggerating slightly to drive this point home: if we only ever recorded what we intended to record (even when we are aiming for a very complex outcome), then we would only ever obtain very inadequate results; because desire is much more banal than reality, and dreams are much poorer than matter. A sheet of corrugated iron, a lampshade, a fan, when diverted from their everyday use, produce unsuspected sounds.

Day after day, we go looking for such sounds, laboriously we discover them, and we preserve the stages of our investigations in the Group's sound library, which charts the progress of our manipulative skills and our imagination. The raw object (i.e., not transformed by electro-acoustics) is the reflection of raw imagination.

That's the great quest. Everybody brings in their own sounds, classifies them, consigns them in the different sections where they will be used. The sound library is at the centre of a star shape. From there, the sounds will depart in many different directions; some will be used for personal works because they so obviously bear the stamp of their authors; others will be sent to the technicians, who will submit them to electronic vivisections; others still, or the same ones, will be analysed or saved on file. For we are very serious people. We can spend a very long time discussing one sound. We do not want it to escape us, we want to identify its smallest details, to pull out its secrets; we compare it to other sounds which appear to obey the same laws. The common characteristics are analysed according to their material causality (shape of the object, type of attack), according to their acoustic causality (sound recording apparatus, spatial movements), and sometimes also according to anti-causalities (i.e., we are confronted with a sound and we do not want to know its provenance).

One may compare an orchestral structure (when you select a fragment, you are already analysing) with a sound object produced by a metal rod for example. Rapid passages played on string or wood instruments can represent the back-and-forth movements of an exaggerated vibrato (the tempo); as for the dry and tight percussions, they represent the grain (rolling of the snare drum), and the brass percussions are the accidents, etc.

This analysis enables us to imagine a work consisting of orchestral structures that would be the deliberate and active continuation of the passive and natural laws of the sound object.

One can imagine infinite combinations. For example an orchestra's modulating sounds can relate to the undulations of a corrugated metal sheet; the clusters of fundamentals would therefore rub together, that friction producing certain oscillations whose knots would be the orchestra and loudspeakers, and whose belly would be the audience. One may also imagine music made solely with food — that would come as a blessing, especially when you think of all the works that bring you more despair than nourishment.

I think I have the "living thing" complex. I am convinced that the ladybird's song is more interesting than a serial structure in its raw stage, even if that structure represents an eclipse of the Polar star.

The challenge is to create a language that is never codified, the danger (both danger and advantage) is never being safe, complying to the law of morphology imposed by the object or giving the object an invented morphology.

Producing sounds, transforming them, superimposing and structuring them—all of this offers untold possibilities. These new possibilities will only enable musical language to progress if one decides to look for new sources or to revitalise old ones, to identify their specific gestures, to explore their limits. All the while carried away by a frenzy of subjectivity.

EXPERIENCES
MUSICALES

MUSIQUES CONCRETE
ELECTRONIQUE EXOTIQUE

par
LE GROUPE DE RECHERCHES MUSICALES DE
LA RADIODIFFUSION TÉLÉVISION FRANÇAISE

sous la direction de
PIERRE SCHAEFFER
avec la collaboration
DE FRANÇOIS MACHE

LA
REVUE
MUSICALE
RICHARD-MASSE, EDITEURS
7, PLACE SAINT-SULPICE, PARIS-6e

Programme for the Musique Concrète concert at the Journées Internationales de la Musique Expérimentale [International Festival of Experimental], 5 October 1958, Brussels World Fair [Editions Richard-Masse, Paris, 1959]

Continu Discontinu

Continuous, Discontinuous

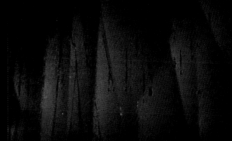

Chamber music for an abstract short 16mm, colour film directed by Piotr Kamler (oboe, clarinet, bassoon, violin, cello, trumpet, horn, trombone, violin, cello, double bass, two percussionists)
INA-GRM

1959
— 9 minutes 6 seconds

Film stills, *Continu Discontinu*, INA

Tête et queue du dragon [14]

Head and Tail of the Dragon

Musique concrète — INA-GRM
WP Festival de la Recherche, Paris, 1960
LP Candide, CE 31025 — 1969
CD EMF, EMF CD 037 — 2003

1959–60
— 9 minutes 13 seconds

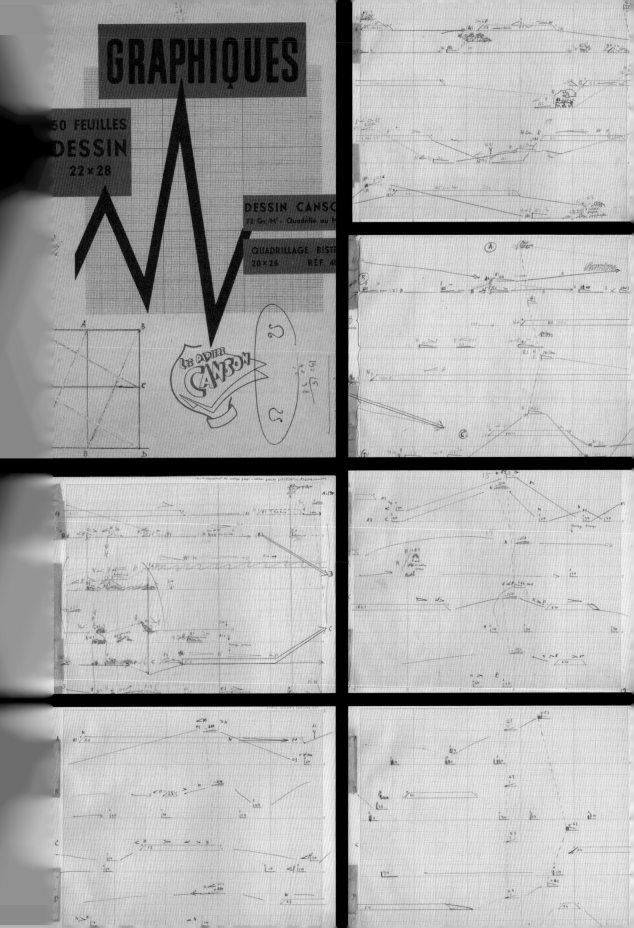

ete et queue du dragon is based on a text by H.P. Lovecraft, whose poetic structure provides the musician with the laws that will govern the organisation of sounds.

One can provide numerous explanations that might appear contradictory, depending on whether one decides to emphasise this or that facet. The difficulty is which facet to choose or they are all connected to form a whole. The work was born from the juxtaposition of different states that bore no relation to one another, except the moment in which they occurred, the friction of said disparate states, and the collision of their heterogeneities. I believe in encounters and I deny chance, which appears to instigate them.

A number of challenges were addressed in this work, which doesn't mean that they were solved. The encounter between the indefinite idea and the outline, between outline and score, score and matter, matter and structure—can only be destabilising. It could be explained by one's desire to modulate things until they enter into a relationship with one another. I could almost say that a form of expression was born from such encounters, that it seems to recapture the source from which the idea initially sprang, and I might be content with that positive outcome.

The aim was to give life to the sounds, without their development having to be constricted by the structure. The overall structure had to be intelligible and not derived from the structure of the sounds themselves; rather, the two structures had to be juxtaposed, perhaps even opposed. That is why a fairly large number of elements were created, as a sort of orchestration, then they were sorted into several families according to shape, matter, substance, or the manner in which they developed. All of these elements are constantly evolving, making repetitions impossible — this is the common characteristic of all the musical objects employed. The manner in which they develop is precisely the criterion used to classify them:

iterative with more or less rapid rhythmic evolution;
samples evolving melodically within a given range;
samples whose dynamic developments produce combined and complex profiles;
even more complex developments that produce a real polyphony of melodies, profiles and masses;
the height of evolution is reached through the rapid succession of small objects which form composite groups that can sometimes be heard as one highly complex object, rhythmically.

Tête et queue du dragon is made up of three sections that segue into each other.

The first section represents the dragon's head and emerges through a discontinuous acceleration of the movements. Fragments of bouncing movements, selected at certain stages in their motion, are linked by sound samples that have similar characteristics. This

horizontal organisation builds up each of the four spacial tracks independently and it causes a certain disturbance. Conversely, groups of very rapid notes restore order and create
a structure named "Vertical unifying principle".

Whereas the first section is spatially linear, the second strives for a spatial rhythmic structure. The body of the dragon is represented through a gradual fragmentation of the note
clusters, within which contrasting elements are introduced.

In the third section, or tail of the dragon, all the elements of the work are scattered, moving
extremely fast. By transforming the slightest fragment of any of the musical objects, one
can confer rhythm to the space.

Luc Ferrari preparing the graphic score for *Tête et queue du dragon*, 1959,
photographed by Brunhild Ferrari

Tautologos I

The title *Tautologos* stands for the idea of superimposed repetitions.
I had worked on repetition processes in previous scores. This was more rigorous.
The section created with the rotating loudspeakers and the generators was part of a spatial cycle related to the rest of the composition.
I like showing up and making do with what is available and present.
There was a piano, and as I was more interested in acoustic sounds than in electronic I worked mostly with the piano. Using frequency generators to create Larsen effects through the studio's revolving loudspeaker and sending electronic sounds through to the loudspeaker, I picked up the output again with swinging, suspended microphones. That's what I called the tautology, hence *Tautologos*.

Electronic music — INA-GRM
Commissioned by Hermann Scherchen, produced at his Gravesano studio
WP concert RTF, Paris, 1962
LP BAM, LD 072
CD EMF, EFM CD 037 — 2003
Maison ONA Editions

1961
— 5 minutes

Overleaf: Luc Ferrari with Hermann Scherchen during the filming of *Grande Repitions*
Photograph by László Ruszka, INA

Tautologos II

In those heroic times, it was called a musique concrète composition.
…A series of beginnings…this idea occurred to me because the beginnings were so challenging.
Rewritten again and again…
This cycle of failed beginnings, which under the rules of the game were meant to get better and better, also illustrated the idea of repetition. This is why I called the piece *Tautologos*, from the word "tautology", meaning unnecessary repetition, a sort of pleonasm or redundant occurrence ("redundant" being understood here as pleonastic parody of the superfluous).

Musique concrète — INA-GRM
WP concert RTF, Paris, 1962
LP BAM, LD 071 — 1962
Maison ONA Editions

1961
— 14 minutes 54 seconds

Interview with Christian Zanesi about recording
at Hermann Scherchen's studio in Gravesano

Interview 1996

CZ. At the end of the fifties, the conductor Hermann Scherchen had an electroacoustic studio built in his villa at Gravesano, in Italian-speaking Switzerland. It was probably the first private studio. The composer Luc Ferrari, a guest at Gravesano, describes that place which no longer exists.

LF: That studio was a crazy dream, but when you got there, you found yourself in a kind of heaven, an ideal place. The property was outside the magnificent village of Gravesano, on a hill, with a unique view over Lake Lugano. You were surrounded by nature, extraordinary. There was an immense garden where one could rest and meditate, a swimming pool where you could cool down, the local weather was beautiful, and the working conditions fantastic.

CZ: How did you meet Hermann Scherchen?

LF: At the end of the 1950s, Hermann Scherchen would turn up in Paris, in what was at the time called the Groupe de recherche de musique concrète [research group on Musique Concrète]. He would turn up with these strange machines, small boxes that produced pseudo stereo and all sorts of things, things that already had to do with electroacoustics, but really off-the wall. These were prototypes he invented himself, and he would have someone else build them. He was fascinated by that kind of thing, it must be said, and had followed the evolution of avant-garde music since Schöneberg, since Pierrot Lunaire [Moonstruck Pierrot] as it were I don't think he premiered it, but not far off). He had also frequented the milieu

or electronic instruments between the wars, like the trautonium, the theremin that kind of thing. So, naturally, he came to see Schaeffer in Paris and I met him at that time.

CZ: What year was that?

LF That was around 1960. He had invited us to Gravesano because he organised symposiums in his studio and it was an opportunity to meet all kinds of weird people. All sorts of disciplines would meet there, cinema, video – which was in its infancy then (I remember video shows on a big screen to demonstrate the Eidophor system, the very first video-projector). There were also physicists, mathematicians, and very few musicians. remember my wife and I drove over with the Xenakises, and if I remember rightly we were the only two musicians at that time. It was a bit like a big family occasion, we had amazing banquets in the garden of the villa and then, a bit woozy on local wine, we would carry on the conversation in the studios.

CZ: But how and why was that studio created?

LF: I think that Hermann Scherchen had had this whim for a long time, to have a studio but also to be able to invite people there. Scherchen was a bit of a talent spotter, he played a part in the recognition of Xenakis, of Luigi Nono, and myself, to some extent; and before the war he had also taken part in all sorts of adventures. He wanted to explore electronic sound. So he had bought that magnificent old house at Gravesano and he had converted the outbuilding, a sort of warehouse into a studio. Quite a profes

...ional studio — in other words, once you were inside, you couldn't hear the birds.

CZ: He was a sort of arts patron, wasn't he? I'm told he built all that with his own money?

LF: He didn't have any outside funding, and he bankrupted himself with that project. He needed a lot of money to eat, to bring up his children (he had a lot of children) and also, and above all, to feed his hunger for culture. I remember his wife telling me with a big smile that he sank all his money into that studio. Also, he had an obsession with loudspeakers and he experimented with spatialization. You know, at the time, hardly anybody talked about stereo, hardly anybody was interested, and incidentally, I'm amazed that, to this day, most of the radio programmes on France Culture are done in mono. I don't mean to sound critical, I'm just astounded to hear that's still the case, forty years on! He was fascinated by anything to do with sound in motion. So were Xenakis, Nono and myself, so we were part of a kind of "sound in motion" family. And Hermann Scherchen had invented a revolving loudspeaker, it was an enormous ball that seemed to rotate in all directions (in fact, in only two directions) and that sphere was mounted with numerous loudspeakers. The main electronic problem was to work out where to run the cables to power the loudspeakers while following the movements of the ball along those two axes. He used to play music through that contraption and it produced a kind of phasing, a bit like an ambulance zooming down the street. It was very entertaining because, through that warping device, we'd listen to Messiaen, Schönberg and Mozart.

CZ: What was his relationship to you?

LF: When he invited me to come and stay, to produce a piece in his studio, we all lived as a family. First of all, he liked Brunhild very much, he found her very pretty, and it wouldn't have occurred to him that I might come without her (I think he was keener to see her than to see me!). We ate together and we stuck to purely convivial exchanges since, out of discretion, he didn't want to know what I was working on — although I did suspect him of asking his technician a few sneaky questions to find out what I had been up to during the day. But he didn't listen to one note of what I was doing until the piece was finished. So the relationship was one of warm attentiveness, very friendly, and at the same time he was the kind of person who liked to play on affection and friendliness as much as on his very impressive stature. I mean, he relied on the fact he was intimidating to exert a kind of power, which he must have found very entertaining.

CZ: Those were the Sixties after all, so did the Gravesano studio lean towards electronic music or musique concrète?

LF: Herman Scherchen didn't wish to take sides in that quarrel, which by the way was a full-blown quarrel between, on the one hand, Herbert Eimert, who had created the electronic music studio in Cologne, and on the other hand Pierre Schaeffer who had invented musique concrète, with Pierre Henry in Paris. It was an all-out rivalry, because it's easier to hate than to like each other, and besides, Schaeffer was difficult to get on with to say the least. So, at the be-

bbcu each other up the wrong way
nd saw each other as competitors, aes-
etic competitors, which was a shame,
ally. And I think that Scherchen didn't
ll into that trap, he was just as interest-
d in creating new sounds based on re-
ordings, i.e. based on the acoustic sys-
m, via the microphones, as by creating
ectronic sounds via the generators.

Z: At the beginning of the Sixties, were
ere a lot of studios apart from those in
aris, Cologne and Milan?

=: Pierre Henry must have set up his
·st studio by then, Studio Apsome,
nce he had already parted company
ith Schaeffer. There was also the Co-
mbia studio founded by Ussachevsky
 the United States, and in Belgium, the
ihent studio was just emerging. That's
ot a lot. So Hermann Scherchen's stu-
o was very interesting because, since
e hadn't taken sides in the Paris-Co-
gne quarrel, you would meet people
·ere from every other studio. It was the
ily symposium that dealt with those
uestions, Darmstadt was concerned
ith other issues.

Z: What did Pierre Schaeffer think of
·cherchen's initiative?

=: Schaeffer was very happy, he en-
·yed that sort of event where you would

munication, and so he would also attend
He had things to say and he was very
receptive to other people's contributions

CZ: Did you compose *Tautologos* in that
studio?

LF I did, it was *Tautologos I* to be precise, because *Tautologos II* was done in
Paris. So I did everything on site, using
whatever was at hand, you see, I like
turning up somewhere and making do
with whatever is available. There was a
piano there and, as I was more interested in acoustic sounds than in electronic
sounds, I worked mostly with the piano
However, I used the frequency generators to create Larsen effects through
the revolving loudspeaker. I would send
electronic sounds through to the loud
speaker and I picked them up again with
swinging suspended microphones. Also
although I had already worked on repetition processes in previous scores, I now
tried to be more rigorous about it. The
title *Tautologos* stands for the idea of
superimposed repetitions. What's funny
and interesting, is that the section created with the rotating loudspeakers and
the generators was part of a spatial cycle related to the rest of the composition
That's what I called the tautology, hence
Tautologos.

CZ: What did Hermann Scherchen think

LF: It was very intimidating, one day, it was late morning, I went to find him in the house. I was on schedule, I'd had a fortnight to work on it, I was even slightly ahead of schedule. When I had stayed here previously, I'd had about the same amount of time to prepare.

So he came into the studio, he listened once, he didn't comment. He listened a second time, same thing, we listened to the piece about ten times, still not a word. The piece isn't very long, seven or eight minutes, but times ten, with the rewinds… the whole listening session must have lasted at least two hours. And I don't remember him saying anything. I was surprised because nobody ever asked to hear a piece ten times — twice was already pretty generous, so ten times seemed a bit much. And I thought: he must find it interesting…(I was an optimist in those days). Either way, over dinner that night, he was very very jovial.

CZ: The Gravesano studio no longer exists. What happened?

LF: Hermann Scherchen had gone into debt in a major way because of that studio and when he died it was a disaster, because there was no more money coming in, no pension, none of that conventional sort of thing, maybe a few royalties for his compositions and orchestrations. So the studio was sold, at least the equipment, his wife had to pay the inheritance tax, the debts, etc. I remember Brunhild went back there to help compile a catalogue of

Gravesaner Blatter, studio journal

Suite Gigogne

Russian Dolls Suite

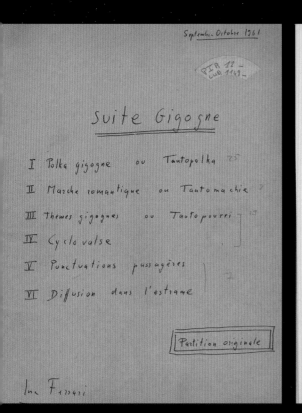

An evolving score in six movements beginning with a 'Tauto-polka' for an ensemble
piccolo, flute, clarinet, cornet, trombone, tuba, banjo, piano, percussions)

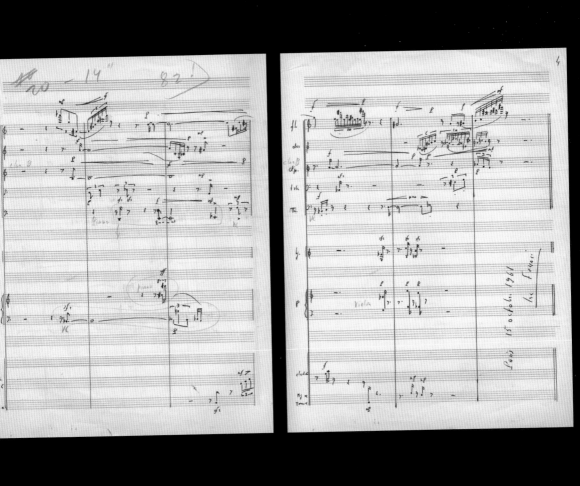

Forme Bleue

Blue Shape

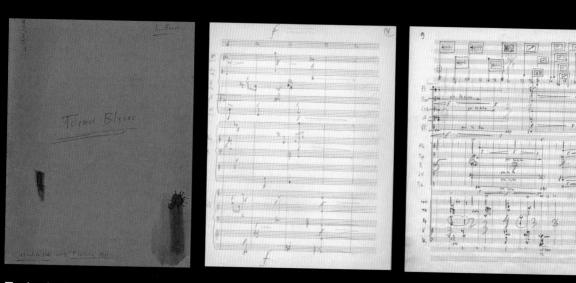

Early drafts of *Forme Bleue*, courtesy Association PRESQUE RIEN

Chamber music for an abstract short film directed by Piotr Kamler (oboe, clarinet, bassoon, violin, cello, trumpet, horn, trombone, violin, cello, double bass, two percussionists)
INA-GRM

1961
— length unknown

Etude I

Study I

Four improvisations on a schematic for orchestra, with the EIMCP Ensemble, directed by Konstantin Simonovic, as part of the instrumental experiment I was in charge of at the GRM.

Etude I, courtesy Association PRESQUE RIEN

Chamber music for an abstract short film directed by Piotr Kamler (clarinet, horn, trumpet, trombone, cello, percussion)
INA-GRM

1961
— 5 minutes 20 seconds

Luc Ferrari at GRM Studio (Photo by Laszlo Ruszka / INA via Getty Images)

Spontané I

Spontaneous I

‡ Improvisation for nine performers

1962

— Time dependent on improvisation

Spontané II

Spontaneous II

Improvisation for ten performers

1962

— Time dependent on improvisation

Spontané III

Spontaneous III

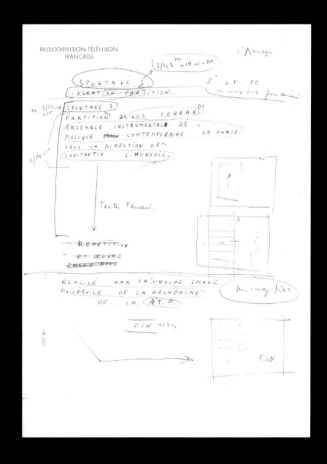

‡ Improvisation for eight performers
Filmed working session, *Spontané III* 16mm short film, directed by Gérard Patris

1962

— Time dependent on improvisation

Original notes for *Spontané III*, courtesy Maison ONA Editions

Spontané IV

Spontaneous IV

‡ Improvisation for eleven performers
Filmed performance of *Spontané IV* (35mm short film directed by Gérard Patris, June 1962)

1962
— Time dependent on improvisation

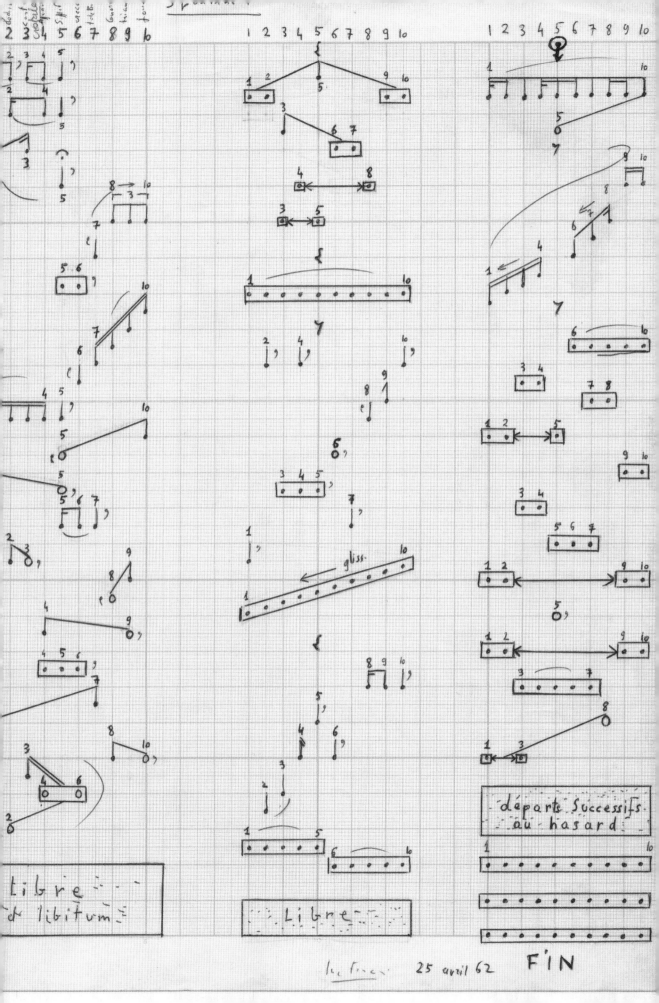

Chastel

CHASTEL
Film d'art

Couleur 16 mm
Durée : 17'

Tentative d'approche de l'œuvre d'un peintre, ce film, au lieu d'analyser les tableaux, d'en classer les signes selon la méthode traditionnelle, s'efforce d'exprimer non pas la toile seule, mais aussi l'œil qui la regarde et la main qui la crée. Il met l'accent sur l'extrême mobilité de l'œuvre picturale, tant pour le peintre qui l'examine et la retouche, que pour le public au multiple regard qui la contemple une fois achevée.

Formé de trois éléments distincts qui se combinent librement, ce film est le fruit d'une triple complicité : celle du peintre CHASTEL, du cinéaste LAPOUJADE et du commentateur Jean LESCURE.

Scénario, réalisation, images, montage . . . . . **Robert LAPOUJADE**

Commentaire dit par . . . . **Jean LESCURE**

Musique . . . . **Luc FERRARI**

Son . . . . **Luc PERINI**

Date de réalisation : 1962

Catalogue Films Service de la recherche translation:
An attempt to approach a painter's work, but instead of analysing the pictures in the traditional way, classifying signs and meanings according to the time-honoured method, this film endeavours to be the expression of not just the canvas but also the eye that looks at it and the hand that creates it. It insists on the work of art's extreme versatility – for the painter who looks at it and touches it up, as well as for the multiple viewpoints of the audience who look at the finished work. Based on three distinct and freely associated components, the film is the fruit of a triple collaboration between the painter, [Édouard Henri Roger] *Chastel, the filmmaker* [Robert] *Lapoujade and the commentator Jean Lescure.*

Music for a 16mm film directed by Robert Lapoujade
INA-GRM

1962
— 17 minutes

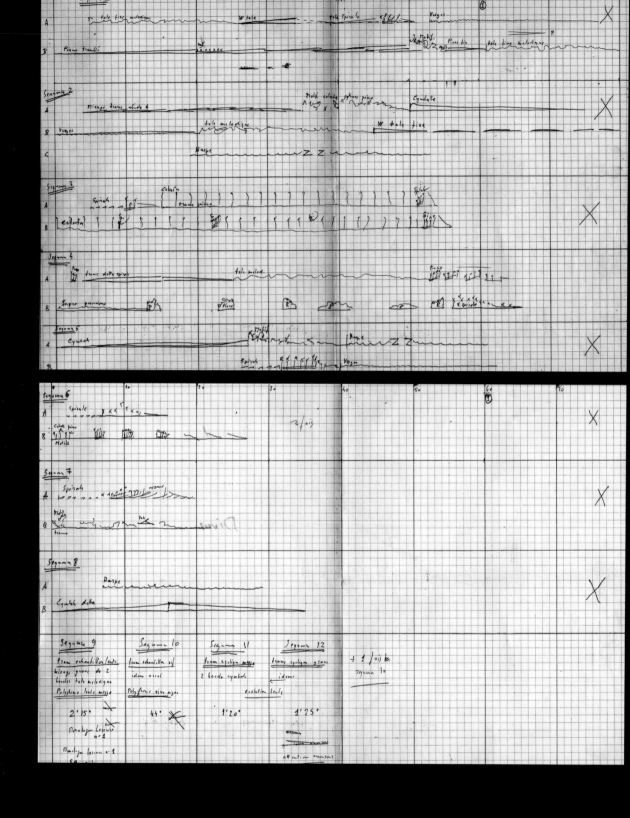

Notes for *Chastel*, courtesy Association PRESQUE RIEN

Egypte ô Egypte

Egypt O Egypt

Egypte, ô Egypte...

Film stills, *Egypte ô Egypte*, INA

Music for a 16mm short film that would become a trilogy directed by Jacques Brissot (flute, oboe, clarinet, contrabass clarinet, trombone, violin, cello, double bass, marimba, percussion). With text and narration by Jean Cocteau.
RFT Service de la recherche
Paris Biennale Prize, 1963
CD boxset INA-GRM - 2009

1959–60
— 21 minutes 24 seconds

Egypte ô Egypte II

Egypt O Egypt II

Catalogue for short films, Service de la recherche

Music for ensemble, for a 35mm colour film directed by Jacques Brissot (clarinet, trombone, violin, viola, cello, double bass, percussion) with a text read by Roger Blin, intertwined with a small orchestra and concrete sounds
INA-GRM

1961–62
— 33 minutes 4 seconds

6 pour 4

6 for 4

-track tape
irst version of the group concert
WP Ranelagh Festival, Paris, 1962
NA-GRM

1962
— 4-track tape

Composé

Composite

Composed Composite

or orchestra and tape (two flutes, oboe, clarinet, bass clarinet, bassoon, double
assoon, two horns, two trumpets, trombone, two percussionists, harp, ten violins I,
ght violins II, eight violas, eight celli, four double bassists)
nal version of the collective concert WP Venice Biennale, 14 April 1963, by the
nsemble of the Zagreb Biennale, dir. Igor Gjadrov Editions EFM-Technisonor

1962–63
— 10 minutes

over of score of Composé Composite courtesy Association PRESQUE RIEN

LUC FERRARI

COMPOSÉ COMPOSITE

(CONCERT COLLECTIF)

PARTITION D'ORCHESTRE

E. F. M. - TECHNISONOR

Autoportrait Jean Dubuffet

Self-Portrait, Jean Dubuffet

Film stills, courtesy INA

Music for a short film directed by Gérard Patris
Production: Service de la Recherche de l'ORTF/Pléiade

1963
— 29 minutes

Les Pèlerins

The Pilgrims (of Bayreuth)

Catalogue for 1962–63 short films, published by Service de la Recherche

35mm colour short film on the Richard Wagner Festival in Bayreuth, co-directed with Jacques Brissot
INA-GRM

1962–63
— 26 minutes

Chaque pays fête son grand homme

Every Country Celebrates Their Great Men

Soundtracks for seven short films co-directed with Jacques Brissot for French television on Frédéric Chopin, William Tell, Joan of Arc, William Shakespeare, Saint Anthony of Lisbon, Johann Strauss II and Wilhelm Richard Wagner

1962

— 7 short films, between 25–30 minutes

Les Bachiques

Baschets pieces

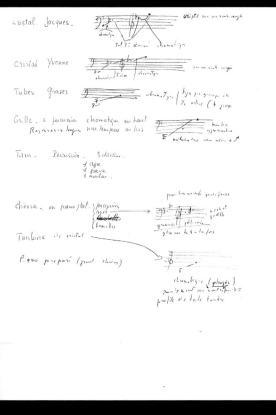

Pages one and two of fifteen, score for *Les Bachiques* courtesy Maison ONA Editions

Music for Baschet instruments

1963

— unknown

Flashes

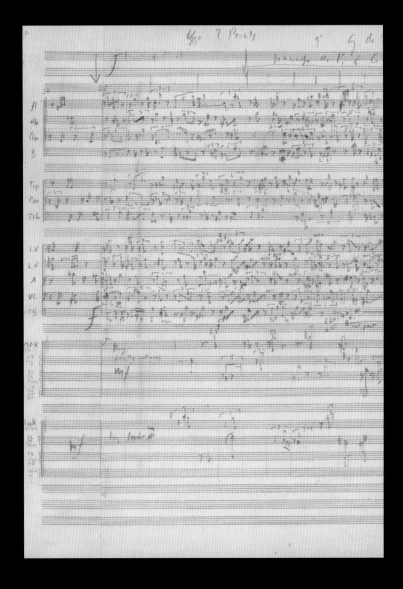

Flashes score courtesy Editions Transatlantiques

Music for fourteen instruments (flute, oboe, clarinet, bassoon, horn, trumpet, trombone, two violins, viola, cello, double bass, two percussionsists)
WP Paris, Olmstedthall, February 1964 by the EIMCP Ensemble, dir. Konstantin Simonovic

1963
— 17 minutes

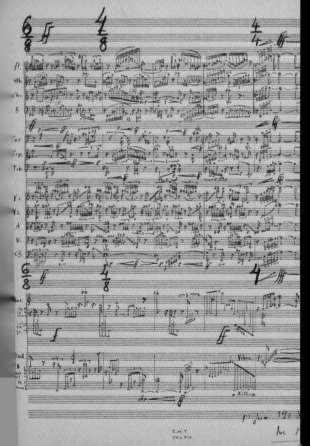

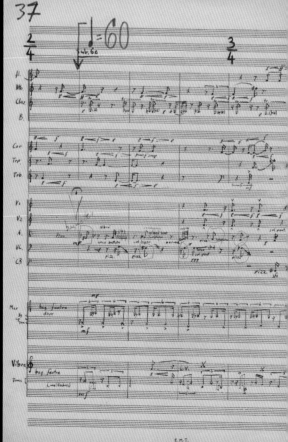

Portrait d'une autre

Portrait of Another Woman

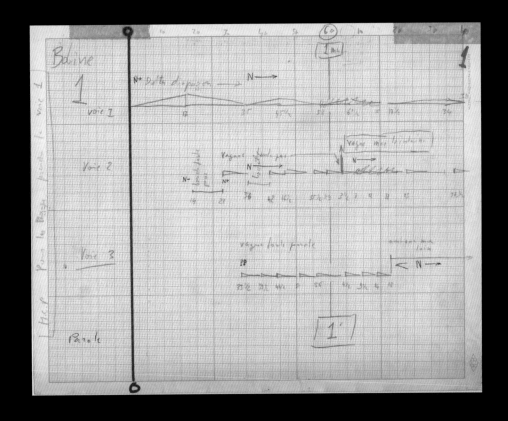

Musique concrète for a 35mm colour short film directed by Marie-Claire Patris
NA-GRM

1963
— 30 minutes

Le Dernier Matin d'Edgar Allan Poe

Edgar Allan Poe's Last Morning

Musique concrète for a 'lost' 35mm black and white short film directed by Jean Barral
INA-GRM

1964
— 30 minutes

Hétérozygote

Heterozygote

One day (for reasons I shall not go into) I went off with a tape recorder that did not belong to me. I travelled, not very far, but for a long time and recorded real sounds. This is how *Hétérozygote* came into being. The first foray into so-called 'anecdotal' music, introducing realist sounds as concrete images, added to traditional abstract sounds and structures. The audience becomes active because they are implicitly asked to imagine their own anecdote. The use of realistic elements allowed me to tell a story and enables the listener to invent their own meaning.

For the different sequences I chose titles that are in no way mandatory, each listener remaining free to choose their own:

Overture, 1st Scene: The Flute and the Big Wheel (*Le great manitou*). Interlude 1. 2nd Scene: Meteors. 3rd Scene: The Beach. Interlude 2. 4th Scene: The Grotto (or Putting into Order). 5th Scene: Arithmetic. 6th Scene: From Dawn to Noon at the Market. Interlude 3. 7th Scene: The Prison. Interlude 4. 8th Scene: Heavenly Geometry.

I'd like the listener to recount *Hétérozygote* and write the plot; in that way this recording would not be a mere abstract object but a living exchange.

Stereo magnetic tape
WP Paris, 1964
INA-GRM
LP Philips, 836 885 DSY — 1969
CD BVHAAST Records, Acousmatrix 3, CD 9009 — 1990

1963–64
— 27 minutes

Graphic score *Hétérozygote* courtesy Maison ONA Editions

La Musique à l'envers

Music Back to Front

Fragment of a group opera
Occasional composition

1965
— fragmented time

GRM YEARS

Alain de Chambure, Jacques Poullin, Pierre Schaeffer and Luc Ferrari

Correspondence with Pierre Schaeffer and the GRM, 1960–68

Paris, January 4th, 1960

My dear friend, Pierre,

I am writing to justify myself, even though I hate doing that, but now and then one has to clarify oneself to make sure misunderstandings don't linger.

You often accuse me of not being mature enough, childish even, but I suspect you of hanging on to this convenient misapprehension to preserve your own integrity. Indeed, you have a very strong personality and others need to put up a furious fight to avoid being put down and belittled, for you do like to throw your weight around more than is necessary. (I won't go into detail.) Having said that, I respect you and you have my complete loyalty and support.

Since I am aware of your shortcomings, I can sometimes get round them.

I have been following you for two years, and over that period, rather than think of myself, I have worked by your side so that *musique concrète* should shed the lamentable reputation it had when I first came to it (through no fault of yours, obviously).

If I had been interested in scheming like my predecessors (even though you now take precautions so that this should not happen again — and we, all of us, often feel the weight of the suspicions "they" have planted in you), I probably could have managed it, despite your watchful eye, and I could have become one of those virtuoso shopkeepers, for that necessitates neither genius, nor intelligence even. But what I am interested in is to help musique concrète gain its rightful respectable place within the field of music so that it should evolve and develop.

(…) Then you accuse me of infantilism, saying Luc doesn't like money. I do like money, but what I like even more is respect for musique concrète.

I also know (despite this barrage of criticism) that you would like us get along, and this is why we need to reassess things on both sides. I know that you accept the responsibilities that are heaped upon you for the good of others, and I admire you for that. You have tried to do me a good turn by placing me in the position of a General, and I have disappointed you.

But I know where my own good lies, and that, if I were to be a General, I could only ever be a "sub-Schaeffer", whereas when I am being a musician, I am Ferrari (and you know only too well the turmoil of creation and the constant self-doubt that goes with it).

I'm asking you to express your discontent toward me, to let me know not your superficial reasons for it, but the profound, innermost causes.

I am trying to provoke, through conjectures that may be very unfair, some fair reprimands or constructive observations.

I constantly sound out acquaintances and musicians in search of useful comments.

I shall aways be rigorous and not moderate.

Having said that, I wish you a fruitful year.

Luc Ferrari

Paris, July 30th, 1961

Once again, the artist is being attacked in his lair.

We should no longer use words like artist, art or creation, which amount to accepting the conventional ideas about creation and God-the-Creator, hence man in His image, that is to say man-as-creator...

Old traditions, old habits.

The artist has a place in society, he is a victim of the function society assigns to him. Better to say that there is no such thing as creation, defined as an event that turns chaos into order. Instead we should say that an exchange takes place.

To attack the artist is still to believe in his existence. Blasphemy is just another way of being religious. (Blasphemy being part of religion, the Vatican's Black Mass.)

We must move beyond such arbitrary contingencies and relics of intellectual-romanticism.

Let us be materialists.

Let us start again from the beginning and assume for example that there has been no creation, but instead, a perpetual transformation. No more creator, but a transformation of one matter into another. Uranium turns into lead after it has released a quantity of energy that may well be necessary to life.

The new scientific society must reveal its secrets to us and make the mysteries of science as accessible as possible. I once saw a photograph of an atom, it was a dark surface specked with a few dots of light, stars surrounded by darkness. I already knew that before seeing it, but seeing it gave me a great shock. What I kew: that matter is darkness speckled with stars, and if you get closer still, the stars are speckled with darkness. We should replace the Arc de Triomphe with that photograph.

Where is the artist in all that? There isn't one.

But let us be mystico-materialists.

Two theories.

Either the world doesn't exist.

Or the world exists, of which we occasionally have evidence.

Between, on the one hand, extreme subjectivity, which would tend to posit that everything is related to me and that therefore there is no world outside of me;

And, on the other hand, extreme objectivity, which would tend to posit that everything exists outside of me and that therefore my presence is pointless;

I can work out an intermediate position which could be defined thus: things exist according to the degree of imagination or energy I put into seeing them; in other words, superimposed on top of objective reality, there is a second, subjective, reality, which is necessary for the thing itself to exist.

I am aware of the thing and I can even go so far as to say that the thing is aware of me, and that I don't exist without that gift exchange, without the (maybe) endless back-and-forth motion of that substance, the life-giving matter.

I could say then that life is neither in me nor in the world outside of me, but rather between the world and me. In action, not in a latent state.

This is where man comes in. No longer the artist, the creator, but man as observer, or man as unintended consequence of that situation.

Let us be mystics and materialists about the power of seeing.

I respect the man who seeks, even if he only seeks his own fortune, for the symbol of life is expressed through this quest, no matter how cruel and venal it may be.

First, I believe that the work of art produced by a single individual has become inadequate and should reclaim its function through collective endeavours. This is probably a means, but maybe also an escape route, or at least a palliative. A possibility (though not an easy option) that remains external.

Whereas in fact solutions should probably be internal; hence the voyage into the unknown, the plague or the cholera in Camus, Artaud, Giono; Beckett's decay, etc.

Why blame the artist? To despise him is still to believe in him, and being an artist is as deserving as picking up cigarette butts, cigarette butts are not so easy to spot.

If we are still intent on using words like art and creation, then we could say that authentic creation consists in seeing, and to see, one needs imagination.

One might say: "Nothing has ever happened in my life", to which we might reply: "you didn't have enough imagination to see what was happening." We walked past a rock without seeing it. A flower opened. I digested.

Hundreds of generations would not suffice to describe the mysteries of digestion: Joyce feeding kidneys to Bloom, who then for a whole day, with acute realistic observations, records the kidneys' slow transformation as he meanders through the labyrinth of a town that is itself like a giant stomach.

The solution is for everyone to do their best, knowing that the things worth taking are those that manifest a capacity for action. Everybody can exert that faculty. I can't tell the difference between real and fake gold like a jeweller would, but I am capable of seeing a rock in my path.

Let us leave the artist to his works. Some display a degree of complexity that says a lot about the world, even unintentionally.

One solution would be to tell society: the world is beautiful, we risk destroying it through sheer stupidity or ignorance.

We could also say: Mr So and So has withdrawn from the world and produced a thing which we no longer call a work, but which in its complexity constitutes an image (a "visage") of the world around us, a part of that thing that can be explained in a thousand ways, presenting a thousand facets, visible in a thousand ways.

No more pedestals, everyone has some power, there is no difference between what we call an artist and a rug merchant who loves his rugs.

How can we think about everything, whether things have a place or not, and how can we think about who we are addressing? And here's the big question: should we focus on our own work or provide others with the moral and material means to work in certain directions? The things we do are important, granted, but what matters even more is how and why we do them.

In this letter, I had meant to talk about opera, but I got carried away and said all sorts of things in my own naive and clumsy way.

Regarding *Opérabus*, I wanted to tell you that, just as a personal experiment, I tried to insert the music — the work I was showing Bayle, which he passed on to you. You need to take it as it was intended, that is to say, I wanted to see based on one section how the relationship between text and music could work. I couldn't take it any further, because the rest of the text didn't lend itself to it. I hope you will take this kind of experiment for what it's worth, and that it will show you that I am very eager, and I'm not the only one, to work on this thing. What matters most is that we agree on the substance, on "the core" as Xenakis puts it.

This said, I send you my best and wish you a good holiday.

Best wishes.
Luc Ferrari

PS This letter hardly answers yours adequately, nor your expectations, but I find myself plagued with so many problems, in this furnace you grapple with day in day out. I mention this because I like the way you explain the purpose of your actions and the profound legitimacy of an entity like the Service de la Recherche.

Paris, October 25, 1962

To Mr Pierre Schaeffer

Head of the Service de la Recherche

Following yesterday's meeting, I feel impelled to write to you, as unpleasant a task as it may be. I would, indeed, rather occupy my time in other ways, or talk to you about other things.

You summoned us to inform us of the new measures you were taking — although they affect the GRM as a whole, the group was not consulted, nor were the people most directly affected (i.e. Mâche and myself), and you made sure to warn us you only had five minutes so there was no point arguing.

And so I didn't argue yesterday, which is why I am writing now, to say that there is no way Mâche or myself, or the GRM, will comply with your suggestions.

Reason:
The wisdom that should stem from past experience. At the GRM, we have tried everything, (too) many things, docilely. In other words, every single mode of operation, in other words all the producers in the group have occupied all the posts, and vice-versa.

Result:
A producer takes up his post but just as he's about to start working, you move him on. It is impossible to work in a state of perpetual motion (For example: I cannot compose if my table isn't tidy, or if someone moves my papers around.)

Change is harmful to work. Since we have explored every configuration, there is no point in making new changes, it would bring nothing but confusion, and will inevitably result in stalling production.

In July, we thought we had reached a degree of stability, and we hoped that, with the arrival of Mâche, things would settle down. But now everything is up in the air again. The GRM had undergone a so-called crisis, following which you received several long declarations, which you apparently didn't have time to read. As for me, I told you, among other things, that I did not believe in these crises; you could have answered: the crisis is that the GRM doesn't produce enough.

Indeed, as I pointed out: how can one produce in the midst of constant change and instability?

For example:
I had scheduled two *Group Concert* meetings which were supposed to be the last before the individual stage of the project. The first of these "production" meetings, yesterday, was interrupted by your notification to attend. The second was due to be held this afternoon but has had to be replaced by another meeting, because you have asked us to devise alternative organisational models.

I mention this very recent example to show you that every time you make a decision, it doesn't help production, it delays it. I could give many more examples.

Result:
Mâche wants to leave, though we were really pleased to have him back, and in a post that suited him.

As for me, I am not prepared to reorganise my current activities, since I am all set to produce and I cannot accept additional responsibilities on top of *Solfège* [music theory] and *Group Concert* (not to mention my personal work).

Another example:
The *Solfège* meeting was a failure because I had been away on the Monday (Donaueschingen). If I had been in Paris, I could have spent the day preparing for the meeting, checking the work and making sure people did it over and over. If I'm again to be pulled into different directions, I might as well be in Donaueschingen.

Besides, at a time when I wish to focus on important interdisciplinary productions, which I suppose are of interest to the Service (otherwise, it would mean that the Service is not interested in its own doctrine, or in good ideas), I cannot find myself swamped by organisational tasks.

Conclusion:
There should be no changes, so we can get on with work, both collectively and individually, in the best — albeit the most experimental — of all possible worlds.

With kind and respectful regards,
Luc Ferrari

Paris, December 14th, 1962

Since my last letter dated October, I have managed to define more clearly the directions I would like my work to take:

Make the most of my music knowledge (ability for formal organisation) and of my heterogeneous interests;
Make the most of my years at the Service de la Recherche and of the experience acquired there;
Steer my activities towards large-scale projects.

Two types of projects:
Artistic productions
Production of information
Artistic productions shouldn't come as a surprise, coming from an "artist", but I think my interest in information is more unexpected — I'll come back to that later.
These two poles make sense in relation to one another, but also to the RTF.

A moral balance.
On the one hand, productions that compromise as little as possible; on the other, productions of non artistic objects but which use the technical know-how and the sensibility of artists, their inspiration so to speak; that is to say the coincidence between what happens,
what you can see,
and the material means
at your disposal to capture it, which isn't that easy by the way (what Joyce called "epiphanies").

1. Artistic productions
I propose to devise a collective show, that is to say a *Group-Concert* experiment, but expanded into a show.

a) Group Concert n°1 will be completed by early January.
b) Work on another group concert will start at the beginning of the year, with a performance scheduled for June, by one of the radio orchestras.
c) During discussions regarding Group Concert n°2, I realised that most of the group's composers wished to take part in a larger-scale experiment, a kind of show. So I said I would look into it. I think that the Service de la Recherche, with its different groups, offers working and creative possibilities that have so far remained untapped. That is to say they have remained confined to individual productions, and it is high time those individuals were given a common goal, fostering a spirit of emulation.

2. Production of information

I have mulled over the information projects for quite a while, so I can now formulate them and be clear as to what form they should take.

Project A
The first relates to musical information.
I am proposing to go on a music information tour, for about three months, in France and abroad (mainly French-speaking countries, plus Germany and Italy).
In each venue, I would present four events:
I would like to prepare 3 comprehensive lectures:
on romantic music
on the great break of 1912 (Mahler, Schoenberg, Webern, Stravinsky, Varèse, Kandinsky, Paul Klee, Dadaism)
on experimental music
and a film event.

Apart from having to prepare the lectures, which is my problem, the project raises two issues:
how to organise a coherent tour, along a continuous route that makes sense.
the technical equipment should be compact, autonomous, good quality, and easy to set up on my own.
I could bring back from this trip some data on audiences, interviews, etc; and the raw material to be used for project B.

Project B
Film on landscapes
Information on the external appearance of the earth. What people see or don't see without realising it.

I have studied landscapes for years (as an amateur photographer, for lack of means) and I have taught my eye to see things. I would like to use this experience to show the beauty of this planet which we'll manage to screw up one day.

I don't know to what extent this landscape project is linked to Brissot's suggestion, but it is close to an idea you once talked about: making a film that explains itself fully through images.

Project C
This project, you're already aware of; it's to do with astronomy, or the internal face of the universe. It's a long-term project that will fit in the three-year plan you mentioned. So I won't go into it now.

Why am I, a musician, interested in those things?

Because music doesn't give information, it just exists like a lump of wood.

(see the end).

By information, I mean a desire to get closer to the audience. Artistic works must have pure intentions, and are too complex anyway to ever be understood; they don't propose, they dispose. Therefore, other productions need to concern themselves with information, itself a form of demonstration.

I would like to dedicate my efforts to information for a while.

The radio or television don't inform, or not properly.
The audience is kept in ignorance;
ignorance breeds anger and disaster.
Information means examining knowledge, or non directive information. Nature has to be explored, you just need to look at it to see that it is a great source of knowledge.
Views of the world evolve:
we don't even know what the first world views were;
we don't even know how to look around us;
and we're incapable of noticing the delicate balance of a rock, its harmony;
I have a lover's disposition overall,
And powers of observation.
I would like to put these qualities at the service of the Service.

Luc Ferrari

Do not count on me to:

I)
Ask the researchers to clock in and clock out.
Make sure they agree to it and don't forget.
Encourage them to agree and not forget.
Do not count on me to clock in and clock out.

Why?

Constraint is the enemy of efficiency.
You don't walk to avoid falling. You walk out of necessity, not constraint.

116

If people aren't toeing the line then instead of suspecting them of dishonesty, which is far too trite a cliché, let's look for the reason.

(What is the risk of looking for the bad: you risk putting it there.

What is the risk of looking for the good: you risk finding it there.)

Nobody becomes a better researcher thanks to a clocking-in machine.

Constraint can slowly spoil curiosity.

Constraint can replace curiosity.

It's like wanting to replace Notre Dame with a washing machine.

Don't count on me to

II)

Decide which researchers should be admitted to general meetings.

Ask them to fill in the questionnaire

Incite them to do so.

Analyse the questionnaire.

Why?

Because common sense demands that I distinguish between what is indispensable and what is just useful.

Between what is useful and what isn't useful.

Between what is not useful and what is harmful.

Time melts away.

Intellectual energy dissolves.

(We don't even feel like arriving on time anymore, this is serious)

We are not the obedient cogs of a machine that just reacts.

To force a reaction is like trying to touch the eye of a snail.

Having said that, I can listen to reason when necessary,

But I instinctively feel we are sinking deeper into a grave mistake.

These crises of austerity,

These crises of violence, are they really useful?

They wear out the imagination and, little by little, kill it.

Luc Ferrari

Paris, November 22nd, 1963

Dear Schaeffer,

I think the easiest thing is for me to write to you, rather than wait for a group meeting, which I would rather avoid anyway, as I no longer really feel a part of the collective body. Since my return, I haven't taken part in the *Solfège* group and, for several reasons, I have no desire to do the work you requested of them. The main reason is a *moral* one.

For several years now, all the sounds and the reels that are circulating have been made or selected by me. I didn't just contribute a hundred sounds, but several hundreds. I did this almost single-handedly, with the dedication and the commitment you have come to know.

So much so that, for much of last year, you called me the *Solfège team*. I performed the most thankless tasks and in the end found myself alone to bear the brunt of your anger. Then, after I left, you asked the GRM, as you had been asking them for a long time, to get involved. The GRM have a long way to go before they can give as much as I did. But maybe my refusal will help them.

I see you coming, with dark threats: no *Solfège*, then no commissions, no contracts, etc. Without wishing to boast, I think I am entitled to some rest, and freedom. Since I started by your side, you have always known that you could ask a lot of me (and you did, which I am grateful for), that my dedication was boundless, as was my commitment, and I may well have been one of the first pillars, or probably at least one of the first stones, on which the Service de la Recherche rested.

I will always be grateful to you for what I have learned at the Service, but now I am asking for a little consideration in return, a little respect for my work, and a little peace and quiet. I can no longer stand your angry outbursts, they sap my energy, which could do without being undermined at a time when I particularly need it to create my own work. Besides, I cannot imagine undertaking large scale works until this Solfège problem is solved.

I think that the group will work just as efficiently as I did, and that you will be satisfied with them, since the spade work has been done.

With my kindest regards, and my deepest respect — though you may sometimes doubt it.

Warmest wishes,
Luc Ferrari

118

Paris, January 12th, 1965

My dear Pierre Schaeffer,

I don't want to let any ambiguity linger over this unfortunate matter, and it is of course my duty to give you a full account of my reasons. You seemed to be deliberately mixing up several issues, so I'll endeavour to be as clear and comprehensive as possible.

You seem to suggest that my refusal to take part in *Opérabus* is an attempt to distance myself from the S.R., that it is the sign of a crisis, if not a rupture. My answer is that I am still very keen to consider myself part of the S.R., and not only do I wish to be kept in the loop, but also to be involved in its future events, and maybe even in its work.

As a matter of fact, I have contributed to the Service so much, so unconditionally, I am inclined to think that the S.R. might in turn show me a little interest. For the last seven years, I have carried out tasks for which I was not really suited. I have learned a lot, but I also gave a lot, if only because during that time, I was taken up by so many different problems that I had to neglect my own concerns. So, over a long period, I have worked exclusively for other people, and composed very little.

Besides, that work left me no opportunity for social interaction, and a musician who loses his contacts is a lost musician. (This is why I'd rather not lose touch with you either, for the reason I have just mentioned, but also because of the affection and attachment I feel towards you.)

Since you show some interest in my music — and I am flattered you do, despite the obvious shortcomings of my work — I think I should mention that last October, I started working on a composition for full orchestra, which is taking up all my musical energies. Aside from the reasons I have already given you, I would be very reluctant to interrupt that work in order to start on another composition, my mind just would not be on it.

When it comes to music, I have always found it hard to compromise, and so, I hope you will understand that it would be difficult for me to work on something I don't fully agree with.

(Moreover, I suffer from a mysterious condition which prevents me from writing, called "hand dystonia", or "writer's cramp", this is my great secret; it is as if my right arm were paralysed and unable to write, and so for the past month I have been learning to write with my left hand. You cannot begin to imagine what it is like to write an orchestral score using one's left hand for the first time; I am rediscovering the world back to front.)

I put this sentence in brackets because it is not the main reason.

Back to the point:

I stepped down from my contractual activities because I disagreed with you regarding my schedule. I refused to get involved with *Opérabus* because I disagreed with the text. (I didn't expect it to cause such a fuss. I hate people thinking I am playing hard to get and want to be coaxed.) You should thank me for my frankness.

I could have said: "After all, who cares, it's a nice little contract, let's just churn out a quick piece and flog it, that way at least my name will be on the bill for several concerts."

This is a caricature of what would have gone through the mind of an unprincipled guy.

Instead, I told you bluntly what I thought, it's pretty funny, you should just laugh it off. Instead, you take it badly, and you are deeply hurt. Why is that? Could it be because I touched a nerve? Because you secretly think I am right?

And even if I am right, what does it matter, nobody is infallible. Once in a lifetime, one can write a substandard piece without it being a disaster. (Let's see the funny side.) And if I'm wrong, never mind. I want to say that I read your letter without an ounce of objectivity, and I think this is what sets us apart (also regarding the *Solfège*): your chief concern is objectivity, and I don't believe in it. This is why I care neither for religion nor for mysticism (and I am not confusing the two), because mystics are convinced that they hold the Truth. Yet if you add up all the mystics, you will still only reach a partial truth, only on a limited scale — the earth, or even just a nation, let's call it: objectivity of temperament —, and it will certainly not equal anything like a "divine" conception, with all the misunderstandings the word implies.

Having said that, I am sure I am right, just like everybody else (XenaStockaBoula), but I am absolutely subjective.

Of course, these are big words for "a bit of banter" — I think that's what you called it. Except this is not banter, because you're talking about a conception of life, about attention, listening, music, etc... So find some other way of justifying what you wrote!

I must say I find myself in a quandary, I don't know what to do or think; I do not want to hurt or offend you, I do not want to fall out with you, because our friendship means a lot to me, if indeed it isn't too late for that. But above all else, I want to be frank, I do not want to treat you as others treat you, that is as someone to be cajoled, indulged whatever his whim, or someone irascible and violent, someone you should be wary of, and be sure not to cross.

So it is out of respect that I am telling you all this.

I could write much more, but one has to stop at some point. So I hope you will respond and, if you are not upset with me (but why should you be upset with me for saying what I mean), that you and your wife will soon come for dinner, we'll have a few drinks.

Yours,
Luc Ferrari

Berlin, July 3rd, 1967

Dear Pierre Schaeffer,

My trip to Paris was a very curious and disappointing experience. It confirmed to me that the music world, about which I might still have harboured some illusions, rejects me categorically. My stay in Berlin gives me an opportunity to assess my position, my human, and musical, condition. And I am troubled. What are the reasons for this rejection — political, academic, qualitative? — the examples abound.

There are about 5 or 6 composers working in France today (maybe 10, but who?), that is not a lot: do those few composers have qualities infinitely superior to mine, that they should enjoy infinitely more recognition? Over the last ten years, I have written some acceptable works, and the critics have occasionally granted me a few comments, but on the whole, they seem more intent on ignoring me, despite the wide range of works I have produced and my multi-faceted activities, which could at least be acknowledged as adventurous, maybe even fit for consumption. (I won't mention quality, but still.)

As for those composers who hold the keys to power, they carefully avoid greeting me (even Messiaen turned away as he said hello!), they think nothing of speaking ill of me, they have built a reputation for me, like a wall, which I keep hitting, and which is certainly not based on close observation of my work.

Furthermore, while I was in Paris, I went to see a publisher regarding that symphony of mine which Bruck is supposed to conduct, and which is on hold for now, because we still need to add some material; that publisher turned me down, alleging a lack of time and money, yet meanwhile he's publishing two composers, mediocre both, but it so happens that their work has been performed at the "Domaine Musical"; one of them attended my classes in Cologne.

I find it rather odd that those who came after me should now come before me. Which means that my public life has not caught up with my work, or that I haven't gained the recognition that could be expected at my age.

So, is the Paris world too academic? For example, that publisher, at one point, looked at me like a priest saying "you are guilty of this or that, you are living in sin." Or maybe my work is inferior to those currently being performed.

At the moment, I do not know whether to feel optimistic and pessimistic. Optimistic because I am making the music I want, in keeping with the life I observe around me, with society (in general), which I try to understand, in keeping with nature and the lessons I am trying to learn from it, with our condition as transient animals living on a planet that is itself transient, etc.

Pessimistic, because all of this is pretentious and maybe even mistaken, and maybe I deserve the situation I am in, and people ignore me because I am even more mediocre than other composers.

Who knows? And yet, when I observe the audience (despite my pessimism and mistrust), their reaction seems quite positive on the whole, maybe even more so than their response to other works on the scene, even to Xenakis; for example there was this concert in Arras where *Visage IV* was encored, or that other concert, in Madrid, where *Flashes* received the prize for Best Foreign Work, even though Xenakis, Amy and a few others were in the running.

Could it be that other composers are disgruntled? Maybe even within the GRM. And what about Claude Samuel, who is careful not to mention the *Grandes Répétitions [Great Rehearsals]* — what am I to think?

Perhaps being a social failure keeps me young and in good health (moral and physical), and it protects me from the sort of complacency that often comes with success.

I am telling you all this is because you are probably the only person I can discuss this with in all honesty, you are also one of the few people who have accepted and supported my work, and helped to make it happen.

And now, I shall tell you why I agreed to make that film for [Hansjörg] Pauli — [Josef Anton] Riedl probably mentioned it to you. Ever since *Hétérozygote* and the new series which I named "Société", and also since the tv programmes I did with Patris, I have been attentive to people's gestures and words. I have increasingly been interested in observing society; this has gradually drawn my work away from music's traditional abstraction (even when it is called *musique concrète*), and it has led me to look for meaning, which I see as a "commitment".

In that sense, cinema is much more convenient than music, probably because music has not yet found the style and meaning appropriate to its time; because we are living in the 20th century with 19th century concepts. The modern world slips out of our hands like a bar of soap. So, my interest for the cinema comes from the fact that it can convey meanings directly (i.e. without having to go through some hermetic aesthetics). That is the main reason I am attracted to that medium. Of course, one has to learn, I have learned a little with Patris, and I want to learn some more. And that is broadly speaking the reason I am making this film. To learn and to find out whether I am capable of making a film on my own — I have been wondering about that.

Living in Berlin, and being in touch with Pauli, his kindness has drawn me into this project, and my curiosity did too. So what I am making here is very modest, just to see what happens, the subject doesn't have the pretensions described above. The reason I didn't mention this to you in Paris is that I wanted to do it first, and then only show the result if it was worth it.

This film bears no relation to music, though there is a kinship with *Hétérozygote*; it's about a group of young women I came across in the street, in Hamburg, neither very beautiful nor ugly, just average, having a good time, walking around and talking.

That's all. (…)

So this is roughly what I wanted to say. I could go on, but one has to stop some time. I would like to carry on doing all sorts of things, as many as possible.

I hope your leg isn't causing you too much discomfort, that you are no longer in pain, and I hope Jacqueline is well.

I very much look forward to hearing from you soon, and I send you my warmest wishes.

Luc Ferrari

Paris, May 9th, 1968

To the GRM

Dear friends,

I received the GRM's weekly leaflet, and I take this opportunity to write you a note, to try and clarify my situation in relation to you.

My first comment is that, when I got back from my travels, nobody seemed particularly keen to establish contact with me.

Judging by this lack of interest, it seems to me that I've become a stranger to the Group I was part of for a number of years, and which received a number of music and film works from me.

Secondly, reading the programme of events for the Journées du GRM [GRM Festival], it strikes me they have been organised as if I didn't exist (and almost as if I had never existed). Amusingly enough, it looks like someone tried to find a gap where I could fit, and felt that the most appropriate option would be to include me in an evening devoted to Stockholm.

For an event that covers twenty years of *Musique Concrète* (and I made that sort of music for ten years), it seems to me that someone could at least have asked for my opinion, or asked whether I did have an opinion, and whether after those few years spent experimenting I might have something to say about it all. There aren't that many people making that sort of music, it would have been thoughtful, and I don't think it would have taken that much time, to consult me.

And so, I have the rather unpleasant feeling, which I hope is mistaken, that this is not due to some oversight or absent-mindedness, or because you are too busy, but instead, a deliberate decision not to consult me.

This rebuke doesn't spring from me merely taking offence — it is consistent with other signs I have been noticing lately, and confirmed by the recent lack of communication.

If I take the liberty of making these remarks, it's also because I have been treated as an outsider even though, wherever I went, I have always showcased the productions of the group.

So, the reason I am writing, at a time when you have a lot on your minds, is to express a sense of frustration I feel toward the Service as a whole, but also to point out that the group seems to be closing in on itself. I think this is not a healthy attitude and it is affecting the work, if not in terms of quality, at least in that it's not moving forward (Parmegiani excepted).

I am taking the liberty to attempt a critique, and also to see if, among the friendships that remain, there is any room for intellectual frankness. You shouldn't see this as a pretentious gesture, but rather as an effort to build a constructive dialogue.

With my best regards, and see you soon.

Luc Ferrari

Société I [17]

Society I

The first so-called "réalisable" [realisable, or "enactable"], totally written in the form of a text. A parlour game based on sound and theatre elements, intended to create a chaotic situation, so that the barriers of convention can hopefully be toppled. So the aim is to attain a form a communication which, having appeared in a given place, could then expand into life itself.

Fragment of a group opera
Occasional composition
Maison ONA Editions

1965
— indeterminate duration

MUSEE D'ART MODERNE
DE LA VILLE DE PARIS
SALLE NEW YORK

MUSIQUE EN THEATRE
ARC

Association subventionnée par la Ville de Paris

à 20 h.30 les
mercredi 22	mardi 28		lundi 4	
jeudi 23	mercredi 29	avril	mardi 5	mai
vendredi 24	jeudi 30		mercredi 6	

1981

création

SOCIETE I
ou
le pouvoir déshabillé
par les écrits perdus
de
LUC FERRARI
une production de
L'ATEM
réalisée par
DIDIER FLAMAND

avec

LIONEL GOLDSTEIN   AGNES TIRY
DANIEL ISOPPO   CHRISTIAN BUTTARD
FRANCIS LEMONNIER VINCENT COLIN JACQUES NOLOT
JEAN RENO   ELISABETH MORTENSEN
ARNAUD CARBONNIER

Assistant de réalisation :
Jean-Marie VERDI

SOCIETE I ou le pouvoir etc...

"Société I" a déjà une longue histoire, bien que cette pièce n'ait jamais été représentée en public. La première version a été écrite en 1965. C'était le prototype de toute une série de "partitions-textes" mais, dans ces temps lointains, elle se doublait d'une partition musicale.
En 1971, j'écrivais une autre version dans laquelle je spécifiais que la partition musicale avait été "volontairement ou non égarée". Je doutais même "qu'elle ait existé un jour". Fort de ce doute et afin de l'entraîner plus loin, je me demandais également si, par hasard, je n'étais pas un menteur.
La réalisation de Didier Flamand part de ce point de vue et semble avoir tendance à faire disparaître aussi la partition-texte qui était la seule qui restait. Le problème ainsi posé, absolument inextricable, est celui de cette absence, et de bien d'autres choses que cela entraîne. Comme dit le candidat : c'est l'aventure.
Les comédiens et comédiennes, qui participent à cette aventure, ont été choisis pour leurs qualités théâtrales. C'est une autre démarche que de choisir des musiciens professionnels qui auraient des actions théâtrales à jouer, ou de mélanger acteurs et instrumentistes comme c'est d'ordinaire le cas du théâtre musical.
Nous avons pris le parti de faire jouer la musique par des comédiens, amateurs en musique. Ainsi, le son musical n'est jamais une architecture abstraite ou une illustration, mais il est complètement intégré dans le concret du drame qui se joue.

Luc Ferrari

PRESENTATION DU SPECTACLE

"De la musique avant toute chose"
Paul Verlaine

En un mot

chercher ses mots, sans mot dire,
c'est toujours la même musique.

Musique des mots
- mots d'enfants,
mots d'auteurs... mots d'ordre,
mots de passe... mots clés,
mots croisés,
mots convenus... bons mots.

Chercher ses maux, sans maudire.

Musique !

P.S. C'est mon dernier mot.

Didier Flamand

REMERCIEMENTS

Ont aidé à la réalisation de ce spectacle : la Société Coca-Cola, la Société Kanterbräu, la Maison Noémie Fromentin fleuriste (9, rue Saint-Florentin, Paris 8e), la Direction des Parcs et Jardins de la Ville de Paris.
La verrerie du bar a été aimablement prêtée par le Cognac Rémy Martin et le Whisky Haig (commercialisés par Rémy et Associés, à Levallois).

LUC FERRARI : ELEMENTS D'UN PARCOURS CONFUS...

J'ai réalisé des travaux qui s'écartent plus ou moins des préoccupations musicales pures et dont certains font appel à une rencontre entre branches diverses de ce qui pourrait être un même arbre. Mon problème était d'essayer d'exprimer, à travers des moyens différents, des idées, des sensations, des intuitions qui passent, et aussi de représenter des observations de la réalité du monde quotidien et social. Ceci peut s'extérioriser sous forme de textes, d'écriture instrumentale, de compositions électroacoustiques, de reportages sonores, de films, de spectacles audio-visuels, etc.
Dans le fond, je me demande si je ne suis pas perdu dans un labyrinthe dont j'explore les différents couloirs. C'est une image, bien sûr : c'est celle de l'individu. La société, elle, voudrait homogénéiser tout ça et, pour plus de facilité, réduire au maximum les choix. Ainsi le pouvoir peut-il s'installer et durer.
Déjouer par la diversité? Quelle prétention!
Le droit à l'hétérogénéité? Quel problème!

Luc Ferrari

DIDIER FLAMAND

Après ses études secondaires, il commence sans trop savoir pourquoi des études de médecine qu'il abandonne pour des cours de photographie. Attiré par la mise en scène, il prépare aussi le concours de l'INSAS à Bruxelles. Sa rencontre, à la Faculté de Vincennes, avec les comédiens de la section Cinéma-Théâtre, lui fait découvrir alors, en y prenant goût, le métier d'acteur sans qu'il abandonne cependant son désir de mettre en scène un jour.
C'est ainsi qu'il suit également des cours chez Tania Balachova et Andréas Voutsinas. En 1974, une double rencontre est le point de départ de sa carrière d'acteur : Marguerite Duras lui confie un de ses principaux rôles dans "Indian Song" et Serge Maets l'engage pour jouer dans "le Pain noir". Parallèlement et ce jusqu'en 1978, il ouvre un atelier d'initiation au travail de l'acteur, à l'Ecole Polytechnique et à la Faculté des Sciences.
C'est avec des étudiants et des comédiens de l'Atelier Andréas Voutsinas qu'il fonde, en 1978, sa propre compagnie, "Retour de Gulliver", pour laquelle il écrit et met en scène différents spectacles dont "Ecce Homo" et "Prends bien garde aux zeppelins".

L'ATEM

L'Atelier Théâtre et Musique a été fondé par Georges Aperghis en 1976, à l'occasion d'une expérience de création originale, produite par le FIC et le Festival d'Automne dans le quartier Centre-Sud de Bagnolet.
Après six mois de travail en relation avec la population du quartier, une première version de "la Bouteille à la mer" fut présentée sous chapiteau, une deuxième reprise dans une deuxième version pour la Biennale de Venise et le Festival d'Automne. Depuis cette première expérience, l'ATEM cherche à mener de front, sous la direction artistique de Georges Aperghis, la recherche d'un nouveau langage basé sur l'interaction du son, du geste, du mot et de l'image, et l'insertion de cette recherche dans la réalité de tous les jours.
Depuis 1976, une dizaine de créations de l'ATEM ont été présentées aussi bien à Bagnolet que dans des festivals et des tournées en France et à l'étranger. Citons notamment : "Marchand de plaisirs, marchand d'oublies" (Fest. d'Avignon et Fest. d'Automne 77), "la Tête dans la valise" et "Méthode pratique pour se perdre" (New Festival de Baltimore 78, USA).

MUSIQUE EN THEATRE
ARC

création

SOCIETE I
ou
le pouvoir déshabillé
par les écrits perdus
de
LUC FERRARI
une production de
L'ATEM
réalisée par
DIDIER FLAMAND

MUSEE D'ART MODERNE
DE LA VILLE DE PARIS
SALLE NEW YORK
16 AV. DE NEW YORK
PARIS 16è
METRO : ALMA-MARCEAU

à 20 h.30 les
mercredi 22	
jeudi 23	avril
vendredi 24	
mardi 28	
mercredi 29	avril
jeudi 30	
lundi 4	
mardi 5	mai
mercredi 6	

PRIX DES PLACES 20F ET 10F (TARIF REDUIT)

Société I
Society I

This score involved a seven-strong orchestra and provided the musicians with a set of rules, just like in a parlour game. Each musician, while following their score, developed an absurd relationship with society, becoming torn between the individual and the collective. They stuck to the score, playing their part without ever being able to communicate with each other. The hierarchical structure given as an example here is that of the orchestra, which is in fact taken as a symbol, or a microcosm, of society as a whole.

Here are some extracts from the original score:
This score should be enacted in a bar or in a cabaret. There is some kind of stage or raised platform and a bar area with tables scattered about, around a centrepiece, named "counter".

A few musicians or actors, real or fake, are on stage and have a score, real or fake.
(I don't know whether this score exists, which is why in its absence it can be replaced by a fake score which would thereby become real. It's just like laws — before you invent them, they don't exist, but once you've invented them, they exist as laws, sacred texts set in stone.)

They also have a list of things to do, called: Action Score.

They can repeat an action several times, or perform a series of actions in a loop, as they wish or see fit, responding to the overall organisation of the ensemble at any particular time.

At the end of the action, they start again from the beginning of the score.
They must bear in mind that one action must hinder the other performers, and if necessary, take the disturbance to the point of disarray.

In its modest way, *Society I* symbolises society as a whole. A certain number of people are gathered in a given place, a playing field where the gestures and movements of a number of individuals are created.

These people have their own private lives, and are therefore independent from one another, but they live together within a society ruled by laws, habits, customs and conventions. So that's the 1965 score. I mention it because it was a starting point.

In the Autumn of 1980, Maurice Fleuret asked me to stage a theatre-and-music show for the Musée d'Art Moderne, where he worked. I suggested putting on *Société I,* and told him I would like to work not with musicians, as was usually the case for musical theatre, but instead with actors. I also suggested bringing in Didier Flamand, a director whose work I had seen and found very interesting.

Didier Flamand and I decided to set up improvisations based on the original score, and to build up a script from there. He gathered a group of actors, each of whom could more or less play an instrument. This is how the orchestra came together.

For three weeks, we rehearsed and wrote the script. I also wrote the music based on the instrumental abilities of each actor. Some could only play three notes, so I composed accordingly. I wouldn't know how to describe the script, if only to say it was based on a few simple ideas but their stage and musical execution was complex:

A foreign orchestra gives a concert one night in a provincial casino. The "musicians" are dressed in "very retro" black tie. They speak an imaginary language. We see the orchestra as a structure in which power emanates from the composer and therefore from the score. The conductor-cum-pianist in charge introduces the work (a caricature of an intellectual study by the author). He uses a made-up, but perfectly comprehensible, language. The actors, with whom Didier Flamand has collaborated for years, are used to working with invented languages – it's a research practice pertaining to the field of communication studies, whereby the language is coherent without any of the words being known.

Luc Ferrari

Société I

Partition
et Texte

1

Sequence I

flûte — ... k ombarde : (comme un accident)

clar — ... (comme un coup)

violon — (8ᵛᵃ) thème folk qui vient comme un accident et sur les notes suivantes :

harpe — (8ᵛᵃ) (comme un accident)

piano — (arco jeté) ... (tête)

violoncelle — (comme un accident)

Batterie — cymb. et peaux (mail. jeux) rythme folk : comme un accident (avec violon)

Perc — (arco piano) petit métal tôle-cloches peaux aiguës (lame d'acier) (comme un accident) sirène + boules

Sequence 2

Même jeu que séquence I
(sans les accidents)

Sequence 1 — Suite

- Colère du Batteur
- "Ligne mélodique"
- Il critique le violoniste
- Le pianiste calme le batteur et rétabli son autorité.

Séquence 2 — Suite

1) — Le batteur regarde la partition
   — "Partition Blanche"

2) Chacun découvre avec effroi sa propre partition blanche

3) On trouve par terre les notes qui sont tombées du papier à musique
   le batteur raconte le maléfice
   Perc — jeu expressioniste

4) Déchirement rageur de la partition
   Discours sur la position : "Perdu le Rythme" "Perdu la mesure"
   "Prendre des mesures"

5) chacun prend des mesures en un jeu qui s'accélère
   "Eureka !..." "Nombre d'or"
   Congratulations générales, grande satisfaction
   Plaisanteries légères

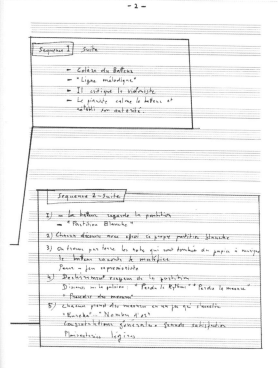

Sequence 3   1: Tempo modéré   2: Rapide   3: Lent   4: disloqué

départ ensemble

fl.

clar

V.   — groupes sur notes I

Vc   — groupes sur notes I

Hp   — groupes et accords sur notes I

Piano — groupes et accords sur notes I

Bat.

Perc — jeu médium   jeu aigu   jeu grave   jeu désarticulé

Sequence 3 | 1 Jeu normal
2 Jeu accéléré
3 Jeu ralenti
4 Jeu disloqué

de + en + disjoint

Lutte avec
les instruments

Sequence 3 suite

- Lutte avec les instruments
- chute des instrumentistes
- Conte fantastique : Explication du Maléfice
- proposition du "Voyage Initiatique"
- "Jungle"
- "De l'autre côté du miroir"
- Saut hors de la scène ...

5

Sequence 4 : Voyage initiatique

fl. Clar. Violon = son bref aigu (comme un signal) + longtemps de
silence (déplacement)

Les autres instrumentistes chacun avec un petit instrument :
Claves - maracas - WB - crotales - guiro - etc...

Pour tout le monde : son bref (apel) + silence et déplacement

Sequence 4 suite : d | Procession (genre folle, mais non affolée)

fl + V

clar   répéter en variant

Vc 9:

Batterie / (cd pentalin)   (timbal)   (peau)   permanent et
régulier

Perc (Tumba pontalip)   petits rythmes d'agrément

+ claves tenu par un instrumentiste   régulier

e | Piano   etc...

f | Piano

6

Sequence 4

Tous les instrumentistes se déplacent et se dispersent dans
la salle obscure et entourent le public.

a) déplacement sonore et habitation de l'espace
b) rencontre hasardeuse par couple et peu sonore
c) jeu de lumière clinotante qui soit et effraie les instrumentistes
d) les instrumentistes s'organisent en procession

d | Les instrumentistes se groupent en Procession
et se dirigent lentement vers la scène côté Piano
tout en jouant la musique page 5 - Seq. 4. d

e | Lorsque les instrumentistes sont arrivés au bord
de la scène, le pianiste qui est déjà là,
joue alors un arpège en do mineur (Lento)

f | Puis il nomme les notes de la gamme suivante :

Sequence 5 | Musique aquatique

Improvisation Piano - Harpe - flute - Violon
sur le mode suivant :

Batterie : cymb. (mail-feutre)
Perc.   : cloches et bois (?)

Sequence 6 | Recomposition

I

Tempo : ♩ = 76

P   développer

V + fl.

Voix femmes
+ Harpe to octave

Rires perlés

Bat.

répétition

Perc.   Toumba

Séquence 5

Les instrumentistes dans un état d'émerveillement juvénile reprennent leur place tout en parlant en chuchotant musicalement entre eux.

Les femmes égrennent des rires perlés et musicaux.

Lorsque la seg. 5 est suffisamment développée le pianiste enchaine à la seg. 6 n° 1

Séquence 6 | suite

Après les rires enchainer 2

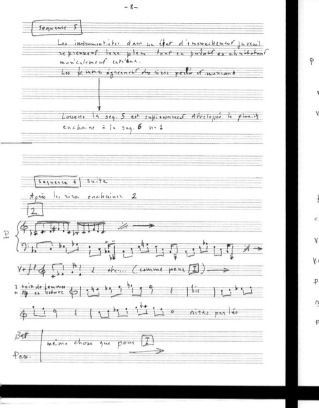

[2]

V+ [...] etc.... (comme pour [I]) →

2 voix de femmes + hp en octave [...] | bis | [...]

[...] rires perlés

Batt. | même chose que pour [I] →

Perc.

Après les rires, enchainer 3 (Séquence 6 = fin)

[3]

P

V. Fl.

Voix + Hp | [...] | bis | répéter si besoin est →

Séquence 7 | accord tournant

fl.

clar. — tous les instruments indépendants avec la même nuance

V.

V.C.

P.

Batt. cymb.

Perc. cloche V.

au tant fort

Pendant toute la séquence 6, les instrumentistes continuent leur jeu joyeux et émerveillé. Continuent à parler entre eux fort en jouant, usant de leur voix d'une façon musicale.

Pendant que se développe le n°3, arrive le "marchand de partition" qui apporte bruillamment une énorme partition

Séquence 7

Les instrumentistes sont progressivement entrainés dans un tourbillon créé par le son lui-même.

Il oscillent d'abord, puis de plus en plus

jusqu'à être éjecté de leur siège

→ Chute des instrumentistes

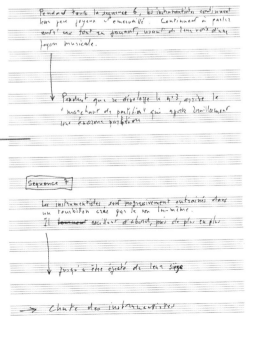

Séquence 8 | informatique

a) Chaque instrument (indépendant) joue un son aigu - un silence long - un son grave - un silence long - etc... généralement piano (musique ponctuelle)

b) Ils jouent de plus en plus nerveusement

c) Ils jouent # des groupes de notes rapides et disjoints

d) grande nervosité musicale

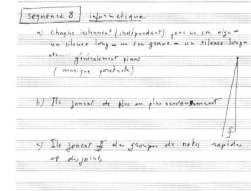

- Colère
- Arrivée de la "partition informatique"
- Explication du mode de jeu.

Séquence 8 | Les instrumentistes déplient progressivement
la partition

La partition commence à envahir l'espace

Ils sont perdus dans la partition
certains s'enroulent dedans

- Colère. Ils se débarassent de la partition
 - "Camarade, organisons-nous"
 - "comité de création"
 - Composition de la partition collective
 - Découverte de la Roméo
 - Distribution de la Partition Collective

13

Séquence 9 | Société I

Chaque instrumentiste donne le signe de départ
Ils jouent ensemble un son bref et aigü
suivi d'un long silence. Ceci 3 fois de suite très
ensemble. La quatrième fois l'ensemble est moins
parfait, puis tout commence à se détériorer.
Chacun joue quand il peut. etc....
Les instrumentistes tout en regardant leur
partition commencent individuellement à
quitter la scène en emportant leur instrument
et leur partition.
Ils entreprennent une série d'actions individuelles
en circulant dans la salle (autour du public)
et dans les coulisses.
Ils jouent des éléments sonores et brefs de leur
instrument et en observant entre chaque action
un temps de silence très long.
Ils prononcent chacun des phrases absurdes
et plus ou moins répétitives.
"- J'ai été sincère" - "Quelle heure est-il"
- "Où suis-je" - "Il n'y a plus d'Européens"
- "Je vous aime" - "C'est ici le chemin de l'opéra"
etc...
Développement assez long et assez lent de cette
séquence.

14

(Séquence 9 suite)
Petit à petit un thème apparait et les instrumentistes
se regroupent en s'organisant autour de ce thème
mais sans jamais le formuler vraiment,
comme maladroitement joué.

Séquence 10 | Procession

Tempo ♩ = 144

Violon [...] développer

clar + fl. [...] déve....

Vc [...] etc...
développer

Tout en jouant les instrumentistes s'approchent de la
scène côté piano.
Le pianiste qui est déjà là commence à jouer le
thème de la fin "Le Lied" et chante d'une
voix de fausset une mélodie (mélopée) très triste

Lent

[...] etc....

S'accompagnant ainsi il chante le chant final pendant
que l'orchestre tout en continuant à jouer avec de plus
en plus d'hésitation montent sur la scène et reprennent
leur place. La musique s'arrête comme incapable de
continuer
T.S.V.P

15

Tous les musiciens semblent de paralyser
Ils lèvent la tête, regardent le public.
Ils essaient de parler, de communiquer,
mais n'y arrivent pas.

Ils restent figés dans leur incapacité

C'est la fin

Noir

Fin

Avril 1981

J.Venni

Les Grandes Répétitions

The Great Rehearsals

The arts should not remain isolated from each other. The idea was to show the rehearsal of a great work captured in its most significant moments. Not only can these films be considered essential documents (given the importance of the subject and the way it is treated), but I believe it was the first time in France that contemporary music was broadcast on television.

Five television documentaries, 16mm dual band
Five portraits of musicians, co-directed with Gérard Patris
Produced by the Service de la Recherche, ORTF

1965–68
— between 45 & 55 minutes

Ce soir
Hommage à
Edgard Varèse
(1883-1965)

Le Groupe
de Recherches Musicales
DE L'
RTF
présente

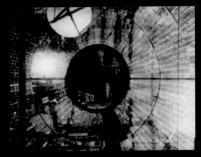

une émission de
Luc Ferrari
·
réalisée par
S.G. Patris

luc ferrari
LES GRANDES RÉPÉTITIONS
s.g. patris

Luc FERRARI

LES GRANDES
RÉPÉTITIONS
Five portraits of musicians,
co-directed with Gérard
Patris

Olivier Messiaen
Homage to Varèse
Karlheinz Stockhausen
Hermann Scherchen
Cecil Taylor

Les Grandes Répétitions
The Great Rehearsals

Olivier Messiaen

Filmed on location during the last rehearsals before the concert, Messiaen explains each movement as he guides the the instrumentalists through his piece. 44 minutes

Cecil Taylor

Joining a rehearsal with bassist Alan Silva, saxophonist Jimmy Lyons and drummer Andrew Cyrille, Cecil Taylor discusses the politics surrounding the emergence of Free Jazz in North America. 44 minutes

Karlheinz Stockhausen

Filmed in a Cologne recording studio, Karlheinz Stockhausen discusses the genesis of his work *Momente*, inspired by love and dedicated to his wife. During the rehearsals he converses with the soprano, the instrumentalists and the choirs of the West Germany Radio Symphony orchestra. 45 minutes

Hermann Scherchen

Filmed shortly before Scherchen's death, this rehearsal shows the conductor directing Bach's *The Art of Fugue* with a contemporary instrumental ensemble from Paris. 57 minutes

Edgar Varèse

In the first half of this film Ferdinand Ouelette, Iannis Xenakis, Olivier Messiaen, Hermann Scherchen, André Jolivet, Pierre Schaeffer, Pierre Boulez and Marcel Duchamp offer an homage to Varèse who passed away days before the scheduled filming of his rehearsals. In the second half of this film Bruno Maderna rehearses *Desert*. 66 minutes

On set photos from *The Great Rehearsals*, courtesy INA
and Centre National de la Cinematographie
Photographs by Laszlo Ruszka, INA – 1966 (above, previous and overleaf)

Und so weiter

And So On, And So Forth

For piano and magnetic tape
Tape produced at the GRM, Paris
Commissioned by Radio Bremen
WP Musika Viva, 1966
LP Wergo, 60046 — 1969

1965–66
— 18 minutes

Page 12 from the score for *Und so weiter*, 1965-66,
courtesy Maison ONA Editions

To put an end to clusters, an ingenious pianist (multiplied by twelve), surpasses himself. He encounters birds and fireworks on his way.

Und so weiter is a composition for electric piano and magnetic tape. It revisits and refines the ideas developed in *Hétérozygote [Heterozygote]*. Pieces like *Flashes*, *Hétérozygote* and *Und so weiter* all encourage the audience to become active listeners. In this work, the sound sources are ambiguous; on the one hand, they are related to different anecdotes; on the other, it's hard to tell who is playing, the piano or the tape.

Current experiments with amplified traditional instruments herald a future rich in musical discoveries, both in terms of spatialisation and of playing techniques, because the contact microphone enables us to hear, and magnifies, many sounds that would otherwise be inaudible. This encounter between an amplified piano and a magnetic tape spells the failure of anecdote. The direct piano, albeit transfigured by electro-acoustics, finds a place within the multiplicity of the recorded piano, but that multiplicity shatters any notion of an origin. Then the sounds are altered and, in this game of failure, the piano totally looses its own reality to mingle with that of the magnetic tape.

This is an encounter between the living piano and the dead piano. The anecdotal potential of the piano is pushed to its last limits. A peak is reached when it is no longer possible to add to the accumulation of maxima, or to further rarefy the minima. The internal musical dynamic of the work rests on a balance between those two poles.

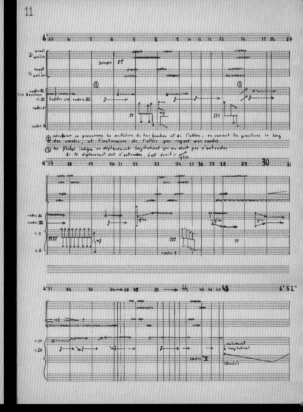

Extract from the score for *Und so weiter*, 1965–66, courtesy Maison ONA Editions

Symphonie inachevée

Unfinished Symphony

And in 1966,
I *un*finished my
symphony.

For full orchestra (Four flutes, three oboes, one English horn, three clarinets, one bass clarinet, three bassoons, one contrabassoon, four horns, three trumpets, three trombones, one tuba, two harps, one piano, four percussionists, ten violins, ten violas, ten celli, six double basses and two conductors)

WP for the inauguration of the Maison de la Culture, Rennes, 28 January 1969, by the ORTF Philharmonic Orchestra, dir. Charles Bruck and Konstantin Simonovich
Editions Moeck, Celle, Germany

1963–66
— 35 minutes 48 seconds

Tinguely

From recordings at an exhibition of Jean Tinguely's 'Baluba' works, named after the Bantu Tribe in Congo. Tinguely expressed his sympathy for Patrice Lumumba, a warrior fighting for Congo's freedom and independence who was murdered in 1961. The savage and ironic dance of these eliminated, rejected expressions illustrated the tragedy of the fighters. Once the 110V Liliput engine is activated sculptures rotate in random and unpredictable ways.

Jean Tinguely's 'Baluba' works, installation view

Musique concrète for a television programme directed by C. Caspari
NDR, Hamburg

XIIIᵉ AUTOMNE DE VARSOVIE

Interrupteur

Interrupter

The first characteristic attempt at immobile music although that concern was already present in *Composé-Composite* and in the music for *Egypte ô Egypte*. This piece is a turning point in my work, in the sense that it 'almost' got rid of post-serial mythology.

I wanted to write music that was as motionless as possible. It didn't quite turn out that way, as it's a pretty busy score. The idea was to have instrumental continuities that ran from beginning to end. One instrument might go up for ten minutes and then come down for ten, while another instrument would go up for three minutes and then come down for seventeen minutes, and so forth. Each instrument had its schematic and every so often, some lines would intersect, producing various unexpected events. That was the basic idea. What interested me was to settle on a duration and to see what concept each instrument would come up with. I'm starting to work with durations again, trying to organise them into a completely aleatory composition; it's all written out, but the compositional data are generated solely by chance. I take the duration and use it as a painter would, like a canvas.

For ten instruments (English horn, clarinet, bass clarinet, horn, trumpet, violin, viola, cello, two percussionists)
WP Barcelona, May 1968, by the EIMCP Ensemble, dir. Konstantin Simonovich
LP EMP, 1C063 11133 — 1997

1967
— approximately 20 minutes

Original programme, 1969 Automne de Varsovie

Presque Rien N°1
ou le Lever du jour au bord de la mer

Almost Nothing N°1
or Sunrise by the Sea

Presque Rien n°1 had come to him out of nowhere, one night when he had placed his microphones on the window ledge facing a small fishing harbour. Some would call this Minimalism, but for him, it was more like a sequence shot, just one take, with minimum intervention. — Brunhild Ferrari

After the total disappearance of abstract sounds, this piece can be considered as a 'sound slide' and the culmination of a whole process. It renders, as faithfully and realistically as possible, a fisherman's village as it awakens. — Luc Ferrari

Stereo magnetic tape
LP Deutsche Grammophon, 2 561 041 — 1970
CD INA-GRM, INA C 2008 — 1995

1967
— 20 minutes

Luc Ferrari 1965, photographed by Brunhild Ferrari

Société II — Et si le piano était un corps de femme

Society II or What if the Piano Were a Woman's Body?

One could say that this piece falls into the category of music theatre in so far as the four soloists vie with each other for the piano's body, which remains desperately cold. If so inclined, but it's not certain, one might almost see this as a caricature of machismo.

For four soloists and sixteen instruments (flute, oboe, clarinet, bassoon, horn, trumpet, trombone, four violins, two violas, two celli, double bass, piano, three percussionsists)
WP The Avignon Festival, 1968, by the EIMCP Ensemble, dir. Konstantin Simonovic
LP Deutsche Grammophon, 2543 004 — 1970
Editions Moeck

1967
— 30 minutes

Les Jeunes Filles ou Société III

Young Women or Society III

I agreed to make this film for Hansjörg Pauli. Ever since *Hétérozygote* and the new series which I named *Société* and also since the television programmes I produced with Patris, I have been more attentive to people's gestures and words. I have increasingly been interested in observing society; this has gradually drawn my work away from music's traditional abstraction (even when it is called musique concrète), and it has led me to look for meaning, which I see as a "commitment". In that sense, cinema is much more convenient than music, probably because music has not yet found the style and meaning appropriate to its time; because we are living in the Twentieth century with Nineteenth century concepts. The modern world slips out of our hands like a bar of soap. So, my interest for the cinema comes from the fact that it can convey meanings directly (i.e., without having to go through some hermetic aesthetics). That is the main reason I am attracted to this medium. Of course, one has to learn, and I have learned a little with Patris, but I want to learn more, and that is broadly speaking the reason I am making this film. To learn and to find out whether I am capable of making a film on my own — I have been wondering about that.

16mm film, dual band
Production: TV Hamburg, 3rd program, NDR (in German)

1967
— 25 minutes

Film stills from *Les Jeunes Filles,* courtesy NDR

LES JEUNES FILLES

Die jungen Mädchen

Société III

LUC FERRARI

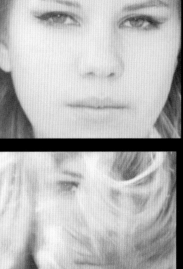

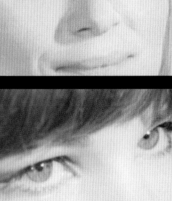

Music
Promenade

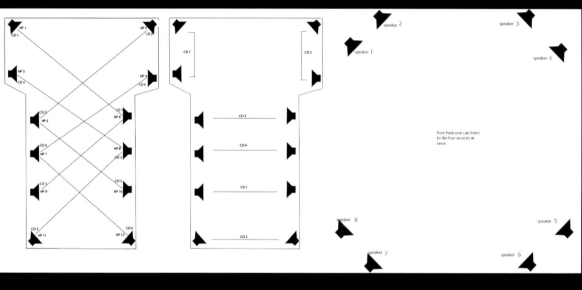

Electroacoustic music
Stereo magnetic tape version
Permanent version for four independent tape recorders
WP Paris, Théâtre de la Musique, 16 March 1970
LP Wergo, 60046 — 1969
CD INA-GRM, INA C 2008 — 1995

1964–69
— 20 minutes

Music Promenade for magnetic tape was created over two periods: a recording period, from 1964 to 1967, and an editing period from 1966 to 1969. A conception that stretches over five years is tantamount to no conception at all. As a consequence the piece gets a hackneyed and insipid title, and it has no formal-stylistic-aesthetic character of its own.
The term Promenade (I'll ignore the word "music" which is only there for decorative purposes, hence I gave it the English spelling, but it would probably be better to say "amusic" or "anamusic" or "paramusic", in the military sense of the term) can be understood in different ways:

Promenade first refers to a number of years spent on tape-recording trips, recording everything that caught my attention.

Secondly, at the editing stage, it's a journey through memory, through those elements that have remained more or less realistic or that have become more or less abstract. For example, a conversation loses its specific human identity to take on a dramatic meaning as sound.

It also includes punctuations (the only musical elements) borrowed from my own earlier works or from other works encountered here and there, and selected not so much on their musical merits but because they provide interruptions.

A Promenade, that is the objective. Devised to run continuously on four independent tape recorders, so that as long as the piece lasts, there can be no exact repetition. It is meant to be placed in a busy location, where people are constantly coming and going, so the audience wanders through it.

Lastly, it is a Promenade through traditional or specialist studios at Radio Stockholm, Hamburg, Paris, Amiens, Baden-Baden.

Music Promenade plans, 1964

So

Musique concrète for the film *Elektronische Musik* directed by Josef Anton Riedl

1967
— 2 minutes 23 seconds

La Famille Bang

The Bang Family

Musical based on a poetico-erotico-sentimental fiction text

1966–69

Société IV —
Mécanique Collectivité Individu

Society IV – Group – Individual Mechanics

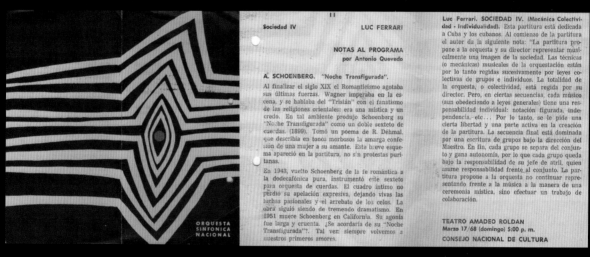

Programme for Orquesta Sinfonica Nacional

For full orchestra (four flutes, three oboes, English horn, three clarinets, bass clarinet, three bassoons, contrabassoon, four horns, four trumpets, four trombones, two tubas, piano, four percussionists, two assistant percussionists, twenty violins, ten violas, ten celli, eight double basses)
WP Havana, Cuba, 1968, by the Symphonic Orchestra, dir. Manuel Duchesne
Maison ONA Editions

1967
— approximately 50 minutes

Theatre action, a "sociodrama" taking music as a starting point, and involving the Majority and the Opposition. Participation or conflict between musicians and audience, encouraged or not by a mediator. This game can be staged like a real show and in a real theatre, but every performance includes unknown elements: what direction will the audience give to the action?

Luc Ferrari **Société V**

"Participation or not participation"

Première mondiale

pour
6 percussionistes
1 acteur et le public

Animateur Guy Jacquet

Percussion Jean-Pierre Drouet, Sylvio Gualda, Michel
Diego Masson, Jacques Carré, Guy Berlioz.

For six percussionists, one actor and the audience
WP Nuits de la Fondation Maeght, Saint-Paul-de-Vence, 1969, by J.-P. Drouet, S. Gualda, M. Lorin, D. Masson, J. Carré, G. Berlioz. MC: Guy Jacquet

1967–69
— indeterminate duration

Directions for the audience
(The following text should be mimeographed and handed out to the audience. The term "musician" can be replaced by another word, depending on the action envisaged.)

A certain number of actions are suggested in the score.
The audience can make a choice and ask the musicians to execute such or such action.
The game leader is there to compère, arbitrate and answer questions.

Participation method
First part: the audience can choose from actions numbered 1 to 20. These numbers correspond to musical actions, which can be heard in this first section. Ask the game leader for explanations, or ask the participants who look like they understand how the piece works.

Second part: the same numbers are available, but this time they are grouped into families. Members of the audience can pick either a number or a family. The number is specific, whereas the family enables the musicians to choose several numbers. All this is explained by the game leader.

Third part: the audience can choose from 4 ensemble actions. That is to say that instead of asking the musicians to perform individual actions, as in the first two sections, the musical elements suggested here are combinations performed by the whole ensemble.

Commands for the ensemble action:
a) imitation; b) participation; c) contradiction; d) reaction.

The musical result should be the "sound image" of the terminology, the composer having endeavoured to find a writing method that enabled him to illustrate those terms through auditory equivalents.

Participation or not participation asks the audience to come out of its silence. They are given a voice, they can choose, complain, proclaim, express their opinion. They are allowed to influence the form and discuss the actions. They can either intervene individually or in groups. Therefore, through their voiced action, they contribute to performing the score.

Critical reflection on a realizable.

(…) having seen the score, he decided to have it done as part of a festival he was running: Les Nuits de la Fondation Maeght [Nights at the Maeght Foundation]. This choice surprised and worried me, but I didn't prevent it, out of weakness (people so rarely volunteer for this kind of experiment), and also out of curiosity, I wondered whether my score was really "realisable". I was sceptical mostly because I suspected Saint-Paul-de-Vence types and Maeght Foundation audiences may be more predisposed to soak up the Mediterranean sun by luxury swimming pools (the beaches are so very dirty) than to take part in a political drama.

The evening was a total flop and the audience, enraged, flung off the foam-cushion that were used as seats and asked for their money back, which I think they got.
What had happened? Was the audience not proficient enough?

I think that the audience is always more or less proficient, but the conditions of the performance should have been planned differently, that is to say, when a thing is risky and involves unpredictable factors, then the practical side really needs to be worked out in advance, down to the smallest detail.

For example, a banal but legitimate criticism was that the audience were being asked to take part in the performance, and yet ticket prices didn't reflect that fact. Another criticism, just as justified, was that the architectural setting should have lent itself to, and even incited, audience participation. Lastly, and this is why I should have refused, the venue was the kind that selects its audiences on social grounds, rather than allow for some diversity. Clearly, that audience was more interested in attending a high society event, complete with hero and remarkable action, than a chaotic event which didn't look like it had started and which, once it was over, gave the impression it hadn't taken place at all.

Still, a lot of things happened there. In particular, and that's fascinating, it showed that my score was poorly drafted, it was badly worded in that it didn't set out the basic conditions of its performability. It stuck to exposing the action, without ambiguity, as if the process only depended on the score. As if the action only involved performers who were music specialists, and therefore venues that were determined musically. Consequently, the excess of prescriptive commands didn't leave the participants enough freedom to really "compose" in varied and contradictory directions.

One last very important thing: I had to choose the participants and, even though they gave it their best, given the shortcomings of the score, I should have gone about it the other way round. The enactors, or a group defining itself as such, should have chosen the score, because it is that choice that matters. The enactment begins the moment that choice is made. There's a huge difference between choosing something and agreeing to do it.

So I rewrote the score, but I think it'd be wrong to consider it complete, it is up to the enactors to make it their own and to compose it based on the circumstances in which it will exist. Having said that, I am not sure the new version is better or more realisable than the previous one. How can I know!

Société VI
— Liberté, Liberté chérie

Society VI – Liberty, Dear Liberty

First page of *Society VI* score, courtesy Maison ONA Editions

For audience solo
Text-score

1967–69
— indeterminate duration

Tautologos III ou Vous plairait-il de tautologuer avec moi [18]

Tautologos III or Would You Like to Tautologue with Me?

For any group of instruments
Text-score
WP Semana Nueva Musica, Madrid, 1969
Editions Moeck
LP EMI, 1C063 11133—1977

1969
— indeterminate duration

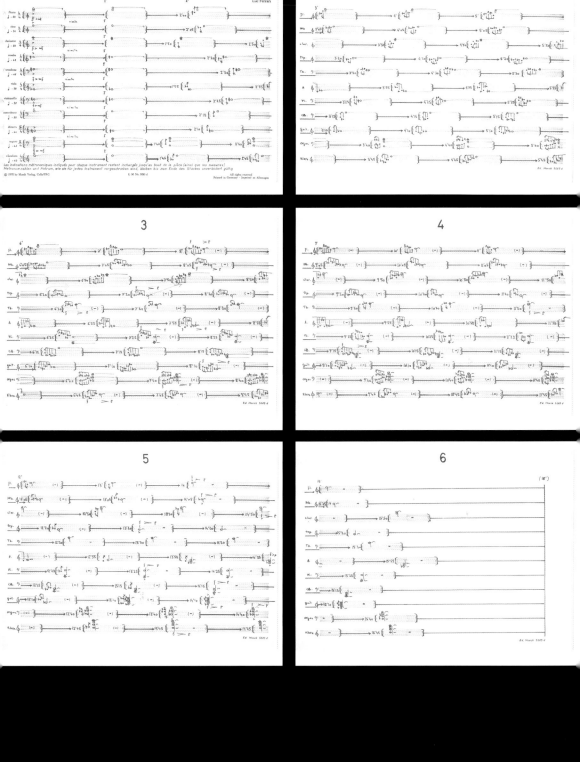

Extract from the score for *Tautologos III*. Courtesy Editions Moec

A systematic explanation of the tautological process I have used non systematically (because I don't like systems) since 1960. This realisable allows professionals or amateurs to experiment with repetitive mechanisms using musical, theatrical or visual elements chosen by themselves. It can also be used as the basis for educational work.

With whom and when can one tautologue?
Tautologos III was devised for any group of instruments, the minimum number being arbitrarily set at seven (seven instruments or several groups of instruments). The score can also be performed by a full orchestra, but with the utmost caution. So it can range from seven instruments up to a symphony orchestra. The audience itself is invited to invent *Tautologos III*, along the same guidelines as the orchestra, in the form of "would you also like to tautologue?"

Tautologos can be done in a traditional concert hall, just like a concert piece, with the musicians on stage, or it can be done in a non traditional venue, with the musicians dotted across the room, or in a concert hall with the musicians dotted around the auditorium, on various locations where the audience comes and goes constantly; or it can be done as a sound environment, with the musicians scattered about, individually or in small groups (if there are enough of them), etc.

It can be done by non professional musicians who, having attended the concert, get hold of the score and decide to tautologue at home. Indeed, one can tautologue with one's friends, using music or words, each person having chosen a sentence. Sensuality is not ruled out. Tautologos can even be done without sound, just with gestures, as one can also move tautologically.

How long should one tautologue?
In a concert setting, the duration of the realisation is variable. It is more or less set by the musicians beforehand. The action can go on for a very long time and thus take on, through relentless tautology, an incantatory quality. (One shouldn't give this word a mystical meaning.) If it's a venue where people constantly come and go, the performance can be quasi-permanent, depending on the abilities and endurance of the protagonists of course.

What is a tautology and what is *Tautologos III*?
It is the superimposition of several phenomena of varying lengths which, through continuous repetition, meet in constantly renewed configurations.

For example:
In *Tautologos III*, the author doesn't impose any restraint, but leaves it up to the participants to choose their own action, and the duration of the gap between the action and its

repetition. The author also leaves them free to choose how to experience time. They can decide to trust their instinct only, or on the contrary rely on mechanical devices, such as a pocket metronome, or on electronic devices, like a computer.

What matters is, firstly, that each action should be chosen for its individual quality, but it should also differ from or combine with, or not combine with, the other individual actions selected.

Secondly, the duration of each silence: each individual silence must vary in length, to allow for a maximum number of overall combinations.

Thirdly, manipulation: whereas the first two elements refer more particularly to the individual, the idea of manipulation refers more particularly to the group.

Durations are fixed individually but when one action comes into contact with another, the participant can (if he feels the need to) react by inflecting his own action in response. That is to say that, while sticking to his individual action, the participant can nonetheless transform one or several of its characteristics. Therefore, in time, the original actions will evolve and may even go as far as to alter the general shape of the realisation.

In short, *Tautologos III* goes from the individual to the collective, touching on notions of action, duration and time, which in turn determine the way actions can be altered as a result of successive encounters.

How should one tautologue?
The author takes the example of a musical realisation, but realisations based on other media, or combinations of other media — speech, gestures, images, etc. — should be organised along the same principles.

One should plan a rehearsal, to enable the participants to discuss, work out calculations, and choose the various elements as a group.

The tautologists can wire their instruments, either with contact microphones or traditional microphones, or with any other electroacoustic device, for simple amplification or for complex transformation.

1) Objects or Actions:

Each instrumentalist will choose an action (A) whose duration is relatively brief compared to the silence (S) which completes the action.

The Action-Silence unit is repeated relentlessly and forms a loop whose duration, in principle, remains constant. The action can be brief: complex attack. It can also last longer: sustained note, melodic or rhythmic formula. So, depending on his instrument and on the group, each participant will choose an action which might combine the different criteria applying to a note (simple or complex) or to a group of notes, and which in this case would only constitute one action.

One should bear in mind that an Action, however brief, can itself be extremely complex, and that even when instrumentalists are performing a realisation, various movements and gestures can be introduced.

One can also create a loop, made up of several Action-Inaction units, using elements from heterogeneous domains, e.g., Sound - Inaction - Gesture - Inaction - Sentence - Inaction - Lights - Inaction.

2) Silences or Inactions:

Each instrumentalist will choose a relatively long silence duration. It will depend on the duration of the Action and on the number of participants. Obviously, the duration will vary widely depending on whether there are seven instruments or 150 — still, the organiser may opt for an extremely dense and profuse realisation.

This is where the notion of "organiser" comes in. The organiser is a kind of conductor, a leader, but without the unpleasant hierarchical connotations of that word — though in fact it would be so much better if we could just do without a leader, in charge of conducting the discussions and the rehearsal, and of overseeing the realisation.

The duration of silences can be set by different metronomic movements, as long as they are not multiples. Without wanting to interfere, here are a few examples of the time — duration = silence ratios, roughly calculated.

Tautologos III insert

(T: tautologist; MM: metronomic movement)

T 1 : 10 time units at MM 50 = 11 seconds
T 2 : 11 time units at MM 48 = 12 seconds and 1/5
T 3 : 11 time units at MM 46 = 13 seconds
T 4 : 12 time units at MM 44 = 14 seconds and 3/5

T 5 : 12 time units at MM 42 = 15 seconds and 1/5
T 6 : 13 time units at MM 40 = 17 seconds and 4/5

3) MANIPULATION

As we said, overlaps and encounters can bring the enactors to alter one or more aspects of their action. For example, within a chosen "register", the musician can dispose of several "pitches", which is one of the possible manipulations. Of course, one can imagine many more manipulations, from the subtlest to the roughest.

The duration and the manipulation must be perceptible. Ideally, the realisation should not be mechanical, but each participant, by concentrating on his communication instinct, should manage to create his own time. Only this state of communication-concentration can create a climate that will be meaningful, and show that the tautological phenomenon is a phenomenon which stems from life.

Those who have no musical knowledge may understand these indications, as they are simple. However, I'll sum up a few fundamental principles one should bear in mind:

- permanent repetition of an Action followed by a Silence, with a notion of individual or independent time. This Action-Silence represents the basic rhythm of the repetition;
- superimposition of several Actions-Silences by a given group, each person keeping to their individual rhythm;
- transformation (manipulation) of the Action depending on the encounters due to the tautological mechanism (of the repetitions).

We should add a few words regarding the staged realisations and the blending of different domains. They should reach a sort of hypnotic state through the laws of repetition; there should be so many tautological elements from the most diverse domains, that the absurd walls which "civilisation" imposes on us will collapse for a while.

– So it must be serious.
– Or rather pretentious!
– What is this?

– So, is it serious or not?
– I don't know.

– Is this music?
– It doesn't matter much.

– Do you think you really have created an original work?
– I didn't create a work, it's up to you to create it if you believe that works can still be created…
– Do you fancy yourself a bit of a philosopher?

– Or a bit of a writer?
– Oh, you know, it's all the same, really, painters and musicians too… No, I trust in very simple and very natural things.
– But you write and yet you have none of the qualities that make a real writer, such as style.
– Style?
– Yes, style!
– Who gives a damn about style?
– Excuse me! But the whole of culture…
– To hell with culture.

Extract from the score for *Tautologos III*, sourtesy Editions Moeck

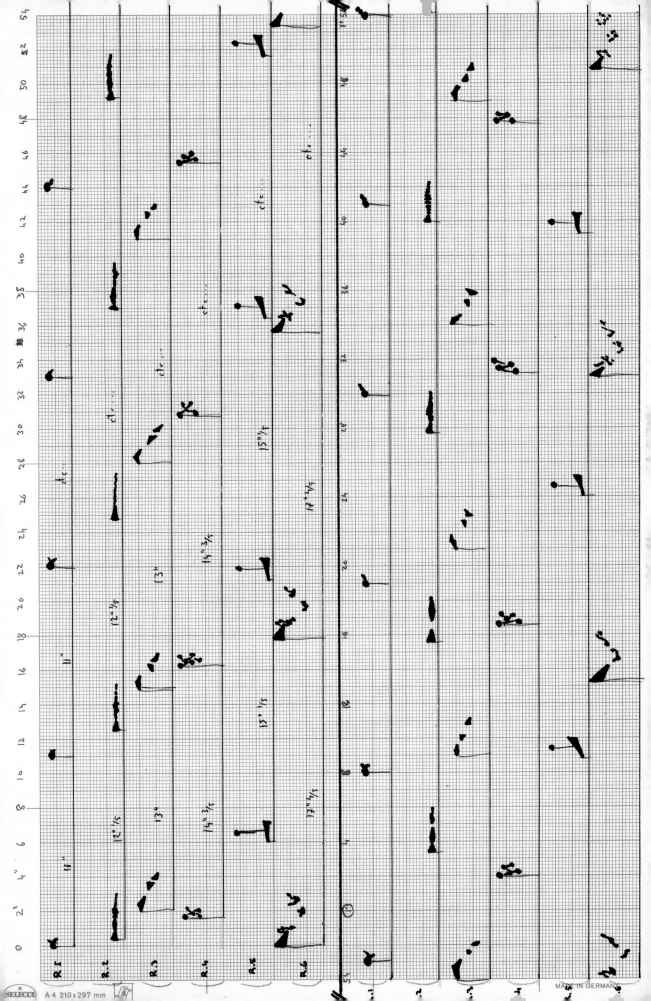

J'ai été coupé

I Was Cut Off

This was made in 1969 from elements that date back to 1962. It is a calm piece in which almost nothing happens. It may even put you to sleep.

I had made a bet with friends that I would entitle my next piece *J'ai été coupé [I was cut or cut short]*. When I went ahead with it, they were surprised I could be so flippant. Then I wrote this text which, in my mind, was to be read while listening to the music. Listening to something while reading a text, the two things having no rationally explicable link, that too was a kind of heterogeneity.

Nothing's going on. We can go to sleep.
And when I woke up, I was cut short.
I don't know whether it's good or bad. Or rather, I do know, but I don't want to say.
This bears no relation to music.
This bears no relation to me, or maybe it bears a relation to both.
Simple as that: I was cut, I'm always being cut.
It's too easy to say: I have never been cut.
Things too get cut, and we are probably too often cut from things.
So, who does the cutting?
There's someone here who cuts, there's always someone who cuts savagely and doesn't say his name, or conceals it, hides it behind his suit.
I was cut.
A lot of other people have been cut too.

Stereo magnetic tape
GRM, Paris
WP GRM concert, Théâtre Récamier, Paris, 1973
LP Philips, 836 885 DSY — 1969, CD SYNOPSYS, SON 4 — 2007
Maison ONA Editions

1960–69
— 12 minutes

J'ai tort, j'ai tort, j'ai mon très grand tort

Mea Culpa, Mea Culpa, Mea Maxima Culpa

A choir where the actors manage, through a surprise effect, to invite the people to a great celebration, joyous and noisy, in which each individual is a component.

imitation-dialogue for mixed-gender choir
Text-score
Editions Moeck (French and German)

1969
— indeterminate duration

Monologos

ould possibly be sung by a
ale singer, but I prefer women.
ould possibly be sung by several
ngers, but after all, why use
veral people when one is enough.
o, *Monologos* was composed
r a female soloist accompanying
rself with a tambourine.

olo voice and electroacoustic device
héâtre Récamier, Paris, 1973, by Elise Ross

970
- indeterminate duration

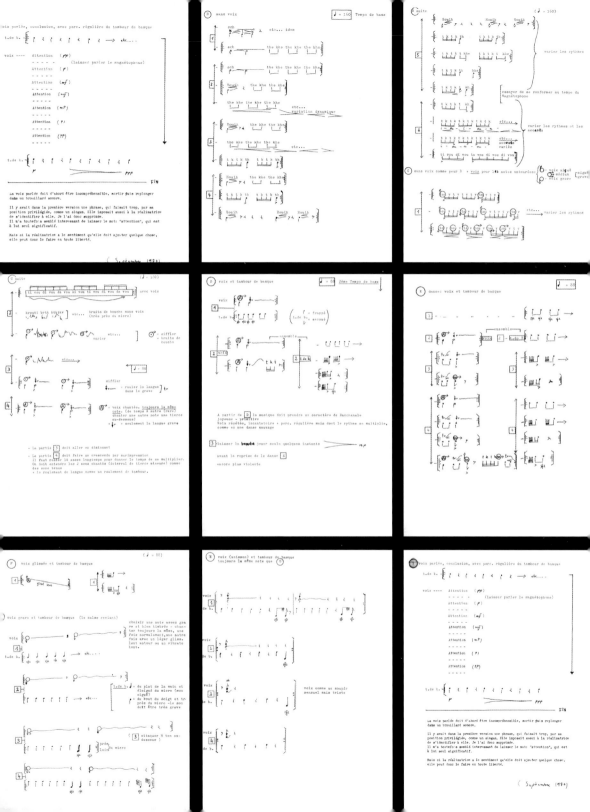

Le Dispositif et son disnégatif [19]

The Device Positive and Negative

How can reading a score lead the musicians to reflect on issues of hierarchy, aesthetics, taken as social constraints. To question the cult of personality. If this reflection could come through in the course of the sound action, it would be really marvellous.

WP/CM Radio Stockholm, 1970

1969–70
— indeterminate duration

Text score, *Le Dispositif et son disnégatif*, courtesy Masion ONA Editions

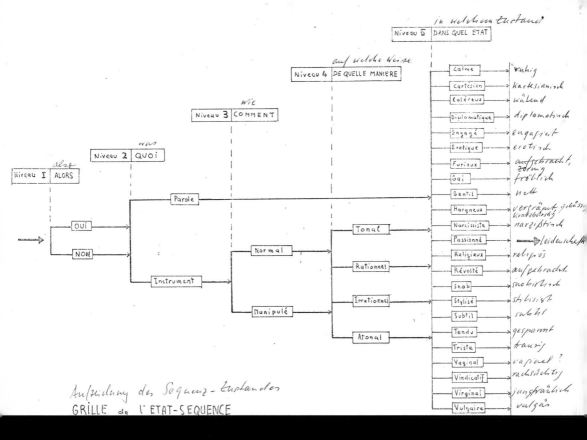

Spazier Musik n°2

Promenade Music n°2

For eleven instruments minimum ("compulsory" core instruments include flute, oboe, clarinet, bass clarinet, horn, trumpet, tenor trombone, two violins, two violas and a conductor with a megaphone)
Must be played while promenading.
Maison ONA Editions

1970
— indeterminate duration

Tautologos III, Réalisation n°3

Realization n°3

To illustrate the text, and as an example of a possible realisation in tape form (n°3) or traditional score (n°4).

LP EMI, C 061 11133 — 1970
CD Blue Chopsticks, BC1 — 1999

1970

Réalisation n°4

Tautologos III, Realization n°4

For 11 instrumentalists (flute, oboe, clarinet, trumpet, trombone, viola, cello, double bass, electric guitar, electric organ, vibraphone)
WP by the EIMCP Ensemble, dir. Konstantin Simonovic
Maison ONA Editions

1970
— approximately 20 minutes

Portrait-Spiel

Portrait Game

The difference that struck me most between a "concert work" and a Hörspiel was the duration: "you can make it as long as you like". I made it 80 minutes long.

The story is told through several recurring elements, some of which evolve through time: there's an absurd dialogue between the composer and his production team, due to the fact the composer was trying to learn German with the Assimil language method. Hence inadequacies and misunderstandings, raising the issue of how to articulate one's thoughts in a foreign language. There are also fragments from some of my 1960s compositions, used either as dramaturgical elements or critically discussed by the audience during public performances. And there's the composer in the city, as sound recordist: at the Musée d'Art Moderne, the football match, the cosmetics factory, the restaurant, etc. Lastly, there's the critique of the process by the production team (typical of the period).

One can see how all these ingredients illustrate what I was describing earlier, and how they are linked to my conception of autobiography, that is to say the author using his microphones as tool for subjective observation.

Stereo magnetic tape
Production: Hörspiel S.W.F., Baden-Baden
Karl Sczuka Prize 1972
Association PRESQUE RIEN

1971
— 80 minutes

Spazier Musik n°3

Promenade Music n°3

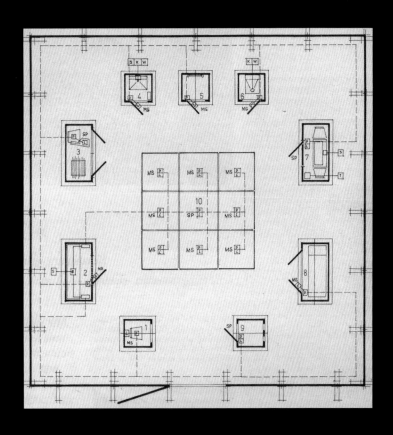

Installation for memorised sounds
WP "Kunstdorf", Kulturwoche, Wuppertal, 6-12 June 1971

DORF II KÖLN
HINGSTMARTIN · DORN
FERRARI · P.D. KRAEMER

Auf einer umzäunten Fläche von 12 x 12 Metern sind neun Häuser aufbaut. Diese Häuser sind aus einem einfachen Grundmodell verschieden
entwickelt. Grundmodell ist die Form 1 qm Grundfläche, zwei Meter
Höhe. Entsprechend den Bestimmungen, die den Häusern durch Abwandl...
des Grundmodells, durch Texte oder einfache Einrichtungen gegeben ...
sind in den Häusern musikalische Rhythmen und rhythmische Sprachstück...
untergebracht. Die sehr aktive Akustik in den Türen, die jeweils be...
Öffnen der Türen laut wird, steht in direktem Zusammenhang mit dem ...
ruhigen, intensiven Klangfeld des P l a t z e s. Der Platz besteht inmitt...
der Häuser aus neun Tonfeldern. Die einzelnen Klänge aus den Tonfeld...
beziehungsweise aus den Türen sind in sich abgeschlossene Kompositi...
die bei gesamter Betätigung durch den Besucher eine gesamte Komposi...
tion ergeben.

In der Mitte des Platzes liegt ein Textfeld. Mit dem Platz ist f...
eine Idylle angedeutet, die jedoch immer durch den Ablauf der Kläng...
und durch den Inhalt der Platzgeschichten gestört wird.

Betritt der Besucher das Dorf, sind alle Türen geschlossen, der Fla...
ist leer, das Dorf ist still.

Erst durch das Betreten des Platzes und das Öffnen der Türen ent...
falten sich die sichtbaren und hörbaren Ereignisse.

Leitung und Objekte   Texte   Musik
Hingstmartin   Anne Dorn   Luc Ferrari
5 Köln 1,   5 Köln 30,   73 rue du Cardi...
Brüsselerstr. 24   Prötelplatz 9

Ein Dorf ist ein Dorf. Ein Platz ist ein Platz. Ein
Haus ist ein Haus. Ein Dorfplatz ist der Platz eines
Dorfes. Ein Vaterhaus ist das Haus eines Vaters.
— obwohl es doch auch ein Mutterhaus sein kann.
Was macht die Dinge vielfach statt einfach? In
jedem Ding spielen andere Dinge mit. In unserem

Dorf kannst Du mit Händen und Füßen spielen, —
niemand kann behaupten, daß Du deshalb ein Handfuhspieler wirst. Du bist der Spielball anderer Gedanken, — es sei denn. Du spielst mit. Komm und
nimm Deinen Kopf in beide Hände und mache Dich
auf die Füße

Kunstdorf-Aufführung

Leitung und Objekte   Texte   Musik
HINGSTMARTIN   ANNE DORN   LUC FERRARI
5 Köln 1   5 Köln 30   Paris 3
Brüsseler Straße 24   Prötelplatz 9   63 Rue du Cardinal Lemoine
Tel. (02 21) 51 35 87   Tel. (02 21) 51 22 44

Elektroakustik Dieter Kramer, Westerwmar

Du erlebst: Gaukhäuschen, Horchhäuschen,
Sauberhäuschen, Schlafhäuschen, Elternbeeinflusshäuschen, Wartehäuschen, Schlürerhäuschen,
Fluphäuschen, Schelthäuschen, Kapellenäuschen,
Bildungshäuschen und den Platz

Bauwelt 32

7. August 1972
63. Jahrgang

Hans Adrian: Hans Joachim Krause:
Weiterkommen   Lebensbereich-Spielplatz
durch Ausprobieren für den Osdorfer Born —
— zur öffentlichen eine dilettantische
Planungsdiskussion Spielplatzidee
in Frankfurt/Main
                    Martina Schneider u.a.:
Das Frankfurter   Jongenisland — ein
Strukturplan-Konzept Insel-Spielplatz am Rand
für citynahe Stadtteile von Amsterdam

Hingstmartin,   Projekt für ein
Anne Dorn, Luc Ferrari: „verfremdetes" Parkhaus
„Dorf" —   in Münster
ein Erlebnisfeld

»Dorf«
Konzipiert, gebaut und eingerichtet
von Hingstmartin, Bildner — Anne Dorn, Autorin — Luc Ferrari, Komponist

Mit vielen Menschen
rede ich, mit wenigen,
von denen einige,
die mitreden,
sind noch weniger da,
die mitreden.
Mit einem Gefühl
ich meine Gedanken
unternraune. Ruhig erwarte ich
das neue Wort
aus dem Munde dessen,
der mir
ins Gesicht schaut.
Aber umgebit
in solchen Freuden
brechen wir alle
an einem Punkt
das Zusammder ab
und gehen davon
mit der leisen
Bedrückung, wir
nicht mehr konnten

»Dorf«

Beschreibung des Dorfes

Auf einer umzäunten Fläche von 12 × 12 m sind neun Häuser
aufgebaut. Diese Häuser sind aus einem einfachen Grundmodell ...

Genaue Beschreibung des Gaukhäuschens

Text
im Wartehäuschen
(spiralförmig angebracht

Anne Dorn
Platzgedichte

Beschreibung der einzelnen Häuschen

Exploitation Du Concept D'autobiographie
Exploitation of the Concept of an Autobiography

I have always, from the beginning, composed as many instrumental pieces as I have electroacoustic or acousmatic works. For the sake of clarity though, and to stick more closely to the topic at hand, I will only speak of electroacoustic pieces or, more generally, pieces that use technology.

Unconsciously at first, and then more and more consciously, I realised that I was working in the field of autobiography. And so with hindsight, I can now evoke the moment when I embraced that concept. It happened around 1962, when I was working on an electroacoustic piece titled *Hétérozygote*. I will try to describe the great significance of a simple act: stepping out of the studio to search for sounds outside.

So, what was the context at the time?
With the Groupe de Musique Concrète, gathered around Pierre Schaeffer and Pierre Henry, the work was being done at the Radio France studios, i.e., in the Institution: a technician would set up microphones to record instrumentalists or diverse and sundry objects. The sounds were then transformed, edited, and reproduced using the technology of the day. I produced my first *Etudes* in 1958.

In the Cologne studios, another Radio institution, the composers gathered around Herbert Eimert, and, with the help of assistants, they busied themselves with the frequency generators, before cutting, editing, manipulating and mixing. Stockhausen was composing his first electronic works at the time. A little later, in the Milan Phonology Studio, yet another institution, Luciano Berio was recording the extreme trilling of Cathy Berberian, which he manipulated and mixed, to compose *Omaggio a Joyce*.

Around that time, 1955–62, music was going through an extraordinary creative period, an effervescence, appropriating technology to experiment with it, misusing machines to create or compose different sounds. I very naturally felt that recording could open the door to other possibilities, outside of the studio. That's when I started using the portable tape recorder to collect the sounds of society and use them in my compositions. This is what we've become accustomed to calling "soundscapes", a term I've always found too restrictive.

Thinking back on it, I feel this was a radically different approach, and I may well have been the first to explore it, which by the way earned me a lot of criticisms and caused a bit of a stir in the early days of electroacoustic music.

As if to stake my claim, I started calling myself a composer of "anecdotal music". It was a joke, a devil-may-care gesture, for this had nothing to do with superficial anecdotes, it was an earnest use of narration in a world that was still in the thrall of abstraction. And above all, there was a more complex, more specific, and maybe newer musical idea, linked to the concept of autobiography.

So I stepped out of the studio, with my own portable equipment, i.e., my microphones and my tape recorder. My equipment and me. Like it or not, my situation was utterly original: my presence, my mode of interaction, my use of instruments, I wasn't aware of it at the time, but all of that turned me into a craftsman creating autobiography. I was there, holding my microphone, pressing "record" whenever I saw fit, I collected fleeting sounds that were happening at the very moment I was selecting them. That sound was my choice, a fragment of my life too, recorded on my equipment. To put it another way, in case the previous sentence wasn't clear, that gesture was compositional in that it recognised a sound however uncertain, it considered the found object as the first state of an emotional frame of mind, which inevitably implied the composer's presence and actions in real time, making him an autobiographer.

In 1970, I started working for the Hörspiel (radiophonic creation) departments of various German radio stations. That's when I became aware of the autobiographical dimension of my electro-acoustic work. To such an extent that my first Hörspiel was entitled

Portrait-Spiel (Portrait Game), and all the later ones bore witness to the presence of the composer as non-critical and unashamedly subjective observer of everyday life. I don't think it would hurt to slip in a few remarks at this point.

I make a distinction between my electroacoustic compositions and my instrumental compositions. The question of autobiography in relation to my instrumental scores requires a different set of explanations, and, as I was saying at the beginning, I'm confining my comments to electroacoustics for now, and therefore to the "gestural autobiography of the man holding the microphone". Moreover, I draw a distinction — or, more precisely, I used to draw a distinction, less and less so now — between "concert compositions" and radiophonic compositions. In a "concert composition", the autobiographical content is generally more diffuse, whereas for me, in a Hörspiel, the autobiographical dimension is more direct, and I'd even say that it is emphasized as a compositional instrument.

The Hörspiel departments of German radio stations encompass anything from radio-drama to extreme forms of experimentation. In France, they used the German word at first, later translating it as "radiophonic creations". When I met Hermann Naber, of the SWF, he told me that compositions like *Hétérozygote* or *Music Promenade* resembled Hörspiels, and he asked if I would be interested in producing a piece for the department he headed. Thus started one of my lives as a Hörspiel composer.

Unheimlich Schön

So Very Beautiful

How does a young woman *breathe* when her mind is elsewhere…?.

Stereo magnetic tape
Production: Hörspiel S.W.F., Baden-Baden (in German)
CD Metamkine, KCD008 — 1993

1971
— 20 minutes

Pornologos

This score is meant for private individuals or private groups, since its public (and non commercial) performance seems problematic to say the least. For the same reasons as above, we'll say that this score is almost unattainable.

‡
Text-score
Erotic realisable

1971
— indeterminate duration

Luc Ferrari

Les Réalisables
et
Journal d'un Autobiographe

(Original)

73 rue du Cardinal Lemoine
Paris 5:
Tél: 633-07-68

99

PORNOLOGOS 2

Dialogue → (Puisque le N° 1 a été supprimé, je décidais d'en faire un second et tout en travaillant je me disais qu'en fait il s'agissait là d'une sorte de ~~Dialogue~~. Le dialogue des corps est hautement significatif. J'ai souvent pensé que faire l'amour avait une portée politique et aussi qu'il était possible qu'il y aient des manières politiques de le faire. Je ne crois pas que la partition de Pornologos 2 aille si loin, mais le fait qu'elle soit ou presque y fait penser. En tout cas fait d'en faire une ou presque pose un problème. Mais lequel ?)

Ce réalisable a plusieurs fonctions.
- Il propose aux réalisateurs de codifier progressivement leurs expériences sexuelles à mesure qu'elles se raffinent grâce aux prises de contacts renouvelées et diverses. (Il est le fruit de l'observation de besoin de changement que ressent aussi bien l'homme que la femme, de la curiosité, et permet de satisfaire le désir de converser aussi bien sensuellement qu'intellectuellement.)
- Il propose de considérer les choses du sexe comme un jeu, dégagé du séculaire poids religieux ou mystique, et tente d'indiquer ce qui aurait toujours dû être: le réalisma d'une fonction naturelle complète et joyeuse. (Dialogue complexe)
- Il propose aux amateurs de mettre en "notes", de fabriquer une "partition", et ainsi d'apprendre par une méthode détournée, comment on peut écrire avec des signes abstraits, des actions concrètes. (J'imagine non sans sourire, un couple ou un groupe, tournant les pages d'une partition et suivant les signes avec le doigt.)
- Enfin il peut être considéré comme une leçon de musique, en passant allègrement par-dessus les préliminaires d'un solfège devenu inutile, que pourtant on s'entête encore à enseigner et avec lequel on rebute les tempéraments les plus imaginatifs. (J'irais même jusqu'à proposer que l'on généralise l'emploi de ce réalisable pour remplacer les cours de solfège devenus caducs grâce à lui.)

En douce, je pense que mettre en partition (en fait ils le sont déjà dans notre mémoire intuitive) les gestes sexuels est bien sûr absurde, mais on pourrait aussi bien dire que faire l'amour sans partition est tout aussi absurde.

(Dès qu'on invente un truc, il y a tout de suite des gens qui se précipitent dessus pour faire l'amour avec, ça a été le cas du disque, de la télé, de l'encens et j'en passe, pourquoi pas avec une partition ?)

La partition comporte des exemples de symboles dont peuvent s'inspirer les réalisateurs, et destinés à aider ceux qui n'ont que peu ou jamais fréquenté la notation musicale, à en inventer une qui convienne à leur réalisation.

(1) pour faciliter la lecture des signes de cette partition j'ai choisi de prendre comme exemple le rapport sexuel du couple homme-femme. Je veux dire par là que la partition est également destinée à tous autres rapports, qu'ils soient homosexuels ou de groupe.

100

P.P.P. ou Proposition Pour une Partition

Principes de base

1) la Verticale (superposition de plusieurs signes), signifie l'instant, ou la simultanéité de plusieurs éléments;
2) l'Horizontale, signifie le temps, ou la succession des évènements.

Notation de détail

a) Comment noter le sexe ?
Plusieurs signes concernent le sexe, son mouvement, sa position et son rythme. Ils seront les multiples du signe de base choisi pour le figurer.
Signe de base représentant:
— = le sexe de la femme.   ⊓ = le sexe de l'homme.

Signes multiples représentent:
1) la Rencontre
La superposition des deux signes précédents, indique le degré moyen de pénétration que l'on a décidé de fixer.
= pénétration moyenne   = pénétration maxi

2) Type de Mouvement
Si on désire bouger, on pourra disposer de plusieurs signes qui indiqueront la direction générale du mouvement, par exemple:

= cette flèche indique comme on le voit un mouvement longitudinal. Ces flèches peuvent se combiner ou se contredire: ......

= cette flèche indique un mouvement latéral. Celui-ci peut se combiner avec le précédent, ce qui donne un latérolongitudinal: ....

= ce signe placé à [droite] indique sans en avoir l'air, un mouvement vertical. On peut le combiner avec les autres ce qui donne un longivertico-lolatératudinal: ....

= ce double losange (si on veut), une contraction (noir), et une décontraction (en blanc) des muscles du ventre. On peut ajouter cette idée aux autres et on obtient un contralatéralverticalementdécontractédans la longueur. Ce signe se place comme ça: ....

---

3) Rythme des Mouvements
Il faut aussi penser que ces mouvements une fois choisis, peuvent se faire dans un certain rythme. On pourra alors utiliser les symboles suivants:

= lent
= moyen   } Rythmes réguliers
= vif
= rapide

= lent
= moyen à vif } Rythmes irréguliers
= rapide

On pourra ainsi indiquer les rythmes pour chaque mouvement différent, comme le montre cet exemple d'une combinaison mouvement-rythme:

R longitudinal,   ← con et décontraction, R régulier vif
R irrégulier
moyen-vif
                         ← R vertical, R régulier rapide

Si on veut maintenant indiquer des combinaisons de Rythmes dans le détail, on pourra noter comme suit:

les pointillés verticaux indiquent des points de synchronisme

b) Comment noter les mains ?
Les mains sont figurées par un symbole carré c'est plus commode, on peut les bouger et rythmer les mouvements qui les animent:

□ = une main
= mouvement d'une main.   Autre mouvement:
= main animée d'un rythme de va et vient rapide

Voici maintenant un exemple dans lequel on retrouve les propositions précédentes, auxquelles on a ajouté les mains:

.....les 2 mains féminines en haut du corps de l'homme
R horizontal et R régulier moyen

les 2 mains masculines au point de rencontre des sexes
R latéral et R régulier vif

(Comme on peut le constater, cette notation d'éléments simples, permet par leur combinaison des actions complexes, libère l'imagination par la dissociation des éléments, propose grâce à leur contradiction des situations irrationnelles originales. Prévoir à sexe reposé, des situations à sexe actif, est aussi intéressant.)

c) Comment noter la respiration ?

(L'idée de jouer consciemment sur la respiration repose sur le postulat que l'absorption de l'oxygène, ou la quantité d'air emmagasiné, peut jouer sur la sensation générale et fait donc partie de l'action.)

○ = indique que les poumons sont remplis
⬭ = indique que les poumons sont vides

Une flèche: ↑ propose l'inspiration
une flèche: ↓ propose l'expiration

Ces signes peuvent se combiner, comme on le voit ci-dessus, mais on peut aussi s'en servir d'une façon plus imaginative. Par exemple le dessin suivant:

= indique qu'il faut continuer d'inspirer, bien que les poumons soient déjà comblés d'air.
= ici c'est le contraire, les poumons sont déjà vides et on propose des expirations rythmiques.

Voici maintenant un dessin qui résume les points précédents:

d) Comment noter le gémissement ?

Les indications concernant le gémissement sont inscrites dans un rectangle, dont la longueur représente le temps, et la hauteur l'extention de la voix:

= sons aigus
= sons graves

Cet exemple décrit donc les inflections de la voix dans un temps donné. On peut naturellement combiner la respiration et le gémissement. Dans l'exemple ci-dessous, on voit les éléments suivants: poumons pleins, gémissement en inspiration, expiration, poumons vides, gémissement tremblé en inspiration, jusqu'à poumons remplis...:

e) Comment noter la parole ?

Il se peut que la parole fasse besoin, c'est pourquoi il faut pouvoir la noter, comme ça: ⟨———⟩

103

Comme elle fait partie du groupe Respiration, on peut donc la combiner avec les éléments précédents. Le dessin suivant,

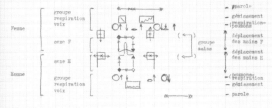

indique comment utiliser la parole par rapport à la mélodie, et par rapport à la respiration

On peut agrémenter la parole avec des accents rythmiques: ⟨———⟩

(Je me demande souvent comment faire l'amour de façon non-autoritaire. La tradition donne à l'homme la direction et la domination, et sa façon de faire est suivant l'expression du pouvoir que la société lui a injustement confié. La préparation de cette partition peut permettre au couple de prendre conscience de cet état de fait conventionnel, et lui donne l'occasion, au niveau de l'écriture collective, d'équilibrer le dialogue.)

Avant d'aller plus loin, voici un dessin résumant la notation expliquée depuis le début.

Indications Formelles

La notation précédente sous-entend que certains éléments se développent par groupes. Le groupe sexe, mains, respiration, peuvent dépendre les uns des autres, ils peuvent aussi être indépendants.

La notation concernant la respiration et la voix, forme un groupe qui peut faire fonction de cycle. C'est-à-dire, se répétant pendant un temps donné, jusqu'à ce qu'une autre notation ne la transforme.

On peut donc dire qu'il y aurait possibilité de superposition de cycles plus ou moins indépendants. Et ceci, étant une référence au procédé tautologique exposé par ailleurs, permet aux réalisateurs de se retrouver sur un terrain déjà connu.

Une autre proposition formelle est celle du libre choix. Ce qui permet au moment de l'action de surprendre le partenaire et d'ainsi jouer sur une nouvelle dimension du dialogue.

104

Par exemple, devant un groupe d'éléments concernant l'instant, le signe: [indique que le choix peut se porter sur un des éléments du groupe.

On pourra aussi donner une préférence à deux ou plusieurs éléments, celui qui sera choisi, pourra alors être joué avec une accentuation toute particulière. Ainsi on ajoute un caractère dynamique à la surprise, qui l'est déjà comblée par elle-même.

Un grand rectangle enfermant plusieurs évènements instantano-temporels, indique un choix d'éléments à jouer dans une succession libre, ou, improvisation sur des éléments donnés.

(Ici apparait l'idée d'improvisation qui, dans la forme, vient se mêler avec les évènements prédéterminés. Ce qui permet de mélanger à la réflection, la spontanéité.)

Un grand carré vide représente, on s'en doute, une improvisation totalement libre. On peut toutefois donner à cette improvisation un caractère particulier, rythmique ou autre, avec les signes que l'on connaît déjà.

Par exemple: une improvisation sur des rythmes réguliers rapides: [ ]

Il va sans dire que l'on peut également travailler sur des rythmes irréguliers, et que si l'on désire une évolution, celle-ci est aussi possible.

par exemple: ⨯ = irrégulier lent, jusqu'à: ⨯ = irrégulier rapide.

Cet autre exemple: | ⟶ ⨯ signifie que l'on peut aller de régulier lent, à irrégulier rapide.

On peut concerner davantage les réalisateurs, en ajoutant aux rythmes, un caractère dynamique

fort ⟶ [ ] = fort avec des rythmes vifs irréguliers.

doux ⟶ [ ] De lent régulier à régulier rapide en diminuant:

et ainsi de suite.

Ces signes d'improvisation, peuvent ne concerner qu'un des membre du couple, c'est-à-dire que pendant que l'un suit la partition fixé, l'autre improvise.

On a pu remarquer que les signes décrits jusqu'ici, sont là comme une incitation à l'invention. C'est pourquoi je laisse le soin aux réalisateur futurs, d'en inventer d'autres. Je remarque que le jeu, sur les quelques bases suggérées, peut être poussé si loin dans la complexité, que l'exécution soit à la limite du possible.

(Je me demande encore une fois, si inventer une notation pour ce genre de chose est bien utile. Difficile à répondre. On peut toujours se servir de ces signes pour composer une réelle partition musicale, dans laquelle les interprètes trouveraient, au lieu de notes écrites, des indications de gestes à faire sur leurs instruments. Je crois que cette notation est vraiment polyvalente.)

Déroulement dans le temps

Après un ensemble de signes, on peut poser l'indication suivante: (2'), ce qui veut dire que pendant 2 minutes, tous les éléments se répètent individuellement, et se combinent suivant le schéma indiqué.

Ensuite si on veut modifier un seul ou plusieurs des éléments, il suffit de dessiner seul, l'élément ou les éléments qui doivent changer.

Si on veut supprimer un élément, il n'y a qu'à le dessiner et le mettre entre parenthèses.

Ceci, bien sûr, en à chaque fois, faisant suivre d'une indication temporelle si on veut.

(Je crois qu'au point où j'en suis arrivé de mes explications, les réalisateurs en savent autant que moi sur la notation musicale en général. Pourtant je ne me sentirai pas quitte, avant de donner un exemple de succession d'évènements, ceci afin de tester l'efficacité et la fiabilité de cette notation là.)

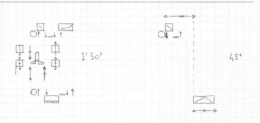

(«→»)

106

10" (bref, pas que fatigant)

2'

7'46"

et... .

(«—»)

(On peut imaginer une autre version de ce réalisable, dans laquelle plusieurs couples feraient l'amour selon une partition (par exemple au cours d'un concert) qui serait dirigée par un chef d'orchestre. Pour rendre l'action plus sonore, on pourrait utiliser des sommiers métalliques à ressort à boudin, le tout capté par des micros de contact. On pourrait aussi garnir un des lits avec des cymbales, un autre avec des grosses caisses, un autre dont les mouvements actionneraient un soufflet d'orgue sur lequel quelqu'un jouerait, etc... et puis il pourrait y avoir des binious partout qui seraient branchés sur des matelas pneumatiques ou dépneumatiques, et des lits aquatiques avec des bulles d'air qui feraient glouglou. le moindre geste déclencherait toute une symphonie idyllique...

On pourrait inventer encore bien d'autres versions.

On pourrait inventer des versions religieuses

des versions culturelles

des versions métaphysiques

etc...)

Cymbales

Ressorts

grosse-caisse

Conclusion

Oui, je peux le dire, honnêtement je crois qu'on peut employer cette notation, elle semble bien marcher.

x x x

(si le lire à faute clec inceitir)

107

LOISIR D'AMATEUR

(J'aime bien ce titre, il est très musical et me fait penser à plaisir d'amour. C'est aussi un rêve d'amour dans lequel les amateurs aimeraient le loisir qu'on leur propose.)

Le Loisir.

Ce terme concerne le temps compris entre le travail et la fatigue qui en résulte. Comment employer le temps qui reste, avant que le travailleur quel qu'il soit, ne tombe de fatigue.

La société se penche sur ce problème, et tout honnête citoyen doit aussi y penser, sinon qu'est-ce qu'elle va inventer?

L'Amateur.

C'est une personne qui dans son temps de "loisir", a un intérêt pour quelque chose ayant ou non rapport avec son travail. L'amateur est celui qui choisit d'occuper son loisir de manière plus ou moins homogène, et dans une activité ayant une direction donnée.

Ce réalisable propose au réalisateur d'occuper son loisir dans le domaine du journalisme, et indique comment il peut employer les moyens que la technique moderne met à sa disposition.

L'amateur doit d'abord observer que, malgré le raffinement technique et l'ubiquité des moyens, les systèmes traditionnels d'information sont insuffisants, et ainsi constater la faillite de l'information, du fait du monopol que le pouvoir exerce sur elle.

Il s'agit donc de se constituer en groupe d'informateurs amateurs, sans souci des normes, et avec des moyens qui peuvent échapper à la pression économique qui est justement celle du pouvoir. Il peut ainsi tenter de démontrer que l'information est possible malgré la pauvreté des moyens, en employant le plus économique, c'est-à-dire celui qui permet d'aborder le plus librement les problèmes les plus divers. La mini-cassette semble convenir à ce besoin, et ce réalisable suggère des idées pour s'en servir.

Imaginons qu'un amateur, scandalisé par le manque d'information, qui malgré les moyens mis en oeuvre n'arrive pas à assumer sa tâche, décide de se fabriquer la sienne, c'est-à-dire l'information la plus subjective qui soit.

Il fait donc collection des questions qui selon lui sont restées sans réponse, ou dont les réponses ont été savonnées.

Dans ses temps de loisir, il part avec dans une main, sa collection de questions, et dans l'autre son enregistreur.

Il enquête partout où il peut.

Avec les réponses qu'il ramène, il réalise un "montage" cohérent, c'est-à-dire, dont le sens soit une réponse aux questions, ou démontre l'incapacité de répondre aux questions, ou que les réponses formulent justement d'autres questions.

Ainsi le jeu continue.

Quand il a réalisé ce qu'il considère comme une "émission", il invite des amis pour l'écouter.

Il se peut qu'après cette écoute, un groupe insatisfait par l'information recueillie décide de partir à la chasse et de réaliser sa propre émission.

Et ainsi le jeu continue encore.

108

On peut compter sur l'émulation pour qu'une chaîne d'"informateur" amateur naisse et se ramifie avec une certaine rapidité. Ceci est possible grâce au matériel employé, accessible du fait de son prix peu élevé, et tant que les moyens traditionnels ne satisferont pas la "clientèle".

On peut donc imaginer que des groupes de réalisateurs se forment et se déforment, qu'ils débordent les frontières, qu'ils échangent les "émissions", comme se fabriquent des réseaux de correspondance par lettre ou par radio amateur.

P. M. T. ou Partition de Méthode de Travail

(Je ne m'immisce pas dans les affaires des autres; j'indique seulement, pour ceux qui ne sauraient pas comment faire un procédé technique suffisant pour ce réalisable, et que l'expérience des moyens sophistiqués m'a enseigné.)

Cette partition intervient au moment où le réalisateur revient de son enquête, avec sa collection de bandes enregistrées.

Il doit pouvoir disposer pour son "montage" de deux mini-cassettes.

Les opérations de ce que j'appelle le montage, et qui en réalité est plutôt un collage par copies successives, se déroulent comme suit:

1) Plusieurs bandes enregistrées représentent la quête de l'information, appelées par exemple, bande 1, 2, 3 et 4.

2) Relevé par écrit, d'un résumé du contenu de chaque bande.

3) Choix dans ces bandes, du matériel devant constituer l'émission.

4) Réalisation d'un plan écrit.

On ne peut pas monter la bande des cassettes, on va donc devoir copier dans l'ordre décidé sur ce plan.

Par Exemple:

3 minutes de la fin de la bande N° 2

30 sec. du milieu de la bande N° 1

6 minutes du début de la bande N° 4

2 minutes du début, de nouveau de la bande N° 2

etc...

Plusieurs bandes enregistrées

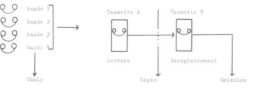

bande 1

bande 2

bande 3

bande 4

Cassette A

Cassette B

Choix

Lecture

Copie

Enregistrement

Emission

---

5) Suivant le schéma:

Employer la cassette A comme lecteur, et y placer la bande choisie pour le début;

employer la cassette B comme enregistreur.

Copier successivement et dans l'ordre du plan, les bandes choisies, en les plaçant chaque fois dans la cassette A

Arrêter l'enregistreur lorsque le contenu de la bande lue n'a plus d'intérêt.

Avec un peu d'expérience, on doit obtenir un travail propre, avec un minimum de défauts ou de blancs, dus aux changements de bande.

6) On peut intercaler si besoin est, des bruits d'ambiance enregistrés sur les lieux de l'enquête, ou des musiques, ou des commentaires personnels, etc...

Comme on peut le voir, j'explique avec des termes ultrasimples, le procédé employé pour la plûpart des émissions de radio. Il n'était peut-être pas utile d'expliquer, sinon que l'auditeur ne doute pas toujours de la simplicité du procédé. En outre, je l'ai fait pour bien montrer que la réalisation était à la portée de tous.

Ce qui est, je crois, le sujet de ce réalisable.

A la suite de quoi on peut imaginer avec la plus grande facilité, qu'un réseau d'information incontrôlable se propage à travers le monde, fabriquant ainsi une information officieuse dont l'information officielle sera un jour obligé de tenir compte si elle veut maintenir sa clientèle.

Ainsi va la vie, il ne fallait pas inventer la mini-cassette....

(Ce réalisable est, on l'a sûrement deviné, destiné à inciter les amateurs à faire des reportages ayant rapport avec leur travail. On obtient ainsi des "comptes-rendus" de l'intérieur que seul le travailleur qui est impliqué dans son activité et qui y a des problèmes, peut faire. En échangeant ces comptes-rendus, venus de tous les milieux possibles (usine, administration, grand magasin, école et même journalisme) on doit obtenir une information réelle que le reporter, de meilleure volonté soit-il, est incapable de donner. Il y a beaucoup de sujets à traiter....)

Les réalisables et le journal d'un autobiographe

The Realisables and the Diary of an Autobiographer

This book charts the strange evolution that goes from realisables that are meant to be enacted (eg., *Tautologos III*) to utopian, and probably impossible realisables. You will find here all the themes that have concerned me and which can be summed up thus: how does artistic creation, when it remains on a solely aesthetic plane, run the risk of masking reality, and of sometimes being no more than a waste of energy.

Collection of text-scores in book form, with various autobriographical reflections
Erotic realisable

1964–72
— indeterminate duration

Collage art from *Les réalisables et le journal d'un autobiographe*

Kennen Sie Schönberg?

Do You Know Schönberg?

16mm, dual band, colour film
Production: WDR 3 TV, Cologne

1972
— 30 minutes

Allô, ici la terre, Chapter 1

Hello, This Is The Earth Speaking, Chapter I

This piece is a sort of audio-visual poem, dedicated to the earth we walk on; it attempts to show nature's harmony as well as the hope of preserving nature's balance.

Play-light and time-show
Screenplay and music: Luc Ferrari
Photographs: Jean-Serge Breton
Commissioned by the City of Bonn
WP Beethovensaal, Bonn, 3 May 1972, by the Beethovenhalle Orchestra, dir. Volta Wangenheim
Scores Ars Viva-Verlag

1971–72
— approximately 2 hours

Score courtesy Association PRESQUE RIEN

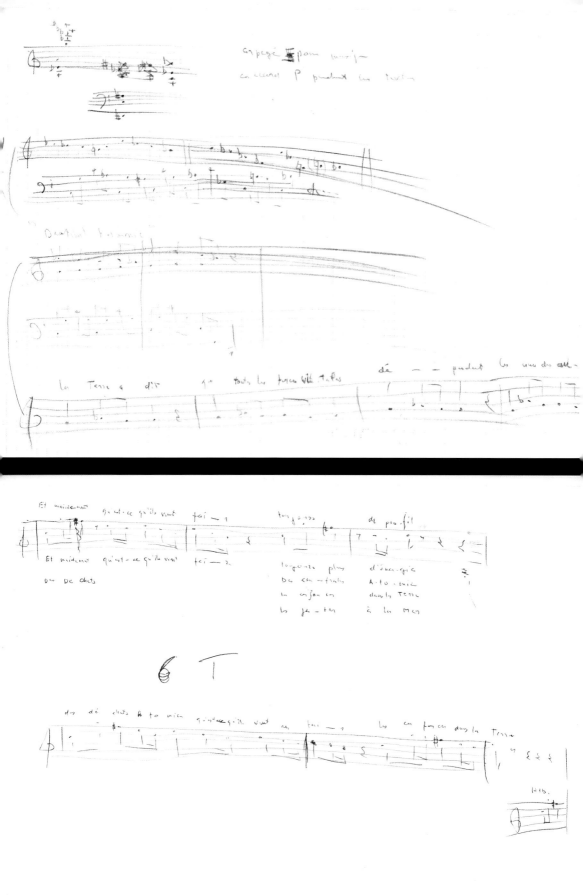

Programme commun pour clavecin et bande

Common Programme for Harpsichord and Tape

For amplified harpsichord and stereo magnetic tape
WP GRM concert, Théâtre Récamier, Paris, 1973, by Elisabeth Chojnacka
LP Erato, STU 71010 — 1977
CD Adda, 581233 — 1990

1972
— approximately 20 minutes

Why this title? The question imposes itself – prior to listening, and post listen. Is there a relationship between my title and my piece?

Just like the great question of Socialism – still imposing itself after the elections. (I am not drawing comparisons, but who could tune out current events?) Reactionaries condemn foreign Socialist regimes before a naïve crowd eager to hear them, and that is the most profitable and easiest solution there is. What is more difficult is to build an original society that would not be based on fraudulent profiteering — and that is something that should be of interest to everyone, even artists.

(I am not into politics, I am merely trying to do a job that should have a place in society.)

Contributing to this search, this quest, has been my sole interest for a long time. It should be said that in my field, actions, however big or small, have their place, so I am not giving up hope.

This piece of music is cheerful, but it also raises a serious question: Can an artist separate their own political concerns from their artistic concerns, either directly as a film allows or indirectly as in this music?

I cannot separate social and artistic aspirations, even if I wanted to, as some too often do in order to protect old privileges. How do we help develop a new society through our artistic activities? That is the question, I for one do not know how to answer, but I am searching, definitely searching…

"This music was also my way of commemorating an occasion in 1972 — my signing of The Programme Commune."
OVERLEAF: Portrait on Rue Rollin, photographed by Olivier Garros, 1973

indépendante
dans une Europe
démocratique
Parti communiste français
che
STRES COMMUN
000 EMPLOIS
AN

Journal d'un journaliste amateur

Journal of an Amateur Journalist

This is a montage of interviews with various social groups on various social issues in a provincial town in France. With the comments by an amateur reporter – it was my first foray into investigative journalism. The ideal circulation of this tape should be to encourage an exchange of information between groups. This tape is a pure product of the 1970s about the intellectual and the people. Highly inadvisable.

Stereo tape
Production: G.M.E.B., Maison de la Culture, Bourges

1972
— 27 minutes

FBM: How have you developed since 1958, the year we met to set up the GRM?

LF: I have spent my time developing, evolving, tackling ever different problems: music, images, theatre, etc.

FBM: What are the landmark pieces you consider important?

LF: I almost never listen to my own work, but there are one or two pieces I am very attached to, for example *Hétérozygote*, in 1964, a part-musical, part-"anecdotal" attempt.

FBM: Do you listen more to other people's music? What do the heirs of serial music represent for you?

LF: I am no longer interested in serial music. For me, the formal issue was never the main point, and musical discourse in general has never interested me.

FBM: Did John Cage influence this standpoint?

LF: Historically speaking, Cage played a very important critical role by questioning the whole of music.

FBM: To the point of nihilism sometimes.

LF: Personally, I am not a nihilist, I think one should do lots of things.

FBM: Even if that means sometimes confining oneself to "Almost Nothing"…

LF: Absolutely! The important thing is

that Cage helped us become aware of the presence of things and time. That's what I tried to do in *Presque Rien*, and what I had started with *Hétérozygote*.

FBM: On this, I think our attitude, yours and mine, were worlds apart from P. Schaeffer's ideas, heretical even. But although we converge in our choice of materials from reality, we use them in diametrically opposed ways. For example, in *Presque Rien*, which I find particularly accomplished, you don't seek to prompt an exclusively musical way of listening: on the contrary, you focus on the suggestive potential of the chosen sounds.

LF: Indeed, *Presque Rien* is driven by predominantly dramatic preoccupations, poetic in the widest sense of the term. Not only do I not call this music, but for for me it contributes to challenging the very notion of music.

FBM: So what you do is more akin to a sort of cinema for the ear?

LF: If you like, yes.

FBM: What is the script in this particular case?

LF: It's a recording of the sunrise by the sea. In this piece, I shed any remaining hint of musical construction, what I'm doing now is no longer composition. It is, let's say, a certain way of looking at things. A way of looking that is no doubt subjective — an objective way of looking would make no sense! — but general.

About *Presque Rien*
Interview with Francois-Bernard Mâche

Photograph by Brunhild Ferrari

Interview 1972

BM: You have swapped your career as a composer for a career as a sound reporter?

LF: Not exactly. It is still the musician who makes choices amongst the recorded things. What is ugly from the point of view of sound cannot be used.

FBM: I thought you were presenting "found" sound situations, the way a tree stump has at times been called a "sculpture"?

LF: Something like that. The Surrealists did that sort of thing. However, in *Presque Rien*, amongst all the sounds that accompany the sunrise every morning, I chose those that kept returning, those I felt were really typical, and I didn't make just the one recording.

FBM: If it is edited, then it's a composition. For example you chose to cut short the cicadas at the end, after twenty minutes of "music", whereas real cicadas stridulate for hours. So you actively interfered with the sound event. You are still a composer, figurative rather than realist.

LF: Let's say that I'm a reducer.

FBM: If you like, but you are a composer: however discreet your intervention, all things considered, it is analogous to Beethoven's development: you're also producing variations through a process of elimination!

LF: Let's not get carried away. Between what I do and "concert music" there's a

marked difference.

FBM: I'm prepared to take back Beethoven, but only to replace him with Debussy, who did "From Dawn to Noon on the Sea". Are you his heir?

LF: Debussy wanted to draw a musical outcome from this spectacle — I am content with showing it. He had no microphone, that's the difference. When faced with the qualities of nature, why transcribe them through an orchestra if you can just replicate them? Debussy was no doubt right for his time.

FBM: If what you're doing is just replicating those sounds, then why not organise a trip, like a tour operator, so the audience can attend this auditory show live, in situ. There are certainly places where every day, at certain times of the year, the sunrise is accompanied by enchanting murmurs. Let's go there, the stereo effect will be even better.

LF: Precisely. I'd really like to work for travel agencies. You could for example install some booths at Orly, playing different kinds of *Presque Riens*, soundscapes, to replace the sounds of the airport.

FBM: But why have booths, why albums? What I'm trying to say isn't at all that the realist practice is pointless or sterile, on the contrary, I share your interest in the beauty of the real auditory world, but this practice has to acknowledge a paradox: you have to admit that if we turn a sunrise into apartment music we are already dealing with artifice, and therefore with art: we're already beyond realism and therefore it's Surrealism.

LF: Why Surrealism? It's still a manipulation of things, though I reduce it to a minimum.

FBM: No, it's closer to the idea of the magical beneath the everyday
LF: But still, and always, to aesthetic ends.

FBM: To revolutionary ends, I would say.

LF: From where I stand, it isn't the same effect, you see. Why be a Surrealist when you can be a Realist? I grew up with Surrealism, which is probably why I hate it so much, and why I'm so much of a Realist.

FBM: Total Realism would be to walk around with one's ears wide open, but not with a tape recorder slung over your shoulder. The minute you start recording, choosing, assembling, editing, you're going beyond Realism. In fact, as soon as you adopt a musical way of listening to the real.

LF: I don't go beyond the real, I'm beneath it. What I do is Sub-Realism.

FBM: Nevertheless, you're still responsible for what you're presenting, whatever the degree of interference.

LF: Absolutely, I feel totally responsible. However I eschew as much as possible a certain type of cultural sophistication — writing.

FBM: So your approach can be explained by a sociological context, not just an aesthetic one?
LF: Of course, I try to make a kind of anti-music, and to challenge the bourgeois myth of the composer, which tends to perpetuate a certain ideology, and a certain culture. But I am not very cultured, you know.

FBM: Isn't the question of the ideological content of music, if it arises, a matter for the sociologist rather than the composer?

LF: Not at all. I think it is precisely the composer's problem.

FBM: So for you, musical quality comes second?

LF: The concept of quality, the importance attached to hard work, it's just another myth we need to get rid of.

FBM: So whatever the composer does, what really counts is the commentary, the explanatory notes, and the composer just needs to turn into a writer?

LF: No, without explanatory notes, the ideological content is inscribed within the sounds.

FBM: It remains to be seen who will be in charge of deciphering it. After all, your audience isn't the proletariate, but a fraction of the bourgeoisie.
LF: That's because the proletariate is a victim of the dominant ideology. But Revolutionary action rests on those contradictions.

BM: *Fresque Rien* is only possible here, in the Capitalist West, it's a cultural fact. I think that if our "realist" works have any revolutionary potential, it is not because they stand up against the rite of the concert, for example, but because they learn to seize the real and see it as a source of pleasure and wonder, and so they seize culture not as consumer goods but as a game with that reality.

LF: Yes, and I try to get people to play. After my various *Tautologos*, I asked them "Would you like to tautologue with me?"

FBM: And what did they answer?

LF: Nothing. Some have tried, quite successfully.

FBM: Had you given them the rules of the game?

LF: No, I'm not a superego composer!

FBM: I don't think it's possible to play for long if you don't agree on some rules. Children are very clear on that point.

LF: Maybe music isn't child's play? Still, there are some games you can play very happily without having to set any rules…

FBM: You entitled one of your pieces *What if the Piano Were a Woman's Body, I think?*

LF: I see you grasped my point perfectly.

Luc Ferrari, Musée d'Art Moderne, 1974

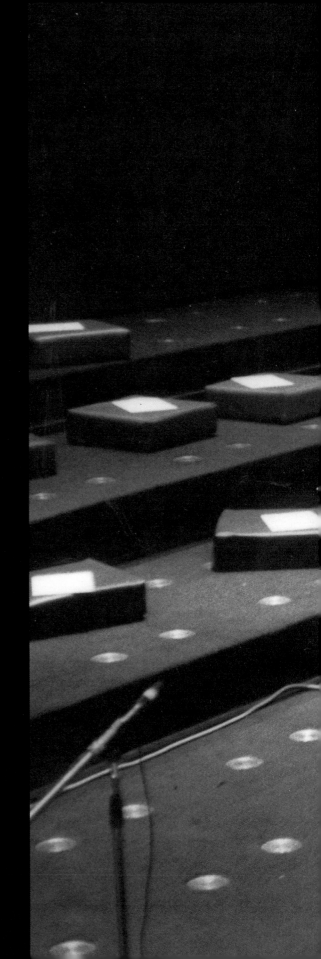

Danses organiques

Organic Dances

In the background there is some generic folk music about which I offer a pseudo-analysis.
Meanwhile, two young women meet for the first time and make love.
…A composer militates in favour of women's liberation.

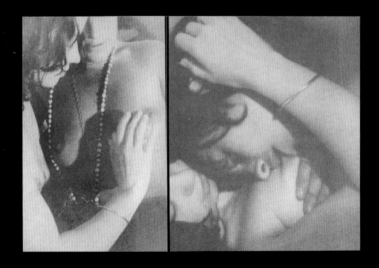

Stereo tape
Premiered in Paris, concert GRM, Théâtre Récamier, 1973

1971–1973
— 52 minutes

Photographs by Philippe Gras

Interview 1979 with Daniel Caux

On May 28, during a concert dedicated to Luc Ferrari and organised by the G.R.M., Ferrari presented his latest magnetic tape work at the Théâtre Récamier in Paris: *Les Danses Organiques* [*Organic Dances*]. To briefly describe what the author considers as a kind of 'comic strip for the ear," let's say that the tape records the first meeting between two young lesbians. The recording is interrupted by laconic comments by the author, who derides the clichés of musical analysis, and by repetitive instrumental sequences – the music is multiplied by obsessional effects, echoing through electro-acoustic devices. As the piece progresses, there is a fusion of music and love games, culminating in a long final section during which the partners reach a climax.

Apart from the ambiguous charm of a situation to which it is difficult to remain insensitive, what strikes us in *Organic Dances* is the simplicity, freedom and natural harmony that emanate from it. But such freshness shouldn't surprise us, coming from the author of *Et si le piano était un corps de femme* [*What if the Piano Were a Woman's Body*] and of *Presque Rien: Le lever du jour au bord de la mer* [*Almost Nothing: Sunrise by the Sea*]? And if the piece is provocative, it is because it was home-made, on non-professional equipment, thus showing that electro-acoustic music can be accessible to all, in every sense of the term.

A few days before the concert, Luc Ferrari had organised a gathering at his home. Apart from the composer and myself, this included: Brunhild Ferrari, the two young women, Rio and Monika, Jacqueline Caux and the photographer Philippe Gras. After listening to the tape a discussion took place. Here are some extracts from it:

Brunhild: I couldn't really say whether the music became sensuous due to the meeting of these two women, or whether the sensuality that was already there in your music prompted you to choose these two women.

Luc: There's already a sensuality in me...

Brunhild: A sensuality, and a degree of voyeurism.

Luc: Yes, why not? Isn't that natural? The audience is a sort of voyeur and, in so far as I'm also part of an audience, am a voyeur. And when the voyeur meets the exhibitionists, harmony arises.

Brunhild: But you're as coy as your composer colleagues: you don't expose yourself.

Luc: I do! Music is a way of exposing oneself after all: what I display is extremely private and intimate.

Brunhild: Yes, that's true. You do man-hide. You say that you don't think when you work... You give free rein to your instincts.

Luc: Sensuality hasn't been discussed much, until recently. Of course, there's a whole body of "private" literature. However this is a general issue, not a personal one. In the piece, we happen to start from a specific aspect, the meeting of two women, very directly inserted in the music, and this gradually leads us to a general issue – how to express sensuality without making it specific, individual. But there's another problem, a more tricky one: the fact that a man is concerning himself with two lesbians; this could be a kind of male appropriation of the female world.

Rio: It all depends on the man's attitude. On the contrary, there can be some complicity between his inner femininity and the two women's complicity. And then it becomes something totally different: it's to do with participation, and not appropriation.

Brunhild: Would you, in the same way, have chosen a meeting between two men?

Luc: No, I wouldn't. Because I'm not gay, I would probably have found it awkward. Having said that, someone else could do it. The piece consists in a jigsaw puzzle system which can be assembled with three overlapping components: my comments, which can be replaced by any other producer's comments, my music, and lastly a group of characters in a dramatic situation. So I could give this music to a gay producer who could do the piece with two gay men, or to a priest who could do it with two nuns, or any other type of encounter, the very first moments of the encounter. The meeting itself, that's what interests me in this piece. I don't know why I came up with the idea, but it's not such a silly idea after all: we so rarely meet in life, we might as well use music as an excuse...

Brunhild: You met these women you found attractive, by whom you could be attracted – or by whom you were attracted – but who are not exclusively lesbian. If they had been, you would no doubt have been less attracted.

Luc: True, but that's because I don't like things that are too systematic. For example, in this piece, there are three fundamentally ambiguous elements. First ambiguity: my would-be "analytical" comments are in fact a caricature of musical analysis, but serious at the same time, because I say a couple of things that might be meaningful... Second ambiguity: these young women act naturally because they are attracted to each other, but at the same time they're not altogether natural because they know they're being recorded: so there's an ambiguity here between acting and reality. Then the third ambiguity is the music because on the one hand it's original, I mean my own, since I made it, but on the other hand, it imitates all sorts of other musics: so there's a game of imitation. And you constantly play on those three ambiguities.

Daniel: At the beginning, you have the feeling that the piece will be a series of nore or less disconnected and hetero-geneous elements, and then gradually, a sort of plenitude takes over and you find yourself in a very different disposition.

Rio: That's right, there's a progression.

Luc: What's going on here, I think, is the discovery of a certain musical technique. At the beginning, I use pretty basic ele-ments, and little by little, I discover the experiment. Through playing, but also through the technical system that leads me to a certain harmony. As I explain in the piece, I chose a horizontal system, so I considered the music as duration instead of working vertically, as you usu-ally do when you're writing or when you edit magnetic tape with "stickies". In this case, there are no stickies, the music is totally horizontal: it's a new technique I started learning three years ago. So there's an encounter with a new musical experiment, started three years ago; the other encounter was much more brief, it only lasted one evening: the meeting of the two young women who didn't know each other beforehand, and who go as far as making love. So there's this par-allel, which is quite unexpected, since you don't expect things to develop that way. Things are so harmonious some-times that you don't expect what's going to happen, even if it's totally natural for it to happen.

Daniel: What struck me, especially at the end of the piece, is this sort of quest for 'beauty". Modern art has been so wary of "beauty".

Luc. After years of very rigorous music arid and dry like serial music, systematic normative (even if these were avant-gar-de norms), I wanted to look for harmo-nies that could combine and give you room to breathe. It's a reaction piece but not in the sense of "reactionary", it reacts against the anti-sensuality inher-ent in that music, and in which compos-ers of my generation were raised.

Luc: I've always been attracted by heter-ogeneity, the mingling of genres. I think that the search for stylistic purity can lead to something very sterile. We have lived in very specific systems: adminis-trations, institutions, thought systems writing systems, working systems, in the arts or in every aspect of society, and we eventually realised a few years ago that all those systems led to total failure failure of the family, etc… We're at a moment when we've become aware of those failures, and we're troubled by the collapse of all the systems…

Monika: There's nothing stable to hang on to…

Luc: Yes, but that means we're totally free to go in other directions. That in-cludes the freedom to become a total fascist, which could happen to us soon-er than we think… Or on the contrary we can discover something marvellous a free society! This may seem utopian but I think we're living in an extraordinary period from that point of view.

Daniel: To what extent do you think the

Danses Organiques fits in with your other works?

Luc: In so far as I don't take a critical stance. I think criticism is so obsolete; observation is more interesting. When you observe, you learn to look, to listen, you learn about life. Centuries of criticism, and all we've learned is death – proof is, we're still beating the shit out of each other... This notion of observation probably implies "defects", but a lot of love too; in the things I do, those defects are very important, because they give people something to react to. I find the desire to make perfect works completely absurd. It's really a form of megalomania, a desire to be like God. But God is over, we've had enough!... No more God, no more right thought, no more perfection, no more sin. The values in which we've macerated all our lives, and still do, are so reactionary and stupid... I'm essentially rebelling against all the things that imposed chastity belts on us all.

Daniel: Had you been thinking about this piece for a while, or about the basic idea at least?

Luc: Not at all. I'd started working at home with my small equipment, and every now and then, something came out of it, little pieces, two or three minutes long. That was usually when I was working on big projects: when I'd had enough, I'd start messing around, to relax. I'd play with my tape recorders and my organ, or my drums, or my flutes.

And so after a while, small pieces started piling up, and they all had something in common: a kind of permanence, either in the rhythm or in the harmonies, and that reminded me of a sort of family, I called it *Organic Dances*. But at the beginning, I didn't have a set idea and I only recently asked myself how I might assemble all this. That's when the encounter idea came up.

Daniel: Can sounds be erotic?

Luc: I don't think so. I suppose with machines, it might be possible to analyse the vibrations produced by certain sounds. But I don't know, I can't say...

Daniel: For example, I thought Rio and Monika's voices were very...

Brunhild: Not just the voices: the music even when the voices weren't involved, I found it very sensuous.

Luc: Yes, but was that because of the sounds themselves, or the way they were assembled? When I started that piece I didn't have a plan, no musical agenda, and so I let myself be carried away by how can I put it, by instinct. Instinct is connected to sensuality and sensuality implies eroticism. As soon as you let the brain play a part that is not cultural but purely instinctive, eroticism automatically ensues. For me, eroticism lies more in the mechanics of creation than in the sound itself. But when the brain doesn't think along cultural lines, it becomes so free that maybe it chooses sounds lad en with eroticism, that's possible. What I mean, and I don't know if I said it clearly enough, is that when you're letting yourself go freely and you don't obey a system, that necessarily creates a sensuous atmosphere: everything just becomes erotic.

What is very odd is that when faced with these two components, on the one hand the two women meeting, and on the other hand, the music, I found it hard at first. I couldn't see how to organise this and I felt I would never manage it. Then I realised that I wasn't thinking, and I said that into the microphone: "When I'm working, I don't think." From the moment I became aware that I wasn't thinking, things started falling into place by themselves. The overlay of music, voice, laughter, happened naturally, and just when something needed to be heard, there was a gap in the music... What an extraordinary mystery, that synchronicity.

Daniel: What are your reactions after listening to the piece for the first time?

Monika: I think he managed to recreate through the music that ethereal atmosphere, two women together...

Rio: Yes, and also that very fresh, very bright, radiant side in the complicity. The eroticism is rather understated, but very bright. In the end, it's the poetry that stands out...

Luc: Do you think other women, who may be lesbians but didn't take part in the encounter, could be touched?

Rio: I think so, of course.

Bunhild: Even non lesbians.

Monika: Everybody has homosexual tendencies. And if we have emotional or intellectual relationships with all the people around us, then why not have sexual relationships too? Man or woman, you're a human being, with other human beings. Relationships should be complete, instead of limiting oneself to emotional relations with people of the same sex, and then confining emotional and sexual relationships to people of the opposite sex. Why this mind-body dichotomy?

Daniel: Do you think eroticism arises from a taboo being broken?

Rio: That's not how we felt, neither of us. On the contrary, it was very natural.

Monika: Absolutely.

Luc: The notion that eroticism is based on breaking taboos seems to me extremely reactionary. We're living at a time when the forbidden is starting to recede, and so another aspect of sensuality emerges: one that precisely isn't based on the forbidden, it is much richer.

Rio: Exactly: it derives from sensibility, from a direct relationship with others. In this piece, the source of eroticism is the encounter leading to intimacy and the way music reveals that intimacy. In my view, that's where the exciting aspect lies for the listener.

Luc: What does that feel like, listening to yourselves?

Rio: It's both embarrassing and… interesting. The sound takes you back to the situation, and you feel you were caught at a particularly intimate moment. But on the other hand, listening to yourself adds an intellectual erotic dimension.

Monika: At the beginning, there was a lot of shyness: we were meeting for the first time, and with microphones. When you listen, you feel the progression, the shyness fading…

Rio: As emotions take over, you forget about the embarrassment.

Daniel: Do you relive the situation?

Rio: You relive it with a different perspective, a different amplitude.

Luc: Do you find it exciting?

Monika: Yes, of course.

Monika: One criticism could be that you didn't involve us in the editing. In the end, it's a piece you made on your own.

Luc: That's a perfectly justified criticism. The society we live in is engrained in my mind, no matter how free and liberated I may feel. I really have to blame myself in a fundamental way. It hadn't even occurred to me to say: come round, let's do the editing together. That's so revealing.

Monika: What you kept from our words is what a man felt like keeping…

Rio: We're not criticising the relationship between the music and the words, but by selecting some words, you also selected some aspects of our encounter.

Monika: That choice of words, and also for example, of laughter – wouldn't you say that's the choice of the male who finds these lesbians so charming?… Because we're in it, there are things we wouldn't have kept.

Rio: A lot of people will probably feel that what we're saying isn't very intelligent. We hadn't prepared anything…

Daniel: And so they'll totally miss what makes this encounter interesting!

Luc: Audience reactions in front of a realistic event like this one are definitely an issue. It's a realistic event, but placed in an artistic, cultural context. It has to be sensational, because to them music is sensational, it's not everyday…. What I tried to achieve has nothing to do with sensationalist journalism. It is the most difficult type of account, of a totally normal, everyday thing, it is moving precisely because it's commonplace.

I am so appalled by nastiness, repression, lies and all kinds of brutality, that at the same time, life fills me with wonder. And an encounter as natural as the one that happens on this tape, with all its tenderness, seems to me a lesson in living.

Presque rien ou le désir de vivre

Almost Nothing or The Desire to Live

1972–73

—— Part 1: 55 minutes, Part 2: 52 minutes

Part I: Le Causse Méjean

This is about the daily life of farmers in a poor region... French farm workers are interviewed by a German couple. This very slow-paced film not only criticises itself, but dangerously allows the viewer to criticise it.

Part 2: Le Plateau du Larzac

This was a record of how the farmers fought to preserve their right to live and to work on land that the army tried to occupy for training purposes. This film is a document, an example of the fight of the disenfranchised minority.

Production: S.W.F., Unterhaltung Musik und Dramaturgie, Baden-Baden

Petite symphonie intuitive pour un paysage de printemps

Little Intuitive Symphony for a Spring Landscape

Stereo tape
CD BVHAAST Records Acousmatrix 3 (1990)

1973–74
— 25 minutes

This is the musical form of the soundtrack for *Almost Nothing or The Desire to Live (Presque rien ou le désir de vivre)*, where I try to represent the impression we felt in front of the landscape.

We were Brunhild and I, in the surroundings of the Gorges of the Tarn. We had the idea to take a small road climbing a rocky mountain up ten kilometres. After the last curve, the landscape at sunset revealed itself to us, unexpectedly, and gloriously. The colours went from the dry grass yellow to the mauve — only a vast landscape of nature was offered to our eyes — without any obstacle. We could see everything. Later, when I projected back to this moment, this place and the feelings I tried to compose music to revive my memory.

The "Causse Méjean" is a high plateau of an altitude of about 1000m in the Massif Central. Farms far from each other punctuate it. Some persons returned their herds of ewe. I had the idea to evoke this recluse and diffuse presence of humans by fragments of conversation I had with some of the shepherds.

The human language is integrated in musical texture; the sound of the voice says much more than what it really says. One of the shepherds said to me one day:

"…I am never bored. I listen to the landscape. Sometimes I blow in my flute and I listen to the echo speaking to me…"

When thinking of him I used the flute and its echo in this music.

Allô, ici la terre, chapter 2

Hello, This is the Earth Speaking, Chapter 2

This piece tries to show the irremediable way in which the organisation of contemporary society is likely to disturb conditions that are necessary to the perpetuation of life. It is a (modest) report at the same time lyrical and informative regarding the state of pollution and it's effect on the natural elements. Contrary to the first chapter, which is an audio-visual piece, the second chapter is an only sound piece, composed of magnetic tapes accompanied by an ensemble of amplified instruments (five instruments & two tape recorders). The texts are by scientists, philosophers and sociologists. Instrumental sequences and realistic waves of noises including rain, sea, landscapes, industry, and sounds of war are used as dramatic elements to the various texts. It is the first piece in which I consciously employ (insofar as the attempt at *Hétérozygote* was unconscious) the sounds as ideas and t hus as real speech. This ground is divided into five elements: Earth, Water, Air, the War… and Utopia.

This piece is quite characteristic of beginning of the 1970s — the beginning of a 'green' reflection…

Commissioned and produced by WDR. Abteilung Neue Musik, Cologne
Premiered in Cologne, Aula Apostelgymnasium on October 7, 1974 Groupe BETWEEN

1973–74

— approximately 2 hours

Portrait of Luc by Brunhild, 1971

Allô, ici la terre
Hello, This is the Earth
Speaking

In the show titled *Allô, ici la terre n°1* (composed in 1971-72), the audience was surrounded by sounds and projected images (3,000 slides, several tapes playing electronic music, and a live ensemble with amplified instruments). I thought of it as a poem dedicated to the Earth. It attempted to depict Nature, while expressing the hope that its harmonious balance could be preserved. At the time, I went as far as to say (and it was already a tad old-fashioned), that the piece was like a love poem, because I was so moved by all that drowning beauty.

The script revolved around nine elements (light, space, landscape, looking, waiting, eroticism, movement, heterogeneity and dance), with an irrational sequence of impressions and sensations.

But there was an underlying tension, betraying the fact that all this could just collapse at any time. This political suggestion introduced the mood of the second chapter (in the same way, the second piece introduced the third). What I mean is (in case the reader hasn't already guessed), that these were three sides of the same idea, each being a show in itself.

Allô, ici la terre n°2, unlike Number 1, attempted to build a rational argument, forming a concrete discourse. All the elements that constituted the piece, be they noises, music, texts, instruments or songs, had to be as charged with meaning as possible.
The script, score and tapes for *Allô, ici la Terre n°2* were done in 1973-74. To analyse the piece briefly, I would say that I gathered texts, sounds, documents, music and songs which were connected though their meanings. There are two kinds of texts (objective and subjective), and two kinds of sounds (realistic and abstract).

The "objective" texts — scientific, sociological, political, and the statistics — are illustrated by songs whose "subjective" lyrics, in contrast, make use of popular images.
The "concrete" sounds and the realistic noises conflict with the abstract musical elements, creating a sense of contradiction that tints the texts and gives them a more perceptible presence.

The piece is made up of five parts: Earth, Water, Wind, War and Utopia. I wasn't trying to give a full account of any of those elements; rather, I wanted to consider them as places one looks at, just because they're there. This is why all the things that are said, and which are neither meant to be original nor essential, have to be considered as found objects.

That is to say, I found this or that, but someone else might well have found something else. And so you have the frustrating feeling that something is missing, but that's compensated by the fact that what you discover feels close and familiar.

Making ecology a political matter is a very complex endeavour. You might say that the only people interested in the consequences of pollution are a rich elite, worried about losing their comfort. But you could also say that a global upheaval would reach well beyond that privileged elite, affecting every single human being. Therefore, every social class should think about those issues. Ordinary people too should ponder those problems, not just a few specialists and professionals. Specialists have always guarded their secrets jealously: industrial secrets, military secrets, research secrets, etc.

Can we call for an end to secrets?
Is it utopic to think that we have to change everything?

That the structures and institutions we hide behind are no longer suited to us, but will instead drive society, and the earth itself, to destruction?

Should the handful of people who lead the world, who create structures and institutions and who protect them, decide what our future should be?

At the end of *Allô, ici la terre n°2*, a woman's voice provides us with a temporary conclusion. The woman is a symbol here. She implies that men are too worn out by wars, by power and speculation, and too corrupted by compromises and the pleasures of easy money. She means, in a nutshell, that the role of men in history is over. Whereas women could, thanks to their freshness and their candour, represent the future.

That voice tells us:
Here starts utopia,
It is still embryonic
We must use our imagination to help it come to life.
Politicians and statesmen have only brought about violence,
our role, all of us,
is to invent the future."

Ephémère

Ephemeral

This piece of music – which as the name indicates, is based on 'effects of sea' – is intended for instrumentalists, prfessional as well as amateurs, and for musicians open to all musical genres. The tape is used as score. As its name also indicates, this tape was designed for one special moment...

Short-lived experiment
Tape alone or to be played with various instruments (Free instrumentation).
CD ALGA MARGHEN plana f. 33 NMN 081– 2010

1974
— 30 minutes

Labyrinthe de violence — "Mais où donc est-on?"

Violent Labyrinth –
"Where are We?"

An endless program for tape and two slide projectors. Images and sounds evoke the violence of the civilised contemporary society. The multi-media piece is closely related to the political situation of that year.

Stereo tape and slides
Premiered at Musée Galiera, 23-25-26 June 1975
Record LP: PLANA-F alga027 - 2009
Dance

1975
— continuous loop

Cellule 75, Force du rythme et cadence forcée

Cell 75, Force of Rhythm and Forced Cadence

Premiered in Berlin Metamusikfestival 1976. JP Drouet (percussion),
and G. Frémy (piano)
Record LP : La Museen Circuit MEC01 – (vinyl)
Maison ONA Editions
CD La Museen Circuit – Musidisc 242232. CD Tzadik USA – TZ 7033

1975
— 31 minutes

This piece for piano, percussion and tape tries to express — successfully or not, I'm not sure — a few ideas related to everyday concerns. The musical means are ambiguous, yet they present the listener with a range of suggestions that may, ultimately, trigger some thoughts.

"75" is the year it was composed, which implies a social context specific to 1975. This doesn't mean the context was different in 1976, just that any creation is grounded in the moment of its conception.

"Cell" relates to the idea of a musical cell of course, but also a prison cell; political prisons, refugee camps, ghettos and apartheid, as well as cultural and intellectual forms of segregation.

"Force of Rhythm" has to do with trying to find in rhythm a liberation through imagination, intuition, vitality, feet firmly on the ground (the opposite of head in the clouds) — through the dynamics of reality.

"Forced cadence" on the other hand suggests constraints. It's also to do with precision marching as a manifestation of oppression.

The ambiguity comes from the fact that the "force of rhythm" and "forced cadence" are based on the same regular rhythms. One is positive and is turned towards life, while the other, which is negative, tries to imprison the former.

These few ideas are probably very far from what one feels while listening to this piece, which is why it is itself like a cell which imprisons meanings.

Panama

One People One Canal

Still courtesy C.N.R.S., Paris

Soundtrack for 16mm sociological film studying US colonial presence in the Panama
Canal area and joint struggle against imperialism by the Panamanian people and the
military regime in power in 1975. Directed by Jean-Louis Berdot.
Awarded Cannes Film Festival Official 1976 Selectio: "Perspectives di cinema Français"

1976
— 53 minutes

Algérie 76 n°1. La révolution agraire

Algeria 76. The Agrarian Revolution

Tape solo or tape and slides
Report on the Algerian peasants who, after the Agrarian Revolution, received grounds and exploit it jointly. Discussions with farmers, illustrated by Algerian music recorded on the spot. (Bilingual: French-Arabic)
Photographs by Djamel Farès
Premiered at Cinémathèque Algiers, 1977

1976
— 32 minutes

Promenade symphonique dans un paysage musical or Un jour de fête à El Oued en 1976

Symphonic Promenade in a Musical Landscape, or Feast Day at El Oued in 1976

The sound of the landscape, the voices, the language, the market and a feast, together form a symphony that recounts a day trip to the region of El Oued; they also place the music within its original environment.

Stereo tape solo — At the origin, audio-visual version
Photographs by Nasser Edin Ghénifi
Record INA-GRM 9104 fe (vinyle). CD Sub Rosa, Belgique SR252 2006
Maison ONA Editions

1976–78
— 32 minutes

Algérie 76 n°2. Belghimouze, village socialiste

Algeria 76 n°2. Belghimouze, A Socialist Village

Tape solo or tape and slides
Report on the establishment of a new agricultural village, known as "Socialist Village".
A co-operative of women who speak about their new life, their work and who sing the Revolution.
Photographs by Djamel Farès
Premiered at Cinémathèque Algiers, 1977

1976–77
— 30 minutes

Tuchan, village n°11350

A series of conversations draw the life of a village of Corbières. The farmers speak about Cathares, their policies, the 'Popular Front,' the exodus of the young people, the vineyards and hunting. For one month, we questioned, followed and photographed some of the inhabitants who accepted the suggested experiment. This is a symphonic report with original music and ambient noise from the village.

Audio-visual piece (music, interviews, slides)
Stereo tape and two projectors for two screens
Premiered in Paris at Musée d'Art Moderne on 11 March 1977
Maison ONA Editions

1976–77
— 1 hour 15 minutes

1977 programme, *Tuchan Village 11350*

NARBONNE

Samedi 28 Mai
à 21 heures
Amphithéâtre
M. J. C.

Le G.A.A.M. présente

2ème PRINTEMPS MUSICAL

Direction Artistique   Henry FOURÈS   —   Jules CALMETTES

« TUCHAN 11350 »

Spectacle audio-visuel de

Luc et Brunhild FERRARI

Réservation :   Bureau M.J.C., Service Relations Extérieures Mairie, Syndicat d'Initiative
Prix des Places :   Adultes 12 F.   Enfants 8 F.

Algérie n°3. La Société nationale de sidérurgie

Algeria n°3. National Steel Company

Algeria N°1, N°2 and N°3 is from a visit in El-hadjar (Annaba) with various discussions with the workers in connection with their work conditions, of socialist management and how the factory is run. It is recorded with the noises and environments of their daily life. Unfortunately the "Agrarian revolution" presented here as freedom from colonialism has since given way to a reactionary religious rift.

Stereo tape or tape and slides
Photography by Djamel Farès
Premiered: Cinémathèque Algiers, 1978

1976–78
— 35 minutes

Place des Abbesses

This is a musical portrait of Abbesses in Paris, intended for a film. It is an electroacoustic piece and is devoid of any technological sophistication. It was composed in a time of my life where, having left all the institutions, I started to build up a personal studio.

It forms part of a family of portraits, which I developed in the 1970s — portraits of society, of villages, people and places. The portraits of people call upon the techniques of report, while the places are rather suggested than photographed. Like poems. For *Place des Abbesses*, it is rather a question of evoking than representation. It is a small place of Paris, located at semi-hill of Montmartre, between the Sacré-Coeur of God and of his Saints, and Pigalle of the liberties and the sex. It is a pretty place and a little old-fashioned, full of ambulant musicians, old philosoper-tramps. Many friends were living in the district.

Music for a film by Erika Magdalinski
Production: INA
CD Tzadik USA – TZ 7033

1977
— 25 minutes

Les Apprentis

The Apprentices

Stills from *Les Apprentis du Magicien*, 1977, a biographical film on French polymath Boris Vian made for television, scored by Luc Ferrari.

Music for a 16mm film by Gérard Patris
Production: Coquelicot Film and Südwestfunk for television

1977
— 1 hour 20 minutes

Loin de l'équilibre

Evolutions Far From Equilibrium

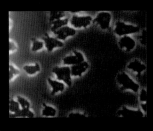

Stills from scientific documentary produced by CNRS Paris

For a 16mm colour, scientific film by Alain Bedos
Production: CNRS Paris

1977
— 30 minutes

Cyclotron

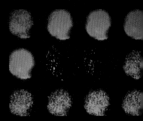

Stills from scientific documentary produced by CNRS Paris

For a 16mm colour, scientific film by Alain Bedos
Production: CNRS Paris

1978
— 18 minutes 44 seconds

Et tournent les sons de la garrigue

And the Sounds of the Garrigue Go Round and Round

Stereo tape and free instrumentation
Premiered : Action Musicale, Narbonne (1977), Le Vivant Quartet
Maison ONA Editions
CD Césaré 06/03/4/2/1 France September 2006

1977
— 25 minutes

How can we convey musical ideas without resorting to the conventions of erudite writing, and allowing the musicians some freedom and spontaneity? Lying down in the gentle heat of the garrigue, the atmosphere seeping through me, I pondered this problem, with the sounds and scents blowing across the landscape. Anywhere between five and ten participants, more even. It would be good to have a piano or a keyboard (with vibraphone, possibly synth), and one or several melodic instruments (the word melodic is used in the vaguest possible sense).

Depending on the type of ensemble and the size of the venue, the instrumentalists, or some of them, can be wired. In which case, the microphones must also be used to amplify micro-sounds, i.e., sounds that would not be audible under normal acoustic conditions.

This music is not conducted in the traditional way. However, it would be preferable to have a leader in charge of the general organisation of the piece, and of the way sound moves around.

This score indicates how to play sequence by sequence, as well as the ambiance, and the general line the music follows. This piece of music is a proposal more than a composition. It is about the communication between the musicians whom choose to carry it out or "to invent it".

This is a score of intentions, or of sound wishes, a tape that points to musical matters and shape. These general ideas give the piece a direction. I found a few quotes written at the time I composed this piece, describing the intentions of the composition and explaining how I meant to create a psychological climate to stimulate the musicians' imagination:

…Over the last few summers, I had extended holidays in Corbières. During the hottest part of the day, I would snooze without really sleeping. In that half-sleep (where I abandoned consciousness to some extent), I found myself steeped in this place, and felt a link with it. The silence inhabited by small indefinite sounds, the scent of lavender or thyme, the harshness of the stones and thistle, their air blowing through the pine needles with a noise that evoked a hand stroking the curves of a large body.

("What did you do today?" I was asked, and I answered, "I worked in the bush.") The gentle and violent garrigue with its complex and diffuse sensuality, so different from the rest of the landscape. I saw in its suspended time the forms and durations of gestures of love…"

The score and the tape consist of six sequences. The chain of the one with the other is done by fades, so that they should be heard. The musical result is thus only one gesture, a slow evolution, only one movement of pleasure.

Seq. 1 (5) eyes, the glance, approach, contemplation, harmonic play, the absence of time

Seq. 2 (3) the kiss, the mouth, immobility, the changing vibration, the chord, time

Seq. 3 ('45) hands, caresses, touches, the beginning of the rhythm, recognition and the superimposition of different times

Seq. 4 (4'45) language, the course, the movement, shivers, dispersion, tension, speed repetition, nervousness

Seq. 5 (4'10) play, rise, convergence, orgasm, rhythm, unit

Seq. 6 (4'30) languor, memory, calmness, the impulse, the harmonic melody

♩ = 144 (environ)

exemples de formules répétitives à partir du mode et des accords

Exercices d'improvisation

Improvisation Exercises

A suite of exercises (five to seven minutes each) that can constitute the basis to/ for individual or collective improvisation for any instrument or group of instruments (eight maximum). Each exercise is based on a continuity: harmonic or melodic colours and rhythms. They are intended for amateurs, professionals or students and can take place in concerts. Interpretations can take after different musical genres and styles from classical/contemporary to something approaching Jazz or Folk. The best would be to try to avoid cliches, supposing it's possible not to fall into other traps by doing so . Rather, look to forget cultural conventions. Having said this, it should be made clear the chief improvisational propositions are of a tonal nature, i.e, each Study has a characteristic 'harmonically vague tonality' which it is advised to take as a starting point around which you can then develop. The hypothetical schema — either a key, tonality, or a mode with a regular tempo — are there to be played with and not be prisoners of; they should be seen instead as a means to physically communicate with the other members of the group. Apart from these propositions (harmony, tempo), performers are completely free to invent the music as they desire. (Though some will say, well, what's left after proposing the key and the rhythm? I say everything's left, that is, invention. I'd go further and add that invention shouldn't be beholden to technique. Each study's proposition being simple and continous (fluctuation, variation), they should be considered as support and instigator of the collective imagination. To get the most out of the excercise there must be simultaneous focus on the proposition and the other players—as should always be the case when making music—which is easier said than done. Focused listening and group reactions from the attention given to others. Everyone speaks and responds in the intuitive intimacy of involvement. The result is musical speech.

For stereo tape and instruments. Maison ONA Editions. Disque vinyle ALGA MARGHEN planam 5 (it) – 2010 by Gol and Brunhild Ferrari

1977

— approximately 44 minutes

Presque rien n°2.

"Ainsi continue la nuit dans ma tête multiple"

Almost Nothing n°2, So the Night Continues in My Restless Mind

Premiered : Paris Festival d'Automne, Centre Pompidou, 14 November 1979
Record LP INA-GRM 9104 fe (vinyle)
CD "Presque Rien" INA-GRM / La Museen Circuit – MUSIDISC 245172
Maison ONA Editions

1977
— 21 minutes

A Presque Rien is one (i.e. not two) homogeneous and natural non-urban place, with particular acoustic qualities (transparency and depth), where one hears far and near without excess, on the scale of the ear like one says on a human scale, without technology, and where nothing stands out, so that the various sound inhabitants each have their own floor, and this small world is never covered over – just an "almost nothing". Or the opposite of sensational

Then something happens and settles in.

When I finished composing *Presque Rien N° 2*, I wrote this:

'The sound hunter sets off to capture a depiction of the landscape at night, encircling the sounds of night with the tape recorder and many microphones. Instead the night takes over, the interior landscape modifies the external night, composing it, and the sound hunter juxtaposes his own reality (imagination of reality); or can one say, psychoanalysis of his landscape of night.'

What is very peculiar in this story about *Presque Rien N° 2*, is that after having finished it I did not consider releasing it, as if this thing were too intimate, as if it concerned only me. Two years later I forced myself to listen to it again, and told myself that I had no reason to lock up this psychoanalysis of the night landscape jealously, that it was necessary to give it its freedom—there was no reason that this secret night should not see the sun.

The premiere of *Presque Rien N °2* took place in 1979 at the Centre Pompidou in Paris, and I remember that at a certain moment, people opened their umbrellas. I took this as a gentle sign of complicity.

A la recherche du rythme perdu

Remembrance of Rhythms Past

For piano and tape (can be also played by adding other musicians)
Premiered: Béziers. 9 May 1978. Henry Fourès
Maison ONA Editions
CD La Muse en Circuit – Musidisc 242242

1978
— 20 minutes

la recherche du rythme perdu is more specifically meant for jazz musicians, which doesn't mean it's intended to be a kind of jazz music. It isn't really a new piece, yet it isn't a new version of an older piece either. But let's be clear: the same magnetic tape was also used for Musique socialiste — programme commun for harpsichord and magnetic tape, a piece that was created in 1972, the year the "Joint Programme for the Left" was signed.

As for the score, although it isn't totally new (it uses the same notes in parts), it contains new and different approaches; let me try to explain. *Musique Socialiste* was meant for the harpsichord, but more importantly, for performers from the world of classical music, and their experience led them to reproduce instrumentally what the composer had written.

In *A la recherche du rythme perdu*, I would like to address musicians from the Jazz world. That is to say, classical musicians usually see notes as a playing code, as ciphers to be reproduced instrumentally, but now instead, those notes function as pointers that describe an ambiance. The story of this score is, one could say, the story of an experiment, hence the subtitle "Reflections on Writing". The experience of classical musicians has to do with the global form of a piece, therefore they're used to a musical course, with its progressions and degressions. For Jazz musicians, the experience has to do with the moment, the detail the rhythm and the intuitive communication between players.

This is why this score contains fewer notes and, more importantly, the notes don't necessarily have to be played, they are more like pointers indicating a general course. If I said this was a new piece rather than a new version, it is because the music that comes out of it is totally different, one can only say that there is an expressive kinship, and dare say (after looking up the word in a dictionary), a lyrical kinship.

A few remarks about the title. I sometimes have the feeling that what I called the code, the respect for what is written (i.e. the law), has overshadowed musical intuition, it has censored the sense of rhythm, and has gradually gnawed at the performer's imagination. Don't think that I consider the pulsation of the tape as a rhythm; just like writing, it is sterile — only the action gives life to the whole.) I would like us to go looking for those lost treasures. Rhythm can't be written down, the small differences that mean that a body is brought to life by a rhythmic reality are so subtle that the coarseness of writing cannot capture them, this is how the phrase "reflections on writing" should be understood.

P.S. A piano soloist can play *a la recherche du rythme perdu*, but it would be interesting for a pianist and percussionist to perform this piece together. In which case the percussion should be a jazz drum kit, with the possible addition of bongos, congas and sundry small

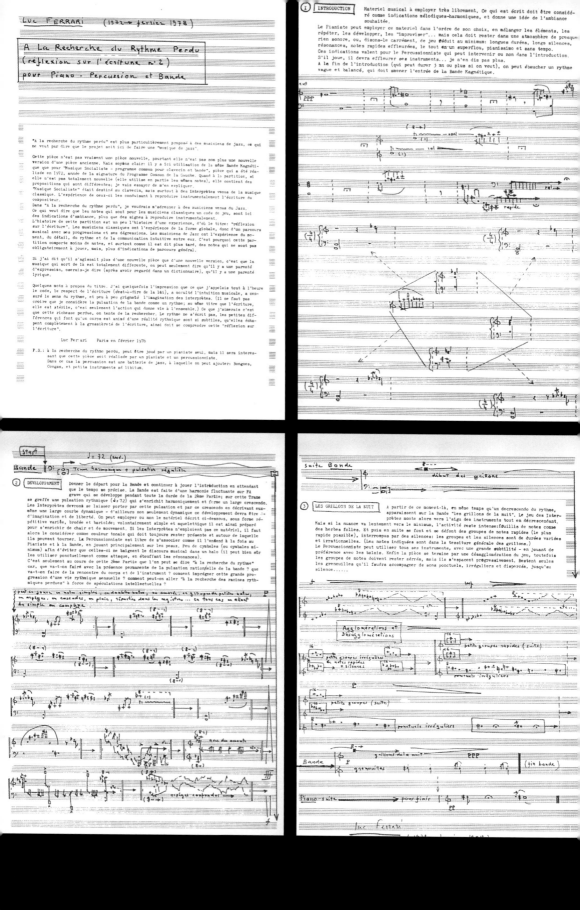

A la recherche du rythme perdu score courtesy of Edition Maison — ONA

Chantal ou Le portrait d'une villageoise

Chantal or Portrait of a Villager

The daily life of a young woman born in a village, aged 22, with one child, married to a bricklayer. She works as a cleaner on minimum wage. She talks about her activities, her hopes, her worries, her women's problems, her search for emancipation.

Photographs by Olivier Garros
Stereo tape, Maison ONA Editions
In collaboration with Brunhild Ferrari

1977–78
— 40 minutes

Interview with Catherine Millet

Photograph by Brunhild Ferrari

Highbrow, Lowbrow

LF: I am not interested in the homogeneity but, on the contrary, in the heterogeneity of cultures and traditions, although it is difficult to define the limits of these notions.

I am open to influences but without seeking to express myself like someone from the East or from the Maghreb. Their knowledge is totally different from mine and inscribed in their way of being, of living, of moving, in their very bodies. Having said that, nowadays we are caught up, even unconsciously, in a gigantic cultural mix. For example, the "repetitive" composers would obviously not have invented that type of music if Jazz hadn't already existed in the USA, or if Hindu music, which they're so keen on, hadn't already been around, etc. Here is an example of cultural "digestion" that can foster the emergence of an original form of expression.

So when I've worked on non-western musics, I've always tried to present the work as a kind of reportage. My report on Algerian music took the form of a piece of music, but with elements that didn't belong to me. It tells a story, the story of my journey through the sounds of Algerian towns and country. I recreated this journey, emphasizing the sounds I heard and recorded. So I don't interfere with those cultures. I don't present myself as a composer, but rather as a "weird journalist." My role, in fact, is to locate, as best I can, that form of expression which doesn't belong to me.

CM: In the realm of the visual arts, at the beginning of the century, artists explored so-called primitive or popular cultures to stimulate avant-garde art: the Cubists did it with African art, the Russian Futurists with religious icons. Were there any comparable moments in music?

LF: I think history is always cyclical. And yet, even when you think you're employing the same formulas as in the past, they are not exactly the same. There is no actual return to Primitivism. You can employ forms that resemble tonality, but it's never tonality the way Beethoven employed it, because the experience of a 20th century composer is very different from Beethoven's. You don't repeat things, but you lean on history to bolster up your own experience. We are not at liberty to ignore our past, our temperament and all of our ethnic baggage.

I would like to insist on the distinction between, on the one hand, a highbrow form of expression, i.e. writing (and we know the few works, created by very few people, that make up History), and on the other hand, the rest, which you could call popular expression. I don't want to give the impression I am indulging in populism, it's got nothing to do with that. For me, popular expression is anything that isn't published, it's all the people who speak. Everybody on earth expresses themselves through speech, not just the masses, but the intelligentsia too, as well as farmers or the bourgeoisie.

Those utterances constitute our culture just as much as those people who engrave it in History. I also think there are connections between those two types of culture, the highbrow writer listens to popular speech, and popular expression draws some of its forms from highbrow writing. Neither is more important than the other. Each has a beneficial influence on the other. Similar influences are at play between unwritten music and highbrow music. If you consider for example Bach's suites based on dance themes, you realise that popular music is in no way simplistic or simpler than scholarly music. On occasion, Bach simplified elements he borrowed from popular music. He simplified the rhythms but he made the harmonies more complex. Another example would be Ravel, borrowing from Andalusian music. If you listen to Andalusian singing, you soon realise that it's ten times more complex than what Ravel did with it. But Ravel had another skill, he knew about orchestral timbre, about the orchestra as substance, matter, and he used that knowledge to give back some complexity to a language he had simplified to begin with.

As city-dwellers, our roots are completely hidden from sight. Maybe we've lost them altogether, but we still have what I would call a temperament. As for me, I was born in Paris, I live in Paris, but my temperament is Mediterranean. My body responds to heat, to the rapid movement of waves rather than the slow movement of the ocean... And I think that this temperament plays an important part because it expresses itself in every aspect of life, in all creative activities.

You can have mixed temperaments, too. You can't really speak of ethnic groups in the case of Latin America, but you can talk of a mix of temperaments — African, Spanish, Portuguese, French, etc. That has given rise to a multitude of very original languages and means of expression. What we now call "Latino-American" is absolutely authentic even though it doesn't correspond to one specific ethnic group. Moreover, in those countries, a few people have been schooled in Western highbrow culture, and so musically, they express themselves in the language of Schönberg, on an internationalist scene that has nothing to do with local artistic expression. However, a whole generation that has gone through the School of Vienna is now returning to its own original temperament, or looking to combine that western culture with their own.

I think it's a shame things are always made to compete, people feel they have to side with one ideology or another. In my opinion, men and women's expressive potential should not be constrained by the straightjacket of any formalism. Scholars and intellectuals often impose a formalist rigidity while denying others the right to express themselves. But you find the same type of extremist tendencies among struggling minority groups who, even if they're not blowing up

lent as bombs. Still, it's understandable, struggles like these are conducive to that sort of intransigence. As for me, I think it is precisely in times of struggle that you should be willing to embrace plurality and diversity.

CM: How does this plurality interact with your own research?

LF: First I went through an intellectualising and a "structuralist" phase, before I realised that form, in and of itself, is rather pointless and that, besides, I was addressing a category of people who were in a minority. Curiously enough, what we often call minorities are in fact majorities. I then got interested in realism, in everyday gestures, everyday sounds. I became aware that freedom wasn't an aesthetic ideology, but that it was conveyed through contradictory desires. This is why I can express myself in musical languages that are contradictory, and it is that contradiction that brings me pleasure.

Ce qu'a vu le Cers

What the Cers Saw

Excerpted from the foreword: The Cers is a wind of the north which blows on the region of Aude. I like that it happens to reference Debussy. What interests me is a subversion of the writing... simplicity is subversive...experimentation of a new simplicity, thus another complexity can appear inside the moment…

Stereo tape and instrumental group
Premiered at Fylkingen, Moderna Museet in Sweden 1979
Record LP: Ventadorn VT 323 (vinyle) CD Musidisc 242262

1978
—25 hours 16 minutes

Ce qu'a vu le Cers score courtesy Maisons ONA Editions

LUC FERRARI

Ce qu'a vu le Cers

Réflexion sur l'écriture n°3

pour bande et instruments

Dédié aux habitants de Tuchan (Aude)
et au Vivant Quartett

Mai Juin 1978

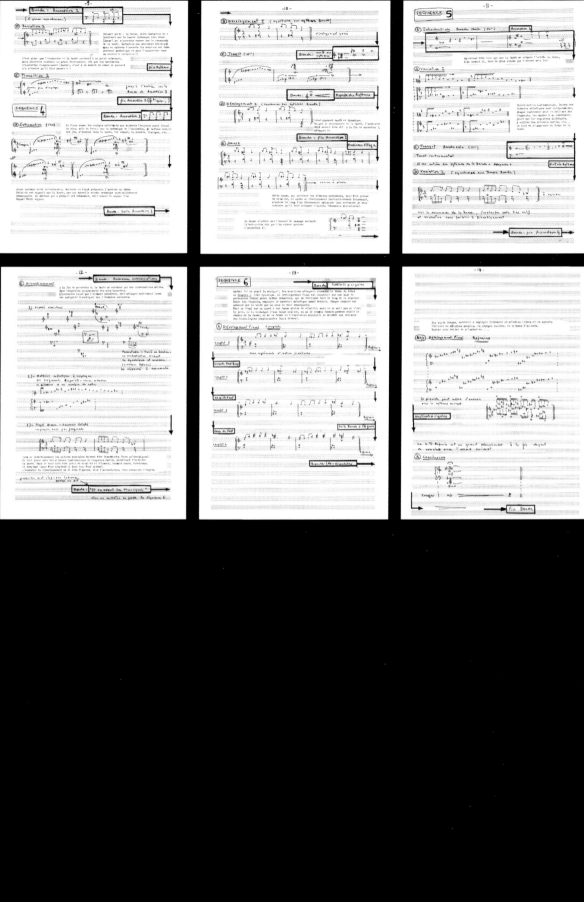

Apparition et disparition mystérieuse d'un accord

Mysterious Appearance and Disappearance of a Chord

A pedagogical score meant for music schools. The realisation is decided by the group, who choose their own path through the score depending on their abilities.

For alto Saxophone-quartet
Alphonse Leduc Editions

1978
— Aleatory duration

Luc FERRARI

Apparition et Disparition Mystérieuse d'un Accord

APPARITION ET DISPARITION MYSTERIEUSE D'UN ACCORD

(texte pour programme)

Cette pièce pédagogique est une suite de variations autour d'un accord.
L'accord-objet (immobilité) est progressivement décoré de guirlandes (rythme-
mouvement), jusqu'à ce que ces ornements prennent toute la place et fasse disparaître l'immobile dans la trappe.
A la fin, l'accord réapparaît comme un diable, et un compromis se cherche entre
stabilité et mouvement.

Introduction

Accord de Base

Travail sur l'attaque et la décroissance homogènes du son. (tenue sans vibrato)
Attaque glissée très cuivrée (effet jazz).
L'ensemble fabrique un Objet Musical.
Répéter plusieurs fois l'accord de base.
Enchaîner sans transition à la Variation I:

Variation 1

Première attaque ensemble.
Travail individuel sur le corps du son; croissance et décroissance homogènes (sans vibrato).
La durée du souffle individuel doit produire la désynchronisation et l'indépendance des instrumentistes. L'ensemble fabrique une Trame.
Enchaîner à la Variation 2, soit ensemble soit indépendamment (c'est-à-dire que le passage à 2 peut se faire progressivement).

Variation 2

Travail individuel sur la nuance d'ensemble et l'évolution harmonique.
L'ensemble fabrique une Trame dont la composition harmonique évolue. Même technique que pour V.I, mais les attaques sffz progressivement diminuent d'intensité jusqu'au P (chacun toujours indépendant).

En diminuant la sffz jusqu'au P

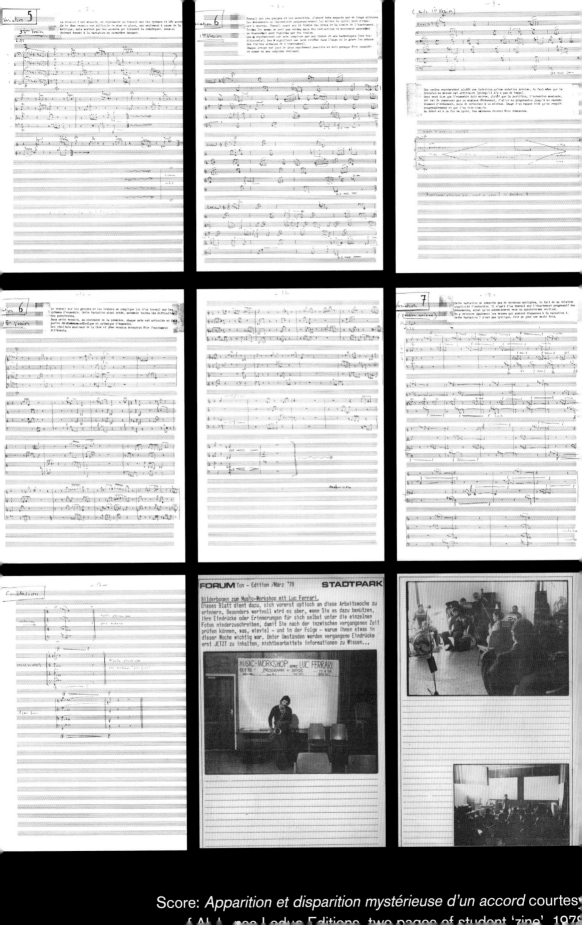

Score: *Apparition et disparition mystérieuse d'un accord* courtesy

Bonjour, comment ça va?

Hello, How Are You?

For piano, violin, cello and bass clarinet.
Premiered at Darmstadt Institut für Neue Musik 29 March 1980
The first version of this score was titled 'The Ministers' Dance at the Pompidous
Salabert Editions

1972–79
— 12 minutes

Bonjour, comment ça va? is a suite of seventeen formulas to be played in the indicated order. The three instruments, being free in the details are bound by the simultaneous fixed and regular tempo. Each formula is to repeat an unspecified number of times. However one could say that the shorter formulas are repeated more often than the longer formulas. The passage from one formula to the other should be done by "fading".

In formula one, the piano begins alone, followed by the cello, then the clarinet. Once the formula is well established, one of the instruments (maybe the piano) gestures (bonjour) and moves on to formula two, the other two finish the formula they are playing and move on to formula two. The passage from one to the next is to be done without a pause. And so on to formula seventeen.

The duration of each formula is free and must only be balanced according to the duration of the piece (10–15 minutes).

One should try to find a dynamic homogeneity for the three instruments. The accentuations are generally not indicated. The musicians can underline and accentuate the rhythmic and melodic effects. The musical writing implies its own accentuation. Inside the formulas every musician has a degree of freedom, they may for example change the rhythms or introduce silences, but must maintain the same tempo.

These variations of detail may intervene especially from formula twelve onwards to facilitate the introduction of noises.

PIANO Tempo ♩= 144 (environ)

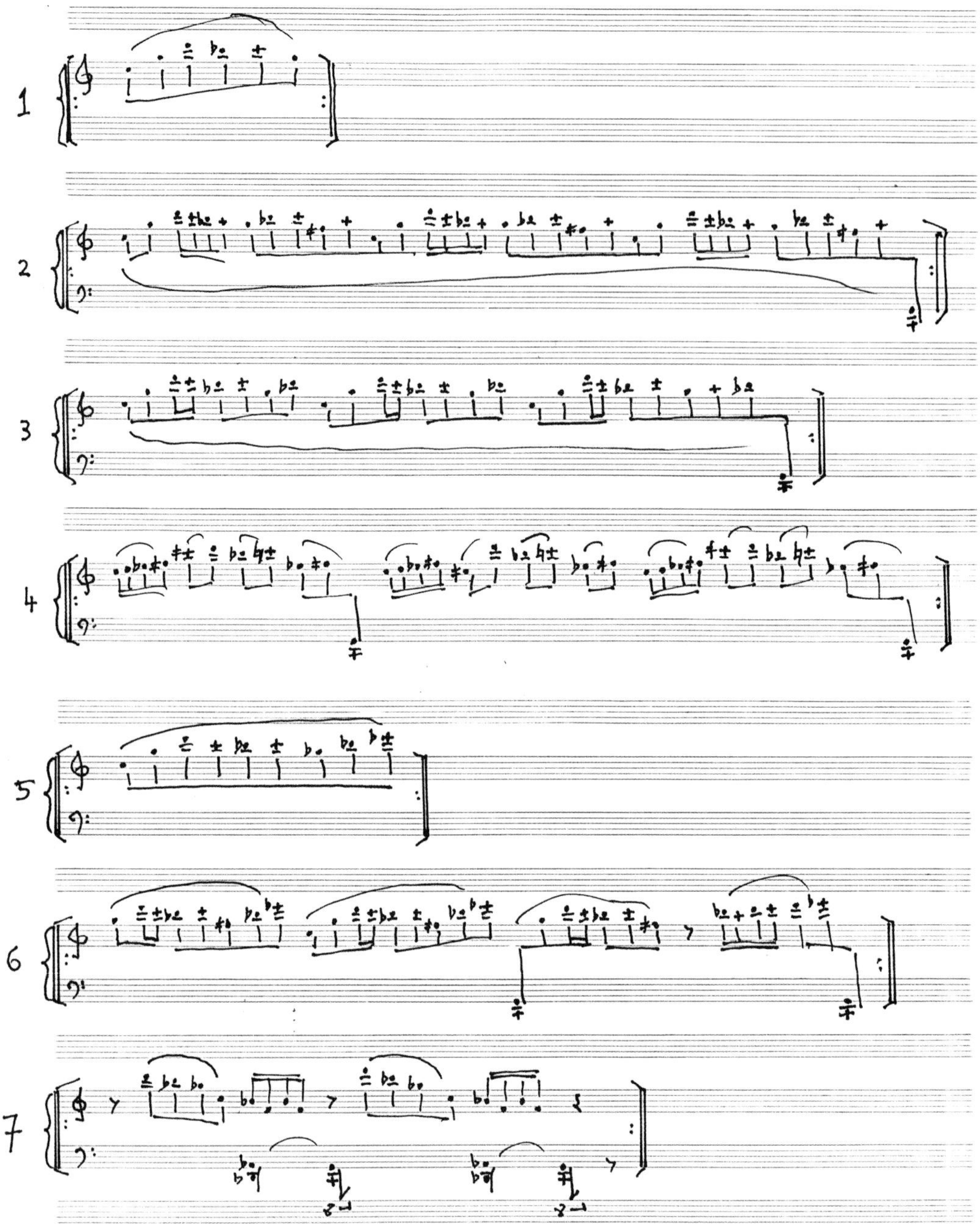

(Piano 2)

x = Taper du pied

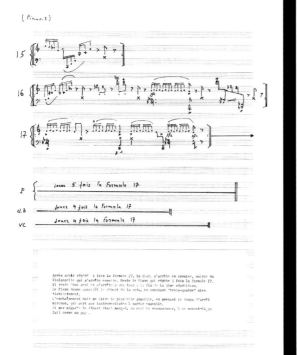

(Piano.3)

15

16

17

P   Jouez 5 fois la Formule 17

cl.B   Jouez 4 fois la Formule 17

VC   Jouez 4 fois la Formule 17

Après avoir répété 4 fois la Formule 17, la Clar. s'arrête en premier, suivie du
Violoncelle qui s'arrête ensuite. Reste le Piano qui répète 5 fois la Formule 17.
Il reste donc seul et s'arrête à son tour à la fin de la 5ème répétition.
Le Piano donne aussitôt le départ de la coda, en comptant "trois-quatre" bien
distinctement.
L'enchaînement doit se faire le plus vite possible, en prenant le temps d'arrêt
minimum, qui sert aux instrumentistes à partir ensemble.
Si par mégarde le départ était manqué, on peut le recommencer, à ce moment-là ça
fait comme un gag .

(Piano.4)

(Tempo ♩ = 144) CODA

Trois quatre

claquement
de mains

CLARINETTE BASSE sib   Tempo ♩ = 144 (environ)
(notes réelles)

0   16/4

1

2

3

4

5

6

7

8

9

10
non legato

(Clar. 2)

11

12

13

14

15

16

17

✗ = Taper du pied

Après avoir répété 4 fois la Formule 17, la Clar. s'arrête en premier, suivie du
Violoncelle qui s'arrête ensuite. Reste le Piano puisqu'il répète 5 fois la Formule 17.
Resté seul, il s'arrête à son tour à la fin de la 5ème répétition.
Le Piano donne aussitôt le départ de la Coda en comptant "trois-quatre" bien distinctement.
L'enchaînement doit se faire le plus vite possible, en prenant le temps d'arrêt minimum,
qui sert aux instrumentistes à partir ensemble.
Si par mégarde le départ était manqué, on peut le recommencer, à ce moment-là, cela
fait comme un gag.

CODA

F non Legato

VIOLONCELLE   Tempo ♩ = 144 (environ)

(VC. 2)

× = Tapez du pied.   ∥ b = Frappez la caisse avec la main gauche.

Après avoir répété 4 fois la Formule 17, la Clar. s'arrête en premier, suivie du Violoncelle qui s'arrête ensuite. Reste le Piano puisqu'il répète 5 fois la Formule 17. Resté seul, il s'arrête à son tour à la fin de la 5ème répétition.
Le Piano donne aussitôt le départ de la Coda en comptant "trois-quatre" bien distinctement.
L'enchaînement doit se faire le plus vite possible, en prenant le temps d'arrêt minimum, qui sert aux instrumentistes à partir ensemble.
Si par mégarde le départ était manqué, on peut le recommencer, à ce moment-là, cela fait comme un gag.

CODA

(Trois quatre)

F non Legato

Le Dernier Soleil

The Last Sun

Music for a documentary film on the Aztecs
Directed by Philippe Lavalette and Charlotte Boigeol
Production: CNRS Paris

1980
— 45 minutes

Still from the *Le Dernier Soleil* courtesy CNRS

le Centre
National
de la
Recherche
Scientifique

CNRS

présente

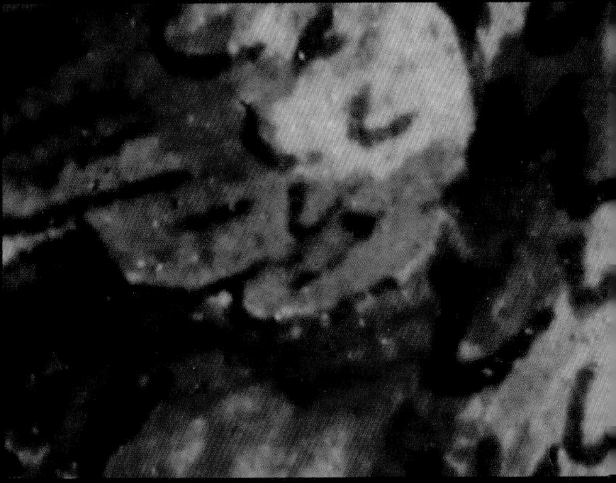

Le Petit Pommier

The Little Apple Tree

Music for a film in collaboration with David Jisse Production: FR3
Directed by Liliane de Kermadec

1980
— 1 hour 30 minutes

Ateliers

Artists' Studios

Electroacoustic music for a short 16mm film on Jean Clerté, directed by Joël Farge

1981
— 13 minutes, 30 seconds

Chronopolis

Chronopolis

Stills from *Chronopolis*, courtesy CNC/Cirque Productions

Electroacoustic music for an experimental animated 35mm colour film by Piotr Kamler. Th
Cirque Productions

1981–82
— 72 minutes

Histoire du plaisir et de la désolation

A History of Pleasure and Distress

The initial idea of this piece is to let oneself go to the harmonics of the devil and the pleasures of sensuality. Pleasure is a journey that goes from logically linked ideas to the breakdown of logic that allows desire to express itself. But the path is paved with desolation, which defeats pleasure. During the composition of this score, I listened to a great deal of music from the beginning of the twentieth century, including Debussy, Ravel, Stravinsky, as well as Bartok and Prokofiev. I allowed these rich orchestrations to permeate in my mind. By comparison, these works seemed more innovative than the works that followed them. Or perhaps it was a new way of listening?

For symphonic orchestra. (Four flutes, two oboes, two English horns, three clarinets, one bass clarinet, three bassoons, four horns, four trumpets, three tenor trombones, one bass trombone, cimbalom, four percussions, piano, two harps, fourteen violins I, twelve violins II, ten violas, ten violoncellos, eight double basses). Commissioned by Radio France for the Orchestra National de France.
Premiered: Paris Radio France Nov. 1982 by the Orchestra National de France, Conductor: Michael Luig. International Prize Serge and Olga Koussewitzky (1990)
Salabert Editions. CD La Museen Circuit – Musidisc 242242 MU 750

1979–81
— 35 minutes

10 décembre 1980

"Harmonie du diable" représente l'idée de donner un sens positif au diable, comme justement celui que représente la chair et la sensualité, alors que la société puritaine a gonflé ce démon historique de tous les maux, de tout le mal, de tous les plus bas instincts puisque les instincts sont toujours les plus bas.

4 janvier 1981

Quel désespoir.
Échec de la vie ou échec à la vie, choix de la guerre.
Échec au plaisir, échec au plaisir de vivre, on choisit la destruction et le plaisir de l'homme devient le plaisir de la destruction, la mort.
L'homme viril, l'homme horrible dans sa violence de mort, d'organiser la mort. L'homme horrible et ridicule dans son pouvoir et dans l'expression absurde de son pouvoir.
L'homme stupide qui détruit avec violence, avec haine, l'homme qui ne connaît pas l'amour, qui ne connaît pas la tendresse, pas la douceur de la caresse sans pouvoir.
L'homme qui mélange le pouvoir et l'amour, au point de ne faire l'amour qu'avec le pouvoir.

Extraits du journal de Luc Ferrari

HISTOIRE DU PLAISIR ET DE LA DÉSOLATION

pour orchestre symphonique

de Luc FERRARI

HISTOIRE DU PLAISIR ET DE LA DÉSOLATION

Pièce pour orchestre symphonique

de Luc FERRARI

Créée le 6 novembre 1982
au Grand auditorium de Radio France
par l'Orchestre national de France
sous la direction de Michaël Luig

Commande de Radio France

FICHE TECHNIQUE

- 4 flûtes	- timbales
- 2 hautbois	- 4 percussions
- 2 cors anglais	- 1 célesta
- 3 clarinettes	- 1 piano
- 1 clarinette basse	- 2 harpes
- 3 bassons	- 14 premiers violons
- 1 contre basson	- 12 deuxièmes violons
- 4 cors	- 10 alti
4 trompettes	- 10 violoncelles
3 trombones	- 8 contrebasses
1 trombone basse	
1 contre tuba	**Durée** : 35 minutes.

Contacts

Michel Dumont - 105, rue Haxo 75020 Paris
Tél. (1) 364.95.64.

Réflexions à propos de...
Histoire du plaisir et de la désolation

« Le propos initial de cette histoire est de se laisser aller aux harmonies du diable et au plaisir de la sensualité. On dirait maintenant à la recherche d'une "nouvelle sensualité" pour faire mode ou étiquette.

Le plaisir est un parcours qui va de la logique d'enchaînement des idées, à la cassure de toute logique pour que s'exprime le désir. Mais le chemin est balisé par la désolation qui ponctue et fait échec au plaisir... Et c'est terrible...

Cette parole narrative se fraie un passage à travers des styles changeants, dont les contradictions sont utilisées pour leurs qualités expressives.

Ainsi le discours se développe le long de trois mouvements enchaînés :
- Harmonie du diable,
- Plaisir-désir,
- Ronde de la désolation.

(...) Pendant la composition de cette pièce, j'écoutais beaucoup de musique du début du XXᵉ siècle : Debussy, Ravel, Stravinsky première manière, et aussi Bartok et Prokofiev. Je me suis laissé imprégné par la richesse de ces orchestrations, par la matière musicale, qui me semblait nouveauté par rapport à celles qui sont venues après. Ou ai-je écouté d'une nouvelle manière ?

Je n'ai pas la prétention de dire que j'ai cherché à faire comme eux, mais j'ai en tout cas essayé de renouer avec un orchestre vu comme un grand corps vivant et charnel, et non plus, à tort ou à raison, disloqué ou découpé en tranches, qui a été celui des trente dernières années.

Ces expérimentations nécessaires ont vécu. La rigueur, et parfois la sécheresse ont piloté le monde musical. Essayons de trouver autre chose...

Et pourquoi pas le plaisir... si c'est possible ? »

LF: Could you tell us how you first came across Jazz?

LF: First, I'd like to say that I'm not used to talking about jazz. I listen to it, I like it, but I rarely talk about it. So I'm really an amateur, in the sense of someone who enjoys something. My point of view definitely isn't that of an expert. So I find it pretty intimidating to be talking about jazz with jazz experts or for a specialist magazine.

FH: Are there jazz musicians who particularly touched you?

LF: Yes, all the time, of course, from the very beginning. What I find interesting in jazz is the sociological and the philosophical viewpoints. It comes from a society that invented its own music, based on a tradition of uprootedness, and under very difficult circumstances. One of the things that interest me is the way jazz emerged, how this creative activity, which in my opinion is one of this century's great musical adventures, came to be.

FH: Do you see this "great musical adventure" within a western context? Would you place jazz in the same category as Contemporary music?

LF: In terms of categories, you could say that the world of jazz and the world of 20th century contemporary music have seldom come into contact. They have imitated each other at times – jazz people were influenced by contemporary music, and classical musicians were influenced by jazz in the 1920s and even before, like Stravinsky, Darius Milhaud, and many others, particularly American compos-

ers. Information and connections bounce back and forth, things connect, but only occasionally.

FH: Is your music influenced by jazz?
Ferrary Indirectly. Jazz is a kind of oral writing, or rather an oral tradition, and that has given me a lot to think about. In recent years, through the 1960s and 1970s, contemporary music started exploring the idea of non-written languages, and the opportunity to create some openings in music, writing and performing; therefore we couldn't remain indifferent to what jazz was doing, nor to the stance of any non-European, non-western music based on an oral tradition. We couldn't help finding direct or indirect connections with those improvisational techniques.

FH: When you say written/oral, do you mean composition/improvisation…

LF: Yes, unavoidably, at one end of the spectrum you have absolute writing, as in classical music over the last two centuries, and at the other end of the spectrum, you have unwritten writing – sorry I mean unwritten music – which is more specifically associated with oriental musics or improvisational music, like jazz. Now, classical music, even when it borders on improvisation, remains a form of writing. In fact, that's what I call unwritten writing; whereas music based on an oral tradition, even when it is written down, remains an oral language. Anyway, for us composers raised in the written tradition, this "philosophical" observation provides a new way of thinking about music.

Jazz at the Crossroads
Interview with Francis Hofstein
Photograph by Brunhil Ferrari

FF. When you say "unwritten writing", it sounds to me like a reproach, as if you were saying that Boulez, for example, could play jazz, since it doesn't really involve any improvisation, or that musicians constantly revert back to set patterns, that invention based on jazz harmonies seldom happen, etc. In short, you're saying that in most cases, what happens is a kind of unwritten writing.

LF: I would actually say that those set patterns are not a form of writing, they are basic principles that enable people to create. The serial principle, for example, is a basic principle that is authentically written. You cannot improvise serial music. However, musical forms remain codes within which we move, and I do not know of any music, no matter how erudite or how informal and irrational, that does not follow codes. We shouldn't regard those codes as more interesting or imaginative than they are; their function is to enable the imagination to express itself. So, what does it matter if we say that certain norms or certain codes in jazz operate across three or four chords, that there are improvisational situations in which one or two people stand apart for a given length of time, or that there are ensembles, and solo parts… I don't mind that. But the central principle still remains improvisation, in so far as all the notes produced come from the body and from immediate intuition rather than from some abstract pre-conceived ideas about writing.

FH: Body sound – that's one of the definitions of jazz. Would you agree with it?

LF: I would go much further: it is the result of a sensuality, a meeting of intui-

tions in the presence of a totally unsustainable event. Precisely at the point when the musical event is being created, a moment of sensuality expresses itself in a crucial instant, it is fragile to the point of being unsustainable. It has to constantly be revived. That's what is so fascinating about these types of music.

FH: What do you mean by "intuition"?

LF: The intuitive knowledge that one is creating something which feels right. By "Right", I don't mean like a judge who decrees that something is "right" or "fair", but like something that is at once expected and unexpected. When you hear a jazz pianist, you feel as though he's always in the heat of the action, he is moved by some extraordinary reason. And sometimes, if he seems to have hit the wrong note, you can see him turn what could be seen as a mistake to his advantage; it becomes a means of renewal. Mistakes or failings, always serve to regenerate ideas. It's very perceptible with soloists.

FH: Could you give an example?

LF: Just when I need them, the names escape me. But I was thinking of Thelonious Monk. He's an extraordinary pianist, you never feel he has technical skills, you might think that his ideas come very slowly, and yet he is extraordinarily agile.

FH: Would you oppose him to a pianist like Art Tatum?

LF: Yes. To me, Art Tatum expresses himself with Chopin-like virtuosity – this is not meant as negative criticism, it is remarkable how the instrument seems to be part of his body, like an extension of the body

With Monk, on the other hand, you rather get the impression of a struggle with the instrument, you feel that he is always good-humoured enough, or violent enough, to create something from that instrument which exists outside of him, like a foreign entity.

FH: You also play the piano, don't you…

LF: Yes, badly. What I'm interested in isn't the instrument in itself, it's the work I do on it. When I write, I prefer to use an instrument, to touch it, because it's sensuous. Sensuality, which is very important for me, brings me closer to jazz, even though I only have indirect connections to it. Also, when I listen to people who are making jazz, I don't listen to them as a musician cum critic, the way I would listen to Gustav Mahler for example. For Mahler, I draw on a whole western culture, and my critical sense; when it comes to jazz, even though there are things I like and others I don't, I listen in a much more spontaneous way.

FH: You make a distinction between a "critical" way of listening and a "sensuous" way of listening. Does this imply a scale of values, or are these just different approaches? To be more specific: today, jazz has achieved "recognition" but for a long time, it was deemed inferior, precisely because it expressed a sensuality, a sexuality, too indecent to be exhibited on a music stage…

LF: Right, you're talking of the early days, the beginning of the 20th century, the 1920s. At that time, a certain group of libertine bourgeois men had every right: they wallowed in debauchery, had young lovers and kept women they despised; mean-

while, society as a whole was puritanical. I believe we've made some progress since then, and we now recognise that sensuality is as important as intellect. There's a renewed appreciation of intuition, sensuality, eroticism, we no longer despise them. Society, culture, have played a part in this greater open-mindedness.

FH: When you talk of culture, do you mean that western ears are more open to all sorts of music?

LF: The role of culture is to open up intelligence, isn't it! Since the end of WWII we have approached other cultures in a much more direct way, and society is less inclined to think that people who don't look like us are savages. It's a small step. We used to see it as "not civilised" music, now it's music by people who are more or less respectable.

FH: Still, more or less…

LF: Yes, that's true. Even if you like the music of a country, you might still retain racist prejudices against its citizens.

FH: Do you think that music – yours as well as Monk's – can have an influence on the social order?

LF: I think that no cultural activity is innocent. Just like jazz, contemporary music – when it's not too elitist – has an influence on society… I don't think we can dissociate the influence of musicians from the influence of their works. Music is a kind of global entity made up of individuals. There are great movements, people who, at the same time, do things that are alike, even from the philosophical point of view. I'm almost certain that there are jazz people black musicians for example, whose ideas are very close to mine. I don't meet many jazz musicians unfortunately, because I live in a very limited circle. When I go to jazz concerts, I feel so inadequate compared to those musicians that I daren't go and give them a hug after the performance, as much as I'd like to sometimes, because I find their work extraordinary!

FH: A whole music current – represented by Archie Shepp for example – has linked musical expression to political expression, saying: for us, playing music is a political act. Would you concur with that, in those terms?

LF: Absolutely. Free Jazz is necessarily a rebellious movement, a political movement. Rebellion *and* politics – sometimes we're rebellious but not political. That's why this movement is very important.

FH: Some people accuse Archie Shepp of going through commercial channels, for the sake of being heard: records, radio, television…

LF: It's impossible for a musician to think they're just playing for themselves. You need to be heard. And for that, you need to go through the communication channels, which are economic channels. But you can't compare the commercial leverage of Archie Shepp and, say, Charles Aznavour. It's totally different, and Archie Shepp earns nowhere near as much as Aznavour! One is a capitalist who indulges in the lowest forms of commerce, the other is a revolutionary artist who makes a bit of money every now and then.

FH: He doesn't make a fortune, but these days, he isn't as "politically" outspoken as he was…

LF: Because times change. In the early days of free jazz, there was a great political explosion – before May 1968 actually. Then, things calmed down a bit. People don't think in the same way, politics have become more internalised, the political situation has changed, and political expression with it. The beginnings of free jazz corresponded to a period when people took a very hardline stance. Black people had a very tough struggle on their hands. Their musical stance was very much like a radical social stance, and the feeling of violence that came through really stemmed from that attitude. Therefore, I would say music and politics are linked in this mode of expression which upset the structures of classic jazz, the chords, the bases, the prevailing codes, the notion of time, virtuosity, instrument – as they no longer used their instrument in the same way –, the notion of solo, of ensemble playing, etc.

FH: Did this upheaval permeate into your music as a result of you listening to jazz?

LF: No, because I don't have a violent temperament, and probably because I've never been in that sort of extreme situation, a harsh racial situation. In the end, as westerners living amongst white people we can't understand that surge of violence one feels when faced with an intractable repressive situation. We can understand it intellectually, but we can only imagine it.

FH: Did the way jazz musicians smashed up the "beauty" of sounds lead you to change the way you approached sound? That new relationship jazz musicians had to their instruments, the way they manipulated, altered, tampered with their instruments, deliberately ignoring notions of "purity" and "beauty", which had been quasi-concepts in music – did all of this filter through to contemporary music?

LF: Yes, in some ways. Contemporary music had this, a way of going beyond the instrument towards the extreme, a sort of non conventional use of the instrument. Everybody went through that stage, more or less, but I don't think this was as a direct result of jazz music, and of free jazz in particular. Anyway, to get back to violence, I think every composer has had, in his life, periods when he's wanted to smash barriers. To smash barriers, you need a degree of violence. But I also think this is temporary: free-jazz musicians who broke down so many barriers, including social, and with such violence, have since moved on to other modes of expression.

FH: Do you sometimes ask jazz musicians to perform your compositions?

LF: Yes, very occasionally. The music I write, the music I think about, that I invent, is conceived for classically trained musicians. But I've experimented with jazz musicians who expressed themselves in both modes, one foot in each camp, so to speak.

FH: When you work with a jazz musician, or a musician who plays both, do you take into account the fact that he plays jazz, or do you choose him because he plays the instrument you need?

LF: Absolutely, I take into account the fact that he plays jazz, that he has a particular way of attacking the instrument, of playing with it, developing ideas, appropriating the intentions and distorting them, an attitude which is typical of jazz. However, what I might write for them is not jazz. But I'm interested in using the way those musicians assimilate the themes and develop them.

FH: In *Bonjour comment ça va? [Hello how are you?]*, performed last year at the Pompidou Centre, the clarinettist Jacques Nourredine attacked the score in a way that was very close to jazz…

LF: Because he plays jazz. But that's a bit of a coincidence. The three musicians who performed the piece were those who agreed to work on it for that concert. Even through it's a very rhythm-based piece, it wasn't meant for jazz musicians. But I'm very interested in the way jazzmen play rhythms, they feel them more than they learn them. That's an issue I have with classical musicians who, conversely, learn rhythms but don't play them. It's very difficult to explain: you can't explain why some things fall into place and others don't. All you know is that some read the rhythms, and others play them, some have technique, others have experience, some get it right, others don't…

FH: And what about jazz musicians?

LF: They have an inexplicable sense of rhythm.

FH: In the programme notes for the Centre Pompidou concert, you wrote: "One shouldn't confuse dynamics and power (...) To take a mischievous example, I would say: the dynamics of jazz, and the power of disco." In the present case, would you talk about the power of rhythm, or the dynamics of jazz?

LF: I would call that the dynamics of rhythm. Because power is institutional, and therefore in a world of its own and that's nothing to do with dynamics.

FH: Maybe you find such dynamics in the voice... In the same concert, Presque rien n°2 [Almost Nothing n°2] was played. In that piece, various sounds are used, and your voices. It isn't a "musical" piece as such...

LF: Let's say it's sounds.

FH: So we can draw a parallel with jazz – for a long time, people said it wasn't music, but noise...

LF: People have always said that about any new music.

FH: But you went through the Groupe de Recherches Musicales, or GRM, where part of the work revolved around noise, noise as sound. There's common ground between your training with Pierre Schaeffer, and a jazz musician's training, or non-training. It's a gradation, with the voice at the basis, the voice of blues singers, then Billie Holliday's voice, which is all the closer to the body as it doesn't go through an instrument...

LF: The blues is the opposite of a sophisticated voice. Of course, it can be invert-

ed sophistication: there's a snobbism of the untrained, unrefined voice... But what fascinates me with those singers, is that the voice is so close to speech and at the same time, totally close to music, without sophistication, that is to say, it doesn't transform the voice, which pertains to the body, into some sort of external instrument. When I hear the great singers of the recent past, for example Maria Callas, I always get the impression that she's singing on the outside; I always pictured her as a completely normal woman, but with a cone in front of her mouth, and a little machine that brought her voice out, as if it all went through a sophisticated mechanical device to produce the sound we hear. That's a weird image, but it's as if their voice were an instrument, like a trumpet. Whereas the male and female blues singers have an interior voice which doesn't need to express itself through strength, or through melody – it expresses itself with all its marvellous imperfections, grainy, rough, imprecise, with all the rich and irrational qualities of speech.

FH: The female blues singers at the beginning of the century sang into a bullhorn.

LF: They sang quietly...

FH: They sang loud, with or without a bullhorn. Opera singers like Maria Callas sing without a microphone, whereas all the singers today, including blues singers, sing into a microphone...

LF: I think that's a shame, but the microphone is another issue. It's to do with fashion, but it's also a necessity. the acoustics aren't as good in venues, and they're larger. Hence this obsession with technology, sound systems, excessive amplification, loudspeakers, all of which are really detrimental to the music.

FH: Is fashion important in music?

LF: Yes, because you can't escape it. It goes hand in hand with business, and the producers say to musicians: this is to-day's sound, these are the orchestrations, the rhythms. Disco is a good example of that, even if it's falling out of fashion: you can say it was all the rage.

FH: When you speak of the power of dis-co, you're alluding to the imperialism of a rhythm, of a music…

LF: Disco isn't a rhythm, it's a machine, a machine to make you buy things. Since everything sounds the same, you no longer need to choose and you just pick a "disco record", it is not the same act as when you're buying an LP by Louis Arm-strong.

FH: It does away with the name?

LF: I'm not bemoaning the loss of a name, but the fact that it also does away with the imagination, dynamics, musicality, and replaces all that with a machine.

FH: Do you see a relationship between a certain use of electricity, the synthesizer, and what was called repetitive music, like Terry Riley or La Monte Young?

LF: I know them personally, and I was in touch with that whole current of American music from the beginning. In my opinion

there's no connection. Terry Riley has never used synthesizers as far as I know and neither has Steve Reich. On the oth-er hand, La Monte Young used electronic sounds, because he worked on harmon-ics and very sustained notes, with minute variations.

FH: Would you see a link between those "repetitive composers" and, for example, the music of John Coltrane?

LF: No, I don't think you can draw such a parallel. I really respect the work of peo-ple like Steve Reich, Philip Glass, etc. even though I think the hype around them is a tad tiresome. It's like a tidal wave sweeping across music, implying that you can't work any other way, at this point in time it's mandatory. Those postures are always irritating. As for those com-posers, their work is totally honest and I find it fascinating. Repetitive music has brought back to the fore some of music's traditional laws: it has always been repet-itive, apart from a few decades – the age of endless variation, of dodecaphony and of serialism. All of Bach's music, Vivaldi Beethoven, Schumann, is based on rep-etition; the theme is repeated, the harmo-nies are repeated, the continuous bases are by definition continuities, and popula music is always based on repetitions, re-peated rhythms, intentions, couplets, al non-European musics are based on rep-etitions…

FH: And what about jazz?

LF: Since jazz is a popular music, in the most interesting sense of the term, it is based on repeated chords, melodies cycles. Let's move away from repetition and talk about cycles, which are natura phenomena, I don't see why musicians should be outside of natural phenomena, like day and night, rest and tension, etc.

FH: As we're talking about cycles, we could also speak of music which evolves according to those cycles...

LF: That's why the history of music has moments of tension and moments of rest... For example, free-jazz is a moment of great tension; in contemporary music, this corresponded to a time of great effervescence, of exploration, of sometimes absurd research; that's also when the first experiments with happenings occured, as well as John Cage's more interesting works, Kagel's music theatre, etc. At the moment, we're living through a period of lesser tension.

FH: So you might say there is no progress as such, but cycles?...

LF: Philosophy spoke of progress, and we believed in it, with the rise of technology. Now, we're not so sure. There's no such thing as progress, only experiences.

FH: So a musician's work follows cycles, with moments of greater or lesser tension?

LF: Yes, but I can't give an example besides myself. In any case, I feel totally susceptible to, and sensitive to such cycles.

FH: You produced a film on Cecil Taylor, in the series titled *"Les Grandes Répétitions"* [*"The Great Rehearsals"*]. Cecil Taylor always seems to be in a state of tension, the tension never relaxes. What

led you to make this programme?

LF: When I heard his music, I was bowled over. At the time my friend Gérard Patris and I were in the middle of devising *Les Grandes Répétitions* for television – the first ever programmes about contemporary music on French television – so we thought of including a jazz musician in the series. In 1965-66, I felt it was important to dedicate one of the programmes to Cecil Taylor and his group. It was quite an adventure, I realised how difficult it was to communicate with someone who, as he put it, didn't come from our community. In the programme, when asked what he thinks of John Cage or Stockhausen, he says "They don't come from my community." And through his attitude, he really made us feel that he didn't come from ours. These communication issues brought a tension and a violence to the film, which was both a flaw and a quality, and which at least gave a good idea of his personality.

FH: So you had problems communicating with Cecil Taylor...

LF: We just didn't manage to talk...

FH: But you didn't have communication problems with his music?

LF: None at all. I had loved his music through the records I'd come across. But we only met him after we had decided to shoot the film.

FH: That brings us back to the piano, Cecil Taylor is a virtuoso, someone who has great technique – what do you think?

LF: That's not what he shows, though

When you hear him play, a moment later, you find yourself thinking: that guy's got a funny technique, but I didn't realise it. The main thing is that incredible strength with which he questions himself as a person, as a musician.

FH: Since we're talking about musicians, what do names like Charlie Parker or Duke Ellington evoke for you...?

LF: Duke Ellington, that's my first contact with jazz, so it would have been after the war, around 1950, and it moved me deeply, in all sorts of ways. I was hearing the big jazz bands for the first time, that is, an orchestra which looked like a symphony orchestra in terms of the instrumental mass, but which didn't sound at all like a symphony orchestra. All of a sudden, I heard amazingly new sonorities, produced by people who seemed like perfect technicians, yet didn't at all play like white people. That's when I realised that rhythm was a totally irrational notion, contrary to what people think, and that it didn't get conveyed through writing.

FH: Did jazz percussion and drums have a particular impact on your music?

LF: Maybe it's thanks to jazz if percussion has achieved such freedom in contemporary music. In the romantic orchestra, percussion was used as backing noise, not as a noble instrument. I wasn't familiar with those instruments at the time, but I hadn't come across Varèse yet.

FH: Were you influenced by jazz when you composed *Cellule 75 [Cell 75]*?

LF: Cellule 75 is a piece that has obvi-ous connections to jazz-like music. It's not jazz, because the thematic improvisation is extremely limited. The cells are scored, and they unfold according to a traditional relationship between instrument and writing, between instrument and score; but rhythmical dynamics are at the heart of *Cellule 75*, whose subtitle is, incidentally, *La Force du rythme et cadence forcée [Force of Rhythm and Forced Cadence]*. What I mean is that there are two poles: on the one hand, the dynamics of sensuality, on the other, *Forced Cadence*, power forcing you to go in a certain direction, to walk at a certain pace. So there is something akin to jazz in this piece, in that Force of Rhythm is based on a pulsation. Even though jazz has for a while now deployed itself outside of pulsation; but its presence is still felt. For example, I recently heard Sunny Murray, who plays very diverse things, very irrational from the point of view of rhythm, but he holds on to an inexplicable sense of pulsation, which is definitely there, in a very subtle, demonically elusive way. Only in jazz can you witness such profoundly intimate occurrences which writing never manages to generate. Only the tone of speech and instinctive gestures are able to transgress the order of things.

FH: How do you choose your titles?

LF: That's a problem. People always tell me that my titles are complicated, bizarre, etc. In fact, they're ambiguous, and they stem from a fondness for literature and a complicity with poetry. I choose them for their meaning, but also for the way they sound, because the sonorities of words combine with their meaning.

...H. In this, you are in agreement with the double bass player Charlie Mingus…

LF: The double bass is an instrument you never hear, and historically, the fact that it should no longer be at the bottom of the hierarchy of instruments is one of jazz's achievement, jazz pulled it out of its cultural wretchedness. It's a shame it's been replaced by the bass guitar, which is an uninteresting instrument. As for Mingus, he evokes for me a type of jazz related to Ellington…

FH: What about Sun Ra?

LF: I would classify him in a "post-free jazz"… We poor Europeans, only came across him around 1970… There's been all sorts of problems around with Sun Ra, demonstrations, bludgeoning, the cops…

FH: Anthony Braxton?

LF: Anthony Braxton puzzles me. I knew his work at the beginning and I thought it was marvellous. It was interesting, different from free jazz, but lately, he's been doing things with big ensembles, very structured, rather cold and intellectual, it unsettled me, I must say I don't like it much.

FH: Would you ask him to record one of your compositions?

LF: I would never dare ask him something like that. It's difficult to ask people who have another way of making music and who don't need some western composer asking them to work on a score that has nothing to do with them. I have worked with French or German jazz musicians, but it's a white kind of jazz without American roots, it's another culture, with totally different ways of doing things. I don't think I have anything to bring to a jazz musician. It is they who bring me something.

FH: You recently recorded an LP with French jazz musicians. How did that come about?

LF: I met this group, the Vivant Quartet [Living Quartet], who work in the South of France. They're not known here because they are Southerners, Occitan people, who don't care much about having a "Parisian career"; they play a lot in the South though, between Montpellier, Toulouse, Bordeaux and Lyon, but they rarely venture further north. I met them down there and we became friends. That's what came first, the pleasure of being together, eating and drinking, enjoying nature, swimming, friendship, then we thought it'd be good to work together, so I wrote a few things, and we tried them out, we brought things to each other, and I started to see how they reacted, how we "combusted" together. We invented some stuff, I did one or two scores which they performed, then I did a score titled *Ce qu'a vu le cers [What the Cers Saw]* – the cers is a wind which, like the Mistral, comes from the North and blows southwards. The idea of this piece is to be in a place and to evoke it through themes that resemble folklore (I called that "imaginary folklore"). We worked on it with the Vivant Quartet, who often played it during their concerts. That's when Ventadour, a record label specialising in Occitan singers, offered to release the piece as their first "contemporary music" record

it was thus adopted as something Occitan people could relate to. It's interesting for me, being released by a record label rooted in the region, rather than by some big, less adventurous, international corporation. However, *Ce qu'a vu le cers* is only one side of that record. On the other side were compositions by Henri Fourès, the founder of the Vivant Quartet. Because of his attitude, his talent and his work, he is also in my opinion one of the most significant and interesting composers today. He has a double training. He attended the Paris Conservatoire where he studied jazz composition and took piano class, so his music is much more "jazzy" than mine.

FH: It's funny, this interview focuses on jazz, and still we see an encounter between the classical world and popular tradition, taken up in a regional context – that really evokes the birth of jazz…

LF: I don't want to compare what I do with the origins of jazz, that would be extremely pretentious. But as a musician, or just as a human being, it is interesting to think about the birth of jazz. It's a totally original and unique phenomenon which can't be compared to anything else. A popular form of expression asserted its identity through means that weren't its own. I mean that those African people, those slaves, brought with them their memory, and not their means. They lived in dire social and cultural conditions, they started to make music with what they had at hand: marches, polkas, religious hymns. They took that western music, with its melodies and its harmonies, and completely subverted

it. They shaped that material with their identity. And the fact that jazz music was born from a subversion is extraordinary – words of rebellion are present in the very expression of that music. This appropriation and that hijacking of a code which was alien to them, can be considered as a political and social revenge: they took from the rich their mode of expression, and they gave it back to them disfigured, without their masters even being aware of it. Theft and grimace. The birth of jazz, that's food for thought, isn't it?

Jetzt,

Oder wahrscheinlich ist dies mein Alltag, in der Verwirrung der Orte und der Augenblicke (Maintenant, ou probablement mon quotidien il est là, dans la confusion des lieux et des moments)

Now, or There Lies My Daily Life, Probably, in the Confusion of Times and Places

Radiophonic composition
Production: Hessischer Rundfunk, Departement Hörspiel
CD Wergo –ZKM milestones WER 2066 2

1981–82
— 1 hour 45 minutes

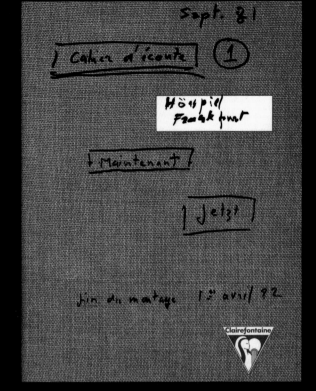

Cover of the original score of *Jetzt*

"Listening is like a dream…"

Besides using my compositions of the 1970s, as in the previous Hörspiel, the subject here is the overlapping of places at a present moment, a moment which itself becomes uncertain through the artifice of composition.

The sounds were collected in Frankfurt: the market, the river port, the Frankfurter Allgemeine printing presses, the corridors and the canteen of the radio station, etc. They were brought back to my home in Paris, where I did the editing, and they were commented upon as they came out of the loudspeakers, in my studio. Another shift then occurred between the particular sound of the speakers and the "real sound" being replayed by the tape recorders and taking the listener back to Frankfurt.

The play on time and place follows the same pattern as in *The Golden Ass* by Apuleius: one story is linked to another story which contains a story that is itself linked to yet another story and so on and so forth, so that in the end you lose track of who is who and who is doing what.

This is a different way of using autobiography as a medium, i.e., a labyrinthine way of conveying information.

Overleaf: Luc Ferrari sampling in studio 1981

Artistic Creation in The City

Text written in June 1981, for the Avignon Conference organised by the members of the Socialist and Republican National Federation, held in Paris (21-23 July 1981)

INTRODUCTION

Making music – just like painting, thinking, creating objects, inventing — is a way of expressing one's freedom.

But in our society, this freedom is hindered:
- by the social constraints that confine it to a narrow circle, with limited distribution channels and small audiences.
- by economic constraints, such as the norms imposed by producers, by the means of production or the media,
- by aesthetic constraints even, because social and economic criteria entail and perpetuate notions of genre or style, thus insidiously but inexorably restricting the freedom of musicians and audiences alike.

All this leads to a particular type of constraint which isolates the musicians, performers and composers from their audience, preventing them from sharing their aims and aspirations, and at the same time amplifying the other constraints. Now, if making music is a way of expressing freedom, then one must try to create more flexible models and organisations designed to allow for maximum freedom.

EXPERIENCING FREEDOM

You can only make music if you experience freedom on a daily basis. That freedom has nothing to do with the so-called "liberalism" produced and exploited by the ruling classes for their own benefit under previous governments.

Liberalism has enabled a handful of people to harness culture. Consequently, society as a whole has lost its ability to exert its freedom, while creative people are forced to operate within a consumerist system with set power relations.

Instead, we should consider creative people as both agents and witnesses: they go through the same experiences as everybody else but at the same time, they stimulate creativity and take it into new directions. This would lead us towards a truly democratic conception of culture.

EXPERIENCING DEMOCRACY

Whichever way you look at it, music today is confined to strictly hierarchical institutions: schools, orchestras, rigid organisations, not to mention the star system. To experience democracy, one would have to place individual and collective responsibilities back in the hands of students, performers and creative people. And to instigate different relationships between them and audiences, music lovers, producers, and the media.

This quest for democracy should make room for ordinary people, because their creativity should not be seen as distinct from the work of professionals. Indeed, music is not the preserve of specialists. It is a part of human nature, and necessary to self-fulfilment.

And so, we should strive for a kind of harmony that runs through the social fabric, and gives every individual access to imagination. At that point, the specialist is no longer the sole owner of the music. There is an exchange between his activity and that of the group. That doesn't mean that we would do away with specialists, but their approach would now be understood by society, because the gap that sets them apart would be bridged by competence, increased responsibilities, exchanges. The listener will hear, understand and act using all their imagination and creativity.

The musician will then be dealing with a society that is no longer passive, and together they'll create a collective listening experience. This is our wish – a society in which each individual, now set free, will create democracy.

Journal intime

Private Journal

Diary
Directed by the author for the Museum of Modern Art of Paris, 1982
Directed by Philippe Adrien, Theatre du Lierre, Paris 1989
Score-book: La Museen Circuit, Paris (no more available)
Score available: Brunhild Ferrari
Musical comedy for one reciting actor, a pianist and a singer
Premiered: ARC, Musée d'Art Moderne, Paris 11 April 1983

1980–82
— 2 hours

Music theatre play in one act
for a female narrator, a pianist and a female singer

"I gave a theatrical form to the reading of my private journal. These extracts were selected for the topics they touched on, and which could be made public, while other passages could only remain secret. Hence the difference between secret and private, or intimate. Fragments of the everyday are read, played, sung; these electroacoustic quotes embodied my concerns over a period of two years or more."

Fake journal of the real private journal or Real journal of a fake private journal

15 April 1982. Baie des Trépassés [Bay of the Trespassed], Finistère.
I am rereading my journal for the first time.
I decide to do something with it and I start sorting and selecting texts.

22 April 1982. Paris.
I look through my piano pieces and I confront the dates with those in the text.
It's amusing.

15 June 1982. Musée d'Art Moderne.
I meet with Christiane Audemard who asks me if I'd like to do something for next season.
I mention my "private journal".
All of a sudden, the title (which is so very original) slipped out of my mouth.

5 July 1982. At home at my desk.
I finish writing out the score. I like it. It swings.

10 August 1982. La Madrague.
I start composing *Sexolidad* for orchestra. I swim in the delightfully polluted Mediterranean.

15 Decembre 1982. Montluçon.
I meet with Jean-Paul Wenzel. I tell him about my concerns and ask him — how do you go about finding actors? He says we know them, but I don't know them, I say. I say I've spent the last two month meeting actresses. Do you like them? He says. Yes, I say, I like them all, but I'm afraid they're not my character.

15 January 1983. Théâtre de l'Odéon.
I meet Claude Degliame. She hurts me, she pleases me, to quote…
Unfortunately she's not available.

20 January 1983.

I meet Laurence Février.

At first she scares me and then she doesn't scare me any more. What agony.

I think she is the character I've been looking for.

29 March 1983.

What is "me"?

Is it him, is it her? or someone else?

Maybe isn't.

And what's a …musician, a composer?

A journal is something that exists, that you encounter…

Is a journal true?

A journal, it's everybody's journal.

As for Elise Caron and Paul Dubuisson, I had known them rather well for quite a long time.

Or I have known them quite long for a rather well.

1 April 1983.

Now the adventure is starting.

The rest is up to you.

Extracts:

The Pianist:

(addressing the audience)

"Between January 20th and 30th, I jotted down a few notes, automatic writing style, without really thinking about it; this is what came out of it."

(he plays while speaking, as if he were deciphering)

"Anyway, I didn't really find it interesting…"

(he plays the next part)

"To be perfectly honest, this last passage, it's the one I used for the introduction… Anyway, I think you had noticed…"

(…)

" - 9 March 82.

Yesterday, Brunhild and I finished doing up the room that's going to be my office. It was Anne's bedroom until she left.

It's been redecorated, I've laid the carpet… The colours all verge on bad taste.

I like flirting with those sorts of limits, it reminds me of Chopin's *Barcarolle* which I've been playing every day lately, with its juicy harmonies."

(…)

The Female Narrator:

" - 17 June 82.

I'm always very moved by the body of a woman. It's an invitation to feast on details. I mean the female body in general, be it a young girl's figure, either too rotund or too thin, or the mature forms of a woman on whose body I read, with infinite tenderness, the passage of time. Those marks of life which troubled me as a boy now speak to me, they tell me of long journeys and difficulties, they narrate the detours. The wrinkles at the corner of the eyes speak of too much light, those around the mouth tell me about all the conversations, the laughter, the worries; the folds on the belly speak of pregnancies, those on the buttocks, of the body's great transformations; the skin's stretched texture tells me of the different stages of life, the difficult times.

This great body, with all its history, is like a condensed summary, on a human scale, of the earth's history. A woman's body is my planet earth, the land that helps me ripen and bear fruit. In that landscape, the landscape I have lived in, I find my genuine and salutary contradiction.

Here I find my difference, and my heterogeneous."

Préface pour piano

Preface for Piano

Piece composed from the introduction of the *Journal intime*. Without extravagance, but can appear without shame in a program, can act as link or as material of improvisation, can be cut up in slices, can be played by several instrumentalists. The interpreters use then the score as material and decide together on its orchestration. The written parts can be played as a kind of homophony and the improvised parts can scatter and become extremely heterophonic.

Composition based on the introduction of *Journal intime*
For piano or keyboards, synthesiser, marimba and vibraphones.
Editions Salabert

1983
— 10 minutes

Luc Ferrari at home, photograph by Brunhild Ferrari

Une Soirée avec Matritia Perséverse [20]

An Evening with Matritia Perséverse

An Evening with Matritia Perséverse programme

1978–84
— 2 hours

Scène du va-et-vient

Coming-and-Going Scene

For piano, bass clarinet; cello and an actress
Maison ONA Editions

1978–80
— 25 minutes

Entrée

Entrance

For fifteen instruments (flute, oboe, clarinet, low clarinet, bassoon, trumpet, trombone, piano, celesta-glockenspiel (keyboard) two percussionists, violin, viola, violoncello, double bass). Premiered: Paris, Festival d'Automne 1979
Ensemble Musique Vivante, Conductor – Diego Masson
Transatlantique Editions

1978–79
— 23 minutes

Sexolidad

This piece explores a tonal language. It is based on a series of tonalities, each associated with meanings linked to the body: a specific tonality is attached to each part of the woman's and the man's bodies. Their movements produce a succession and superimposition of tonalities.

Premiered: Festival de Lille, 1983
Atelier instrumental d'Expression Contemporaine, Conductor: Benoît Renard
Salabert Editions
CD Elica, Mila

1982–83
— 30 minutes

For nine instruments (trumpet, two saxophones, singer, piano, double bass, three percussionists)

Composed for the Bal de la Contemporaine.

Premiered: Musica 84, Strasbourg (1984).

Bal de la Contemporaine Voice: Michel Musseau

Salabert Editions

CD Muse en Circuit – Musidisc 291302

1984
— 25 minutes

Les yeux de Mathieu

Mathieu's Eyes

Music for a film by Nicolas Cahen
Filmed on location in the Poitevin marshes with the sounds of nature. A train arrives with a group of dancers fitted with contact microphones for sounds of breath.
A choreographic conception of Susan Buirge and Claude Hudelot
Production and distribution FR3, Poitou-Charentes

1984
— 26 minutes

Dialogue ordinaire avec la machine or Trois fables pour bande doucement philosophiques

Ordinary Dialogue with the Machine, or Three Gently Philosophical Fables for Tape

The composer and the machine, or how to approach it… The questions asked and how to answer them… These machines that are the everyday surroundings of the indoor composer, what do they say… And how do you make love to a drum machine?

Stereo tape
(Song : Michel Musseau)
CD Elica, Milan
Maison ONA Editions

1984
— 30 minutes

Luc Ferrari in his studio 1983, Photograph by Volker Müller

Collection de petites pièces,
ou 36 Enfilades pour piano et magnétophone

Collection of Short Pieces, or 36 Enfilades for Piano and Tape Recorder

No sooner have they started and they're already over. Sometimes, they don't even start, they have no beginning. So, is this a suite? Maybe it's theatre. Is it that old dream — to never finish, or to always start over again? In the end, all those small pieces form a whole one…

Premiered : Montpellier Festival International de Radio France, Jardin de la DRAC, 27 juil. 1985. Paul Dubuisson
Muse en Circuit MEC 01 (vinyle), CD Muse en Circuit – Musidisc 242232 ED13171 – 2004
Maison ONA Editions

1985
— 45 minutes

An excerpt of *Collection de petites pièces* score courtesy Maison ONA Editions

Strathoven

Strathoven (a composite of Beethoven and Stravinsky)

That's it.

Stereo tape
CD BVHAAST Rehorn ds Acousmatrix 3 (1990)

1985
— 3 minutes

Portrait of Luc Ferrari in Paris by Brunhild Ferrari

Les Emois d'Aphrodite

Aphrodite's Frisson

These are episodes in an invisible woman's life. I'm quite fond of Aphrodite, she's so far away that you can't see her, and yet she has endured through time, despite people finding her immodest, despite being burned several times during the Inquisition. So, I humbly started evoking her frisson, though I end up forgetting her in the web of the music.
A first dance: a piece of fear –
Second dance: a movement by her –
A third dance: a good portion of carnal trip –
Finally: the wild dance of Aphrodite

For piano, clarinet, percussion and tape
Premiered: Paris Péniche-Opéra 1986 (P. Dubuisson piano, François Cremer clarinet, P. Cueco percussion)
Maison ONA Editions

1986
— 35 minutes

LUC FERRARI

LES EMOIS D'APHRODITE

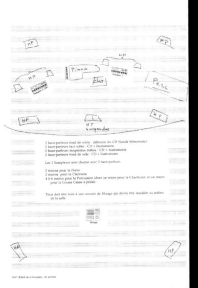

En un tournement d'amour

In a Whirlwind of Love

It is a love which torments. It is always repeated, but never the same. Ideas come and go. Stemming from it great symphonic continuities *(Cellule 75)* and meeting fragmentations en route *(Collection de petites pièces)*, this composition is a great form made of discontinuities that spin and whirl.

For an orchestra of forty nine musicians (two flutes, oboe, English horn, clarinet, bass clarinet, two bassoons, two horns, two trumpets, two trombones tenors, tuba, timpani, three percussionists, piano, harp, eight violins I, six violins II, six violas, four violincello, four double basss)
Premiered: Belfast 27 April 2005 BBC Symph. Orch. North Ireland,
Conductor: Philippe Nahon
Salabert Editions

1986
— 30 minutes

Je me suis perdu ou Labyrinthe portrait

I Got Lost or Labyrinth Portrait

A novelist speaking about her book...And a composer lost in a labyrinth meeting characters and becoming one of the characters himself. This Hörspiel is about the reality and adventures of literary creations.

Hörspiel, Bilingual (French-German). Production Südwestfunk
Realization: Muse en Circuit. Paris – Atelier de Création Radiophonique 1988
With the voices of Hanna Schygulla and Jean-Baptiste Malartre
With texts by Colette Fellous
Karl Sczuka Prize 1988
Stereo tape

1987–88
— 88 minutes

Calypso imaginaire
Imaginary Calypso

A mixed-race calypso composition by a white man who cannot make up his mind between 5/4 or 4/4 time, but you can still dance to it. Part of *Labyrinthe Portrait*.

Maison ONA Editions

1987
— 4 minutes

Conversation intime
Private Conversation

There are no words here, no interpretations, literary or otherwise, but simply a desire to hear a conversation between two very dissimilar instruments. So they needed to mingle intimately during the conversation; this is what I tried to achieve in this score.

For (harpsichord) piano and percussion
Premiered: Maison Radio France, Paris (1989). Elisabeth Chojnacka, Sylvio Gualda
Salabert Editions

1987
— 20 minutes

Tango-Pas
Tango-Step

Another interbreeding of tango and paso-doble, and extracts from *Patajaslotcha* in a new orchestration.

For piano, clarinet, percussion, synthesiser and voice
Premiered : Madrid, IV bienal Madrid-Burdeos (1988)
(JM Golse piano, S.Frydmann clarinet, M.Delafon percussion, M.Musseau voice)
Maison ONA Editions

1988
— 8 minutes

Créamaille 88

Radio documentary on the preparations for a fashion exhibition and a Young Fashion Designers international competition, both organised in Troyes, the French capital of the knitting industry.

Stereo tape
Realization: Brunhild and Luc Ferrari
Maison ONA Editions

1988
— 45 minutes

Musique dans les spasmes
Stereo Spasms
1986–89

It is a sort of novel, made up of memories, of reflections on life and music, and of fantasies. The text, with its dated sections, is a kind of sequel to *Journal intime*.

Friday 30 September 1988
With literary writing I don't feel the urge to have a specific identity, as I might have with other creative activities. My specificity is that, since I am not involved in that particular world, I feel totally free. That's the way I feel now anyway, that might change, but I hope not. Also handling time comes naturally to me. In other words, my creative abilities are defined in relation to time and rhythm, both of which are constitutive of writing. Might as well take this as self-evident from the beginning. There, that settles it.

So what shall I do now? I don't feel like doing anything. This morning, I was thinking everything bores me. What a pain!

I was thinking yes, everything bores me, but if everything really does bore me, what will become of me. I shouldn't get used to that state, maybe it's just a phase, grin and bear it, everything is going to be all right, it's just because I'm ill.
So yes, now, enough.

20 October
I wonder.
I can see it when they say hello, that I don't belong to their world. Through no fault of mine, they have always kept me at arm's length, as if to let me know that I wasn't for real, just that every now and then I was allowed in, next to them, but not too close. Except those who are bright enough to know about the multiplicity of worlds. The others look at me in disgust or amusement, or they file me in a category not unlike pornography.

24 October
I should go back in time, against the grain, visit the various stations of my angst, those that made me change tack. I pick up my book of time to help me understand
I pick it up, and I go backwards.

Donaueschingen, I've already mentioned that place.

Before that, I find a brief but intense station, a three-day seminar in Poland. I had to tell forty starving students about twenty years of my life. At the end, someone asked "And what are you doing at the moment?".

A harmless enough question followed by a deep silence. I didn't know what to answer, I couldn't lie, that's when I spotted, on the table next to me, my latest composition titled *Je me suis perdu*. By way of answer, I held up the score.

In August, Tuscany was a moment suspended in time.

In July, a week of concerts in the Savoie, and at that point I thought: "If I lose writing, I have to find speech again." And so I spoke, and lost my voice.

Turkey was a symbolic voyage. There, I was torn up with pain. The tissue healed, but the scar is still there.

Going further back still, I get to another year of travels and concerts in distant places, every time, they felt like humiliations; and above all, an illness that could not be cured. Concerts can never be taken as medication. Zurich, Frankfurt, Strasbourg, Vienna, etc… on the edge of contempt.

A concert in Nice in April 1987 was a mixture of dense events, including moments of friendship, but it probably caused my life to reach a tipping point; a symphonic concert in Germany, two months earlier, had already triggered off the process, without me being aware of anything.

If I could talk about all that, I'd understand it better.

But now that the tipping over is done, I can't be bothered to go into it.

It gets on my nerves!

I was never lazy, I always worked like a maniac.

That reminds me of Stockhausen who used to say to me "Luc, you are lazy", but I am not. Today, yes, in my new life, I feel like being lazy. And yet, just now, I was in the kitchen, eating a slice of onion tart in peace, and I just had to come here, sit at my typewriter, and write this on this sheet of paper.

27 October

When I compose I turn everything on full blast. Joy, love, anguish. All that sensuality — it takes time, it's hard. It hurts. And what do I get in return? The high dignitaries of musical standards, those who, for a few miserly moments, lend an ear to the wretched; those who collude in the conspiracy of silence. The contempt I have faced on my musical journey kills me, exhausts me, it wounds me deeply. What shall I do with the suffering, the sorrow, the ache of composing, all that time spent in pain? I found that there was too much of a discrepancy between what I gave and what I received. I couldn't take it any more. I stopped composing.

30 October

I had been awarded an international prize for a radiophonic composition and, for some unknown reason, it didn't get mentioned on the radio. It's the equivalent of nobody in the literary world mentioning the Goncourt Prize. Naïvely I thought, I've won the prize, an international prize, the radio commissioned this composition, they're bound to want to talk about it. Well, they didn't. And I was sure it had nothing to do with reasons like "It's garbage, we really can't broadcast such a piece of shit on our airwaves", no, there was some other reason which escaped me. I think. That reminds me of an image linked to this story.

It had happened a little previously — a concert at the radio station. During the interval, the producer of a very popular programme came up to me and said he would be inviting me on his show, to talk about that composition, the one that had been awarded the prize. Next to us stood the director general in charge of music, he had heard us. The place was crowded and we got separated, but then I saw the director talking animatedly to the producer, who looked very surprised, like he couldn't believe his ears. After that night, no music programme producer ever invited me to partake in the grand ceremonials of radio communication. I no longer existed.

21 November

I have a complex relationship with orchestra conductors. Having said that, I don't often think of them these days, or distantly, as if from another world, but it so happens that the other night, at a meeting, one such specimen was present — though in an absent sort of way, as if eager to make his getaway: "I'll be in the room next door if you need me…" without punctuation, no time. And yet, if I was unkind, I'd have been tempted to say that this particular conductor had no reason to act like a superstar. Our conversation was thus

meant to phone me since June, it's already the end of November and the concert is in February. He won't ring me, conductors never ring: "it's not very difficult…" he says, already turning away, "yes, I say, taking my time to try and steal a bit of his, I made sure there were no difficulties for the musicians, but it's a very difficult piece to conduct." I was determined to say this to him, and I softened the blow with a cunningly friendly little smile. And that was it. Good bye see you next time.

Everything is done at the last minute during the few, far too few, rehearsals — count yourself lucky to be getting that many — it's a way of letting you know that your score doesn't deserve any more time. Because we didn't meet up beforehand, as that was not possible we know we won't be talking at this late stage, it's safer that way, but how frustrating and dispiriting. To make themselves even more elusive, conductors have an assortment of phone numbers, and no matter which one you call, the person who picks up doesn't know anything. It's almost musical, like a theme. It's a defence mechanism. There was this conductor, I would spend about one day every month trying to get hold of him on the phone. When I eventually got through, he sounded almost out of breath and said Yes, absolutely we must meet up, but let's say next month. And so of course by the time the concert came we still hadn't managed to meet. I hadn't had a chance to warn him that the score was difficult, even if it didn't look it. The concert was a disaster.

At this juncture it may interesting to explain what a disaster can be. A symphonic score takes months to write, and in my case, because I work very slowly, maybe up to two years I don't know if that's slow. But two years, every day, that's something, and it is so "abstracting", to keep writing without ever hearing the piece, it's a superhuman effort, almost unbearable, yes, it tears you apart, but slowly. And that score is about to be performed for the first time. It matters, all that accumulated potential, all that energy reduced to notes and ciphers that must come to life. So how can anyone take this lightly, how can they not grasp the drama, two years discarded just like that. Isn't it humiliating? All I'm asking for is a short meeting, to explain myself, not just notes on a score, I'm asking for a little bit of their time since I've given so much of mine. But when I get there, I'm amazed: sorry we don't have time, not that we don't consider this important, but you see, we're snowed under.

But then, when the audience hears the piece, they don't know about the preparation being perfunctory, or nonexistent. All they know is that the conductor is very well paid, therefore he must be good at his job. So they think it's just bad music. Whereas I spent a big chunk of my life, a heap of energy — that's really something, two years' worth of energy, of imagination, of despair, all the doubts, the frustrations, yes, that chunk of life, like a piece of flesh, torn off your body, that is what is going to be played badly, that's what the conductor didn't want to talk about, and wasn't prepared to spend enough time on.

And I, sitting through that disaster, surrounded by people — when I listen to that performance, I too am torn apart. Nobody knows that pain.
Ignored and alone. The sickness.
Yes, now, I am sick.

28 November
The radio people had told me that he was excellent, that he would do my creation justice. yes, why not, do give him a call.
I'd been told he was a well-known conductor.
—   Hello, could I speak to M. So and So please.
—   What is it about?
—   My name is Thingy and he's conducting a piece of mine...
—   Yes, the Maestro has received your score, it's all fine.
—   Precisely, I was hoping I could meet with him to discuss the piece.
—   If you have any observations, you can pass them on to me.
—   But I was hoping to meet with him to...
—   That won't be possible I'm afraid, the Maestro is very busy.
—   I thought that some time in the next five months...
—   You'll be able to see him if you come to the rehearsals.
—   But by then there will only be three days left...
—   That's the only option.
—   I was hoping to explain to him...

How could I steer this to my advantage? How could I turn the situation on its head, smother her with humour? At that point, I had run out of humour! I was finding it hard to remain calm and restrained, to seem casual and unconcerned.

All the same, I didn't think I would need to explain that, since I was alive, I couldn't really be treated as though I were dead, and that the very fact I existed gave me a right to speak and a right to speak to those who were about to delve into my intimacy. I felt watered down, dissolved, denied. That conductor, up there, untouchable — I suspected him of not wanting to know what lay behind those notes.

And every time, it was the same. What do these people do to my compositions? When I hear them played, yes, the notes are there. Or sometimes they're not there yet. But even when they get to the notes, they never have time to get to the music.

And who is going to come first in that race, the concert or the musicality? Never enough time. That's why I ask for a conversation, because thinking things through in advance is part of the experience, and afterwards, it benefits the technical part of the work. Maybe I'll

Chansons pour le corps

Songs for the Body

The Chansons pour le corps are made up of two elements. A tape which is a sort of symphony of women being interviewed about the body, and a composition for instruments and voice, based on texts by Colette Fellous. A Song-Opera, maybe, or a lieder-melody, or a sung melodrama, or a little ditty-oratorio, or an aria, so many things can weave their way through a labyrinth.

Conte Sentimental n°1—11

Sentimental Tale n°1–11

The idea for this series was to take an existing composition and to tell the story that had inspired it. This French and German "sentimental" tale is intertwined with the music.

Stereo magnetic tape, Hörspiel commissioned by Hermann Naber
First tale in a series of 11, all directed by Brunhild and Luc Ferrari, with Südwestfunk, Baden-Baden
CD Shiiin, shiiin 8 —2013

1989
— 29 minutes

Extraits du corps
Extracts from the Body

Extracts from nine scores dated 1953 to 1985, subtly edited into a sort of concerto for piano and orchestra in three movements. This edit was devised at the specific request of Michel Redolfi, director of the Manca Festival, and the performance was never repeated.

For fifteen musicians, solo piano and magnetic tape
WP Festival des Manca, Nice, 2 July 1989

1989
— 1 hour 30 minutes

Photophonie I et Photophonie II
Photophony I and Photophony II

Stereo magnetic tape
Commissioned by Musica 89 for Alain Willaume's exhibition of photographs
WP Musica, Strasbourg, 17 September - 15 October 1989, Maison ONA Editions

1986 & 1989
— continuous loop

Le Freischütz
(Die Wolfsschlucht)
The Marksman
(The Wolf's Glen)

One day, a theatre director and a playwright came to see me and said: we're staging a new fantastical production of Carl Maria von Weber's *Freischütz*, for the Munich Opera. As it happens, the composer had refused to write music for one of the acts because he felt the technical means just didn't exist then. Weber had described very precisely the noises of a mysterious forest inhabited by more or less mythical animals. As a specialist of realistic fiction, I was asked to get into the ring.

Magnetic tape on three tape recorders
WP Bayerische Staatsoper, Munich, 21 February 1990

1989–90
— 20 minutes

Presque rien avec filles

Almost Nothing with Girls

For fifteen musicians, solo piano and magnetic tape, stereo
WP Festival des Manca, Nice, 2 July 1989
CD BVHaast Records, Acousmatrix 3 (1990)
Maison ONA Editions

1989
— 14 minutes

Photograph of Luc Ferrari 'sound hunting' by Brunhild Ferrari,1989

Labyrinthe Hôtel

Labyrinth Hotel

Based on *Calypso*, a novel by Colette Fellous. Following a misunderstanding between the novelist, the director and the composer, this chamber opera can no longer be performed. A new musical version exists, under the title *Chansons pour le corps*.

Rehearsal photograph by Jörg Landsberg

Chamber opera for one actress, three actors
Texts by Colette Fellous
WP (oratorio version) Bremen, 11 May 1990, directed by Luc Ferrari, with Elise Caron, Peter Bonke, Michel Musseau
WP Musica Festival, Strasbourg, 27 September 1990, dramatised and directed by Farid Paya

1989–90
— 1 hour 30 minutes

Solitude Transit

The script and the composition were developed in close collaboration with the choreographer during regular work sessions with the whole company. As a result, the music was not just stuck on, but conceived, tried out and amended over a period of six months, allowing for a genuine creative collaboration.

Stereo magnetic tape for a ballet
Based on an original idea by the choreographer Anne-Marie Reynaud
WP TEP, Paris, 1990. Maison ONA Editions

1989–90
— 1 hour 10 minutes

Italie mon amour
Italy, My Love

A sort of musical, mingling dialogues, sketches, dances, light-show, slides. I directed this show with the MUSE EN CIRCUIT's musicians and actors, and some local amateur groups.

Five musicians, one actress, about twenty extras
Light design: Gilles Chatard
WP Biennale Sport-Culture: Italie-Passions, SIM Jean Wiener, Echirolles, 15 June 1990

1989–90
— 50 minutes

Odeillo Research Centre

Stills courtesy C.N.R.S., Paris

Film directed by Marie Cahoreau-Gallier about the Odeillo solar furnace, the world's largest solar furnace. It is situated in Font-Romeu-Odeillo-Via, in the department of Pyrénées-Orientales, in south of France.

1990
— 13 minutes

Comme une fantaisie dite des réminiscences
Like a So-Called Fantasy of Reminiscences

This is a thorough reworking of the *Scène du va-et-vient* (1980), based on the same themes and ideas. The composition unfolds with particularly swinging elements; meanwhile, reminiscences of Bach's *Well Tempered Clavier* (a sort of bedside table book) appear in the warped mirror of memory, sampled and manipulated into a random cycle.

For two pianos. WP GMEA, Albi Municipal Theatre, 16 April 1994, by Christine Lagniel and Michel Maurer. Editions Salabert, Paris
CD Auvidis Montaigne, MO 782110 —1997

1989–91
— 25 minutes

Berceuse d'illusions
Lullaby of Delusions

For three instruments: keyboard, high-pitched and low-pitched woodwind instruments
WP Manca Festival, Musée d'Art Moderne, Nice, 4 December 1991. Commissioned for a laser book with twenty other composers, co-published by Albin Michel, the CIRM and Paris-Musées. Maison ONA Editions

1991
— 3 to 6 minutes

L'Escalier des aveugles

The Stairway of the Blind

A "collection of short-stories". I had been invited to Madrid, and decided to make a sort of sound-portrait of a city I didn't know. Since I didn't want to be alone, I asked to be accompanied by young women whose role was to show me round the city, acting as my interpreters. The rules of the game were strict: "beauty and a place", the way you'd say "beauty and the beast", so each beauty was to choose a location. I was thus led through the city like a blind man turned voyeur. The second rule was that each short-story should be a portrait of both the location and the young woman who had taken me there. And lastly, regarding the composition, I was only allowed to use sounds recorded in that particular location, nowhere else. The notion of autobiography is implied by the constant presence of the author, inextricably linked to the microphone. I could even say that the key subject of each short story is the relationship between the voice of the portraitist and the microphone, and between the voice of the women portrayed and the microphone, since that peculiar acoustic relationship aims to describe the invisible.

Stereo magnetic tape
Collection of short-stories
Commissioned by Radio Nacional de España
Coproduction: Ars Sonora RNE2 / LA MUSE EN CIRCUIT
Italia Prize 1991 (RAI Special Prize)
CD Musidisc, 291302 — 1991
Maison ONA Editions

1991
— 35 minutes

Clap - Pour Mauricio Kagel

Clap – For Mauricio Kagel

All the elements that constitute the tape are part of a group of interviews I r[ecorded in] [t]he winter of 1967–68, with a French television crew.

For piano and tape
Piano solo with an interview of Mauricio Kagel and background noises, com[posed on the] occasion of Mauricio Kagel's birthday.
WP WDR, Cologne, 1992, by Volker Banfield (piano)
Maison ONA Editions

1991
— 9 minutes

ahier du soir

ing Notebook

ty pieces for fourteen instruments, one actress and slides (flute, oboe
clarinet, bassoon, two percussions, piano, synthesiser, two violins, vic
nd an actress). WP Musica Festival, Strasbourg, 2 October 1994, by th
mble, dir. Olivier Dejours, actress: Anne Sée
ert, Paris

1–92

Spoken opera

On stage, fourteen musicians, one actress, a conductor. And some slides. But is there a link between all these? A riddle maybe? And what about that woman conversing with the slides, and with the music it seems? Who listens, who speaks to us, confides in us and ponders? What shall we call this evening, as intimate as a private journal, where text and music mingle but without becoming theatre, involving machines and images without being multimedia? Unclassifiable, some would say. And still completely ordinary. It's the story of feelings that unfold.

Extracts

The female Reader:
I wonder (she wonders).
(she reads) Isn't composing a futile activity in this world of ours? Isn't it inconsiderate, surrounded as we are by violence and terror?
But if I stopped composing, who would notice, amidst the deluge of scorching news, the ruins of civilisation, women slashed, small children eviscerated, people tortured, discarded...
Is there a gap, a respite, between ruins and desolation?
That's where I compose, in that minute recess where civilisation subsists.

Seriously, if I did stop composing, who would notice?
And after all, it's still what I do best.
... in the heart of the storm, I want to be very gentle.

(...)

Without ideology, men are barbarians.
With ideology, men are barbarians.
Which barbarism do you prefer? (she ponders)

(...)

This piece I'm working on, I now realise, compels me to reflect on music theatre. Quite a discovery. But I must stress this is not musical theatre, it's theatre and music. On the one hand, there's speech, and on the other, there's music. Is there a link between the two? Apparently not, but in the depths of sensibility, there probably is.

I think music remains music, with its own problems, its games, its innuendos, but above all with its musical substance. The same applies to the text, which must do its own thing. I trust in each element having an emotional capacity, each contains an emotion which will be released when they come into contact.

What interests me in this idea is that it takes you back to the theatre in Molière's day, when the play was interrupted by ballet or musical interludes which didn't necessarily have anything to do with the plot. But then of course, opera, with its utopian notion of a total art (and the word "total" always includes an element of dictatorship) came and smashed that juxtaposition, shattering the adventurous heterogeneity of "music theatre".

INTROMOMENTS

As I write this score, I increasingly see the questions it raises: what is a group of musicians who get together to play music? Who are they, what links them, and is the ensemble, that rather conventional configuration, sufficient? Couldn't you say that a score is a fragment of life confronted for a moment to the life of a group? Yet, it seemed to me that an ensemble, which is a common and convenient configuration, is a way of infantilising people instead of giving them a sense of responsibility. A way of keeping them in the dark as to the ideas and overall meaning of the score.

I believe that, with my score, I set out particular conditions of responsibility. Regarding the notes of course, but also regarding the relationship between the participants. Each instrumentalist, instead of keeping his text to himself, is confronted with others. He is no longer just a person who formulates his own sentence as best he can, but he is constantly attentive to the totality of what is being played.

One tries to adopt a different approach to such interactions, from a different angle, a different psychological perspective, with different sensations, different configurations seeking to explore different hierarchical relations.

Musical ensembles, ranging from small groups to symphony orchestras, are structured according to a hierarchy, and that architecture, in a way, induces the writing of the score.

Stage layout for *Cahier du soir,* 1991-1992

Loose sheet, notes inserted in the narrator's script. *Cahier du soir,* 1991–92.
The handwritten text reads: "In music, some subtexts are buried so deep that you can't hear them."
Loose sheet, notes inserted in the narrator's script. *Cahier du soir,* 1991–92
The handwritten text reads: "On the Rue Mouffetard, outside a tripe shop, a group of Japanese people in hysterics take photographs of the calves' heads in the window display.

The composer is hostage to the orchestra's hierarchical, administrative or legal structure (just as, aesthetically, he is hostage to the Opera as economico-architectural structure). The musicians are thus protected from all dangers, they don't need to know, they don't need to understand, they don't need to agree, they don't need to grasp why they are there.

The score, in all likelihood, was born out of some sentimental, social, philosophical, or, why not, scientific necessity. So how can you work on it with a group of people who've been led to believe they're not there to think? What kind of puritanism also implies that music should not meddle with that sort of thing, because that's what opera is for; furthermore, speaking over "pure" music is inappropriate, not to say trivial, and anyway the audience wouldn't understand.

Still, no one can deny that the work we, composers and musicians, do together, requires intelligence, that our relationship is an intimate one, based on responsibilities broadly set out in the scores. How can one escape this basic fact? Isn't writing music a truly intimate act, even if that isn't explicit? Of course you address adults, of course you address intelligence directly, and sensibility, and sensuality; of course you deal with profound, difficult, contradictory, and why not hypersensitive, entities.

Yes, this score recounts a relationship. Yes, it contains shyness, provocation, yes, it is profound and funny, with incongruities, intense moments, surprises, complex or superficial feelings, everything you find in life itself, serious, tragic, scary things, but also a desire to play, to share, to convince of course.

Responsibility and exchange — maybe that's what I fret over when I'm writing. These things, here on paper, how can I share them with the musicians whom I entrust with a deep part of myself, and how will they convey all that to the audience? That is, we both have responsibilities and if we don't share them, the danger is, there will be no emotion.

can't say, and it wouldn't be my place to say, whether the score is any good, or interesting, but what I am sure of is that it is traversed by emotions; these abstract notes contain some very concrete sensations that swirl and hang in the air. Is it pretentious to put it that way? An ensemble of musicians isn't an amalgam. This score isn't an amalgam of instruments that don't ever need to know what the others are doing. I have inscribed these ideas about relationships in the score itself. They are there. They need to be deciphered, clarified, and materialised.

This score also raises the question of the conductor's place. Traditionally, that place is conceived in terms of hierarchy. Indeed, he is the head because he has all the elements in hand. Yet what if the conductor were to share those elements with the musicians? What if his presence, instead of being central, became unobtrusive? The point is not to curtail the responsibilities of the conductor, but to find out how he can enhance them through sharing them.

The conductor is an acoustics moderator. Calling him that isn't to belittle him, on the contrary it is a way of making him part of a subtle sound space. He is also the person who ties together the strands of the musical drama, he stages it. Indeed, whether there is a text or not, music is drama, it is performed and unfolds over time, and the specific role of the conductor is to handle time, rather than an instrument. I like that idea, so let me emphasise the conductor is the acoustics moderator who touches time with his magic wand. He is a spokesperson too, best placed to uncover and discuss the score's meanings and philosophy. He is also best able to convey the general form of the work.

This score is made up of fragments of texts and of fragments, or "moments", of music, all of which is bound to mean something. These elements can't simply ignore each other. They need to coexist, and that raises another problem. That's a lot of problems, it seems — too many maybe? Or maybe not interesting enough? Again, it is not for me to say. I just ask questions, as one does in society, and in life. Society is also constantly searching for its own identity, often through violent means, unfortunately. As for me, gently, very humbly, contribute to that search, to the experience of looking, looking again, looking at how, looking at the inner workings of intimacy.

imagine the conductor seated at a table, a little to one side. He is the spokesperson for the composer, he may even be the composer. Most of the time, he intervenes with discreet signs, modulating time, indicating nuances and cues, with the easy gestures of someone close to you. If the whole ensemble is to play together, he can move centerstage to think. The fourteen musicians are scattered across the stage, they are not arranged compact entity but they nonetheless form a defined group. The orchestrations vary, of the musicians don't play in some of the pieces, so they could very well step o come back when they're due to join in. Even if that is not feasible for material reason event calls for people to move around, in a calm rather than agitated way: it's like a at home or at a restaurant.

At this party, at this restaurant, certain moments are spectacular, the orchestra play passages that tear through the acoustic space, but most of the time it's an event at a secret is being told.

Or maybe it isn't told…

Extract from *Cahiers du soir*, 199

Fugue de J.S.B
Fugue by J.S.B.

or flute, clarinet, bass clarinet, cello, vibraphone and piano
rchestration of *Fugue n°4, Book 1* of the Johannes Sebastien Bach's *Well-Temper*
lavier. WP Théâtre de la Villette, Paris, 15 May 1993, by M. Ghisalberti (flute), Sylv
ydman (clarinet), Carol Mundunger (bass clarinet), Christophe Roy (cello), Jean-Mic
ollet (vibraphone), Michel Maurer (piano)
aison ONA Editions

1992
— 5 minutes

Conversation Pieces

Music for a play by François-Michel Pesenti
WP Les Bernardines, Marseilles, 1993

1993
— 13 minutes 45 seconds

Ouvert-Fermé
Open-Closed

Part of a group composition entitled *Un Impossible Pari(s)*, with the composers of LA MUSE EN CIRCUIT.

Stereo magnetic tape
Part of the Metropolis series produced by Akustische Kunst, WDR, Cologne
CD box-set INA-GRM — 2009
Maison ONA Editions

1993
— 11 minutes

Bistro

Stereo magnetic tape
Composed for a choreography by Anne-Marie Reynaud
Recorded by Le Banquet ensemble, dir. O. Dejours
WP Le Théâtre du Lierre, Paris, 25 November 1993

1993
— 60 minutes

Porte ouverte sur ville

Open Door Onto the City

Paris, 26 October 1993

The tape for *Porte ouverte sur ville* is partly composed of random radio fragments. When I get in the car and turn on the ignition, the radio comes on and I immediately turn it off: just for a second, I catch a portion of the world, a snippet of conversation, of music, of emotion or of pointless jargon. This irrational moment is trapped and embedded into my present, it's an apparition. The tape also includes the opening and closing of a door or a window, letting the city show through. A fragment of reality erupts. Someone meanders through the scattered sounds, symbolising the observer's presence. Lastly various "abstract" musical sounds are mixed into the web of sounds from reality, creating a sense of distance or depth of field.

For oboe, clarinet, bass clarinet, percussion, viola and magnetic tape
Commissioned by WDR Department of New Music
WP Music Triennal, Cologne, 16 June 1994, by the Le Banquet ensemble
Maison ONA Editions

1992–93
— 32 minutes

As for the musicians, they are playing a genuine counterpoint, approaching or incorporating the sounds of the tape, conversing with them or, on the contrary, ignoring the tape or even contradicting it to demonstrate their independence of spirit.
We don't know whether *Porte ouverte sur ville* is opening or closing. Probably a bit of both, which accounts for the disorderly and somewhat pessimistic character of this composition.

Cologne, 24 March 1993
I read this text:
"... When I open the door and walk out onto the landing, I will know that the street begins down there, (...), a swarming wilderness where every moment can drop on my head, like a magnolia flower, where I will look at faces and they will come to life (...) and that step by step I will be risking my life just to go and get the paper from the newspaper stand round the corner. (Julio Cortazar, Cronopios and Famas)

Paris, 31 January 1993
... where the noise of the media is so invasive that you can hardly hear the noises of life.

Cologne, 24 June 1993
The rumbling of the city has been replaced by heavenly voices. Radio and television are now the true word of God. People are enthralled by the divine word. No more or less so than in the past, when they believed in churches/religions, but what makes people even more dependent and fragile now, is that the Word is not stable, it changes all the time and falls out of fashion.
Lost in that maze, people try to find their way, try to think, to act, to play, but can they still have feelings, feel pain, isn't pleasure a thing of the past, are words still possible?
And at the end of the visit, they get thrown out because there's no room left for memory.

Cologne, 29 March 1993
The other night, I was in a Spanish restaurant, there was the usual restaurant ritual, people coming in and others leaving, some ordering and others paying, conversations flowing and starting again. But one thing remained unchanged: a man, sitting at the bar, just having a drink, nothing more, and every ten minutes, like a perfect tautologist, he would get up and go to the gents.

Also, there was a Spanish song playing over the tannoy, I remember, it kept repeating: "love is over love is over love is over", nothing else. And I thought of our late 20th century, where love is over.

Portraits de femmes

Portraits of Women

L'Escalier des aveugles and *Chansons pour le corps* appear alternately. The combination of the two works makes up a concert programme.

For female singer, two clarinets, percussion, synthesiser, piano and two tape recorders WP SonMu, INA-GRM, Paris, 18 March 1995, by Elise Caron (voice), Carol Mundinger and Sylvain Frydman (clarinets), Michel Maurer (piano), Michel Musseau (synthesiser), Christine Lagniel (percussion)
Maison ONA Editions

1994
— approximately 80 minutes

Portrait de Michel Portal

Portrait of Michel Portal

Memorised sounds, including interviews with Michel Portal and musical tracks for him to improvise to during concerts. Commissioned by Radio France
Composition created for a day dedicated to Michel Portal on Radio France, 27 April 1995

1994–95
— 45 minutes

Fable de la démission et du cendrier

The Resignation and the Ashtray, A Fable

In 1982, I founded an organization. A few musicians from a variety of backgrounds got together in a studio. We called it LA MUSE EN CIRCUIT. After twelve years, I thought it was time to let it carry on without me. This is why I resigned my position as President.

Over that period, I composed a score for two pianos and two clarinets, which followed all the twists and turns of this episode. At the same time, I was also inventing a formal process which I called, rather impertinently: Post-Computer Hyperserialism!

For two pianos and two clarinets
Commissioned by Radio France
WP Festival Présences, Maison de Radio France, Paris, 3 February 1995, by Christine Lagniel and Michel Maurer (pianos), Carol Mundinger and Véronique Fèvre (clarinets)
Editions Salabert

1994
— 25 minutes

Quatre femmes hollandaises

Four Dutch Women

Portraits of four Dutch artists: a painter, a director, a writer, an actress: Jacobien de Rooij, Barbara Duijfjes, Anne Vegter, Hendrien Adams.

A suite of pieces taken from the music theatre work titled *Journal intime*. Each piece now bears a title that links it to its previous theatrical form, and therefore to the text, without one needing to know it.

Radiophonic piece
Commissioned by Piet Hein van de Poel for the Dutch radio station NCRV

1995
— 25 minutes

Hold still keep moving

Music composition using six CD sources, eight slide projections and two videos generating infinite aleatory encounters in a permanent environment.
Audiovisual installation
Commissioned by the PRIMe Foundation for the Groningen Fine Art Centre
Montage of slide and video projections created by Ellen Kooi on the occasion the Luc Ferrari retrospective, "Luc Ferrari en Pays Bas", October 1995

1995
— continuous loop

Je courais tant de buts divers
I was Pursuing so Many
Different Goals
1994

A n autobiographical text that recounts a part of my life, and which could become the first chapter of my memoirs, if only I could bring myself to write them.

Some nonchalant explanations

…..yes, I was chasing so many different goals, and felt the time had come to tie them all together, into a synthetic whole. The thing is, at first I was convinced everything was clear, that none of it required any explanation. Moreover, I enjoyed confusing people, putting them off the scent, contradicting appearances. I thought there was no point in explaining myself, that everybody would understand anyway. And so I carried on ploughing my furrows, in my mildly obsessive way. I really should have explained myself more fully, because I was chasing all these different goals, with this incredible thirst — when figuring out just one goal is hard enough.
I didn't explain, I was wrong.

It seems that nobody, or very few people, understood my motivations, directions, projects, and the eccentric ideas I was bringing. I'm not saying this out of bitter resentment —after all I myself am guilty of fiddling the deck — but to explain why I am explaining myself now.

Still, I have spoken on the radio often enough, and written a substantial amount both for myself and for others, which is why I sincerely believed I had revealed quite a lot already. have also annotated my scores and composed text-scores, so I felt I had made my thoughts quite clear. Still, to explain oneself is probably something else again, you need to do that in the right arena, where you're supposed to, where you need to gain credibility — you can' take that sort of thing lightly, and must never indulge in derision. I, on the contrary, believe one cannot speak seriously without that ironic touch which combines seriousness with a sense of complicity, and couples reason with its inseparable counterpoint, error. One is expected to explain things using the appropriate terms and to make everything fit into neat categories. Still, to explain, to show, to comment, to clarify without justifying oneself — that is no mean task.

I have to say I have never attempted to found a doctrine or to wear a particular hat. I have never had any military, religious or mystical leanings, nor been involved in any particular political party; I have never followed a school of thought, nor advocated a given aesthetic. Which obviously hasn't prevented me from having a mind of my own, and my own thoughts on those issues.

When I attempt to synthesise my ideas, I identify traces, features that recur throughout my life, points where unrelated ideas meet, where diverging lines converge, persistent ideas, casual brushes with established systems... Whatever the barbaric violence of history, the fears and the laughter, two obsessions of mine have endured, and I will never disown them because they are the vital force that runs through my work. On the one hand, concerning form, I am still wedded to notions of repetition or cycle; and regarding meaning and inter-pretation, I flirt heavily and almost constantly with story-telling and narrative.

I'm quite happy to have found this shortcut for, in the light of these two central ideas, I can at last explain most of my works — scores, films, memorised sounds, multimedia and theatre works, symphonic or solo pieces, somnolent, platonic or aphrodisiac... at last I can disentangle it all. Well, nearly.

UNAPPLIED REPETITION

I have always been interested in repetition, from very early on.
It has become a recognised genre, adopted as an American phenomenon of the '70s, so it's difficult to tell now, but I suppose the ideas of Robert Ashley, Terry Riley and Steve Reich didn't suddenly come out of nowhere, they are the result of a reflection and of an intuition. I was probably going through the same process as them; in my youth, I felt that same need to repeat, for I saw repetition as an alternative to the perpetual variations that drove serial composition.

Of course, I grew up with the post-war serial movement, which for me represented inno-vation, radicalism. As a young man at least, I was part of it, it was the avant-garde; in it I sought my identity. Yet it was probably that very impetuousness which led me early on to assert my independence, to transgress the rules of that system, and to combine the series with a sort of obsession with cyclical forms.
It was hard to express this clearly at the time.

Looking at the score for *Visage I* (1956), one can now see how those two methods, serial and repetitive, are confronted, and how a series evolves across superimposed cycles. But the series expands (it includes not only notes but also sound objects), or it extends and affects the cycles themselves, with that series of pitches resurfacing on occasion, like a submarine or the Loch Ness monster.

What did the idea of "series" mean to me at the time?
Maybe it was to do with varying the pitch in order to get the most variation, or with devising a kind of numbering system that enabled me to wreak havoc with the tonal system and to smash my way out of it. Or it was to do with shedding the straitjacket of academic form and finally stepping into forbidden territory — after all, the conservatories railed against such "disharmony", "music of noises" and even, as they put it, "vandalism".

And when I thought of repetition, what did I have in mind?

As with dodecaphony, I found repetition for its own sake somewhat insufficient.
At this juncture, I think it's important to say — if I don't, it won't be possible to identify the sources which have shaped my life — that I have never let myself be carried away by any method, or be guided by a system, like one obeys a totalitarian idea. Instead, I used methods and systems as means through which other things could be achieved — to tell a story for example, to convey fleeting images, to unfold a sound adventure; all of which allowed me to use the word narration.

At the time *Visage I* was composed, repetition represented for me not so much a tool as a way of observing the social organisation of time. Thus observed, time organises itself in layers and according to various points of view— social, political and emotional. It is in this sense that repetition fascinated me.

So, repetition is a place that allows similarities as well as differences: if I repeat the same sentence twice, it exists differently in two different moments. People's thoughts vary, and even if they have the same thoughts as the day before, those thoughts are a day older, and are therefore modified. Thoughts thus function as a transformation of repetition.
One can hope, even if one is prone to pessimism, that our ability to think does enable us to garner some experiences, it constitutes a memory, and that when our thoughts are superimposed with a purely mechanical repetition, the mind experiences that repetition every

...me as a new occurrence, rather than as redundant. In society, repetition can be inept and meaningless if it is taken as an obligation, a form of alienation, but if repetition is deliberate, really thought through, it acquires a vitality.

When I mention repetition in relation to *Visage I,* we should assume that these ideas were intuited or anticipated, but not yet clearly expressed. They were present as an undercurrent, as one indistinct impulse among others, yet barely audible. Moreover, we should talk of cycles rather than of repetitions, of cycles that change again and again through repetition. One could speak of a series of cycles, or a sense of a more generalised series which would tackle a variety of things besides parameters of sound, besides musical form even. In the 1950s, I was convinced that a single cycle taken on its own could not be interesting. I hadn't come across John Cage then, he detonated into my life in 1957, the bearer of completely new and radical forms. I didn't know you could repeat a chord or a phrase for such a long time. I didn't know you could make a silence last so long. But somehow my very vague aspirations came into focus. I didn't mean to mention John Cage, but it doesn't hurt to stress again the influence he had on that period.

So, the year before I met him, I was composing *Visage I,* a score based on superimposed cycles. I imagined the cycles as individuals who lived at different speeds. When they didn't run into each other, they were independent, but when their temporalities overlapped and they encountered each other, then they would undergo a transformation, either through influence or confrontation.

I said this was a serial work, with the series made up of both objects and cycles, and that a twelve-tone serialism also operated within the cycles themselves. However, I couldn't apply this method systematically, because I didn't want the random encounters brought about by repetitions to systematically alter or transform the individuals. I wanted desire to take precedence and determine what value such transformations should have . At a time when structure was deemed the only legitimate concern and any trace of feeling was to be banished, that emotional-cum-narrative tendency was incongruous.

DIFFUSE NARRATION

So, I was discovering how time unfolded, finding out that my perception of time was a manifestation of my subjectivity, and that my creative activities were a way of expressing that subjectivity confined within a society that conflicted with it — or at least, a society...

within which subjectivity had to find its place, or carve a place for itself. I discovered that every day brought new experiences, not necessarily progress, but something that could be identified as benchmarks. Day after day I kept records and I came to understand that what interested me in the composition process was this very succession of indicators. These marks, the progression, the accumulation of memory, together created the kind of narrative I needed and which endowed even the most obstinate abstraction with a very concrete grounding in social, political or emotional life.

In that way, the everyday, be it realistic or transfigured, became my raw material and its regular monitoring became the tool of my trade. And in my compositions I sought out the everyday, convinced as I was that it gave meaning to creation and that this meaning was being wrought out each day. I don't want to say I didn't have a plan. In fact I even had very intricate plans, sometimes describing in great detail what course to take. But when it came to the actual composition process, I had to start at the beginning and gradually make my way towards the end.

I know that many composers work differently: starting from a set plan, they go from one place to the next, from one moment to the next as Stockhausen used to say, which, by the way, led to the open forms of the 1960s. Although I had been there too — it was in the air I suppose — I am not making a value judgement when I say that I proceeded differently, it's just that such was my inclination. My nature, my sense of individuality and independence predisposed me to embark on an adventure which followed time rather than skipping it. And so, I recognised that maybe I was displaying increasing dexterity when using the ingredients I had chosen for myself, and that I was consistently improving with regards to that particular type of work. I felt that following that specific progress made music more palpable with every passing moment, it made time perceptible, and gave rise to a kind of suspense. And for me, this was narration. There, the musical discourse would be woven like a private journal telling of lived experience and of how dexterity had been acquired in the course of creating the work. I even came to find it interesting that one might detect a degree of awkwardness at the start, and watch that clumsiness wane and give way to dexterity.

This makes me think of *Tautologos II* (1961), a musique concrète composition as it was called back in those heroic times. I wanted to roll out a series of beginnings, explaining to anyone who would listen that this idea came to me because I had found the beginning so lousy that I had rewritten it again and again until it was better, which doesn't mean it was good. This cycle of failed beginnings, which under the rules of the game were meant to get better and better, also illustrated the idea of repetition. This is why I called the piece *Tautologos* from the word "tautology", meaning unnecessary repetition, a sort of pleonasm o edundant occurrence (redundant being understood here as pleonastic parody or is superfluous).

Of course there was an element of derision, for I didn't think those beginnings really were complete failures; yet the explanation pointed to a possible fragility, while at the same time being an example of self-deprecation, and this was unacceptable to many. It must be said that at that time, most composers held unquestioned aesthetic opinions, they wore them with an air of certainty, and were never bogged down by such things as contradictions. They were infallible. To flaunt one's uncertainties was just not done. I was off to a bad start. I was voicing my feelings, I told stories surreptitiously, I was already veering off serial composition — in short, I was playing the scoundrel.

Form and content organised themselves in a peculiar way, following a path akin to a light caress, incriminating themselves through contact with the world. I had come across mu sique concrète and, working with electronic sound and microphones, I had come up with what I now call *son mémorisé* [memorized sound]. I won't go into how I got involved into all this. Or maybe I will one day, because it's a charming story.

This is how I came to use a pen-recorder. The first Nagras were just coming out too, and the first Eclair movie cameras (portable and silent, and with synchronised sound). This was a revolution and everybody wanted to combine pen recorder and images — the triumph of truth. A camera that could penetrate secrets. With my tape recorder, I was at last able to leave the recording studio, which hadn't been possible until then. I went out into the landscape and collected a rather wide variety of sounds.

Thus was born *Hétérozygote* (1964). From 1963 on, I listened to all the sounds I had recorded, and found that they felt like images, not only to me, who could remember their source, but also to the innocent listener. I must offer images, I thought, contradictory im ages that gush into one's mind even more freely than if one could see them for real. And should play with images like one plays with words in poetry. Some images that make no sense at all, and some that do, frail images and inescapable ones too. I had before me a whole range, from abstract to concrete, enabling me to concoct an absurd discourse

Fragments du journal intime

Fragments from Private Journal

A suite of pieces taken from the music theatre work titled *Journal intime*. Each piece no
bears a title that links it to its previous theatrical incarnation, and therefore to the text, b
t's not necessary to know this.

For piano

Madame de Shanghai

The Lady From Shanghai

During these recordings, done with the help of Li-Ping Ting in the 13th arrondissement of Paris, aka China Town, I meet Madame de Shanghai and Orson Welles.

Inside the Asian shopping mall on Ivry avenue (Paris), Madame du Shanghai enters a video store and asks in Mandarin if by chance, the Orson Wells' movie, The Lady from Shanghai is available. There follows a conversation with the merchant, probably in Mandarin and Thai, which ends with something like: "Konn" or "Konn Madame" After which Madame du Shanghai sweetly laughs.

For three flutes and memorised sounds
Tape produced at Ateliers UPIC
WP Théâtre du Renard, Paris, 28 February 1997, by the Trio d'Argent: Michel Boizot, François Daudin Clavaud, Xavier Saint-Bonnet
CD Musique d'Aujourd'hui, MDA M7 847 — 1997
Maison ONA Editions

1996
— 15 minutes

Score courtesy Maison ONA Editions

Selbstportrait oder Peinture de sons ou Tonmalerei

Self-Portrait, or Sound Painting or Tone Painting

Bilingual Hörspiel (French-German)
Produced at the Studio Post-Billig
Commissioned by Südwestfunk
CD SONOPSYS, SON 4 — 2007

1996–97
— 55 minutes

Tautologos IV

In this composition, I was returning to the idea of cycles and of their random superimposition, which I had explored in the 1970s, particularly in *Tautologos III*. It was a way of revisiting old concerns while at the same time expanding them and even damaging them.

Bloc — Interstice — Tautologie
Symphonic suite for full orchestra and four samplers
WP Dangereuses Visions, Lille, 9 March 1998, by Art Zoyd and the National Orchestra of Lille, dir. Jean-Claude Casadessus
Editions Salabert

1996–97
— 30 minutes

Tautologos IV

If I'm going to give the piece a name like that, then of course I also have to provide some kind of explanation. I expected as much, so here we go.

Tautologos is a title I've been using for a long time, first in 1961, at the beginning of my experiments in the field of musique concrète, as it was called at the time. Meaning I was among the young avant-garde crowd that messed around with technological experimentation. For me, "Tautologos" meant : cyclical repetition. But even before that, I was interested in cycles, and those ideas were beginning to emerge in my instrumental scores. This is why, when I met the "American repetitives", in the early 1970s, I wasn't surprised. It was like a mysterious kinship, various individuals going through different experiences, yet unknowingly taking a step in the same direction.

Now, if you take *Tautologos I* and *II*, from 1961, you'll hear very little repetition, or just in the widest sense, in a vague way. Only with *Tautologos III* did this idea get systematically probed. But I'll try and explain what distinguishes the use I make of it from the type of repetitive music which arrived on our shores at that time.

Take for instance Terry Riley's *In C* (1965) and Steve Reich's *Piano Phases* (1967): short phrases are repeated in a loop according to very specific, though different, processes. There's a very clear aesthetic intention here, which distances itself, to put it mildly, from serial aesthetics, particularly through its use of pitch and rhythm. However, both seriality and repetition, at least at that time, fitted in the history of contemporary ideas under the heading of "pure", or "abstract", music — musical works that elaborate and explore a musical phenomenon.

Whereas my ideas on repetition, because I draw on the concrete and the real, were derived from observations external to music: for example, the way daily actions, gestures, feelings, social relations and their cycles, are organized; or from autobiographical preoccupations, or from the idea that musical composition should be considered as autobiography and biography as cycle.

...sidered as an aleatory magma of actions repeated within long cycles, and separated by varying distances. One person, who disposes of a provision of cycles, is confronted with other people who also dispose of provisions of cycles. So in an instant, we witness an apparently random superimposition.

Picture a Métro station at a given instant during rush hour, and imagine all of those people each with their own distinct cycle who, at that precise moment, make a gesture, like an ensemble, but a gesture which has nothing to do with harmony or aesthetics. Without being aware of it, they are playing a score. That instant is made up of superimposed individual actions, repeated cyclically, but which never reoccur in the same arrangement.

Tautologos IV, which came about over two decades after *Tautologos III*, is in the same vein, maybe taking greater liberties, maybe less systematic — not that I've ever had a talent, or a soft spot, for systematicism. Little by little, things evolve, cycles fall in or out of synch. The cycles have come a long way, and diversify some more, in the most secret domains where silence causes you to forget the initial object of the cycle.

Interestingly, by revisiting old ideas which had been used in the intervening years without really being identified as such, and by deliberately focusing my attention on them, I was led to make a kind of music that was very different from the music I had made so far, I think.

BLOC [BLOCK]

If I speak of formless magma, it is to define the character of this musical action and the psychological situation of the listener.

In the first movement, the idea is to create a very loud sound, as loud as possible, and which should seem to last for a very long time. Ten minutes exactly, not a second longer. To create a totally radical sound item. A very particular sonic state, like being in a bath. Or a wall that would surround the listener, seemingly immobile (though "immobile" contains "mobile").

"Block" is closer to a sculpture than to something that evolves through times. To sculpt

For me, an interstice is something that is "in between" but which happens inadvertently. With speech, an interstice is something unintentional, unplanned in the discourse. It's a passage, a gap, the intake of breath that allows you to think of what comes next, or it's like feeling dizzy, or afraid.

You don't create the "interstice", you just find it, it's like a "presque rien" [almost nothing]. Speaking, except in the case of newspeak or in political truisms, is improvisation. In newspeak, there are no interstices. With improvisation we lose track of where an idea is going, we hesitate, seek inspiration, sometimes anxiously: this gap between two ideas is enchanting because of its fragility, it is a sensitive plate, not to say the developing agent, it is the gap between hope and despair.

Noises also have their interstices, metaphorically like passages: like a staircase, like the rustling of clothes is a passage, a caress is also a passage, like the murmur of draperies, the crackling of silk; I mention this because these are noises you find in the composition. This is what "Interstice" is made of.

TAUTOLOGIE [TAUTOLOGY]

The third movement is made up of 21 relatively short musical phrases, unfolding in a familiar harmonic atmosphere. Each phrase is followed by a relatively long silence, of varying but calculated length. Each phrase is therefore repeated in a cycle. This is what I call a tautology, in this case, the result of 21 superimposed cycles over a given time.

Each musical phrase is allocated to specific instruments. The random superimpositions resulting from the variable durations of the different cycles may give rise to some instrumental impossibilities, in which case either the objects or the instrumentation have to be modified. This is what I call constructive tautology. It is possible that the encounter of several phrases may produce a new idea, I call this spontaneous tautology.

This explains why the piece, which is the result of a calculation that produces some aleatory and some spontaneous effects, should be understood as a friction, ideas rubbing against each other, somewhere between the reality of cycles and the interference of elements

Symphonie déchirée

Torn Symphony

This symphony carries within itself a revolt against all kinds of racisms and nationalisms, and it more generally stands up against purity in all its forms

For seventeen amplified instruments and memorised sounds (flute, oboe, clarinet, bass clarinet, bassoon, trumpet, trombone, saxophone, piano, two percussionists, two violins, one viola, two celli, one double bass)
Memorised sounds produced at LA MUSE EN CIRCUIT and CC Mix
WP November Music, Vooruit, Ghent, Belgium, November 1998, by the Champ d'Action ensemble, dir. Zsolt Nagy
Editions Salabert

1994–98
— 60 minutes

Symphonie déchirée is a suite of eight movements for seventeen instrumentalists and sons mémorisés [S & M, or memorised sounds]. Each movement has a separate instrumentation and deals with different problems pertaining to composition, aesthetics or meaning. The symphony oscillates between rebellion and voluptuousness, between realism and abstraction, between impulsive and formalist urges.

Started in late 1994, it went through several upheavals due to crises of confidence, self-questioning, and the passing of time, the days that come and go.

Here are a few "analytical" explanations regarding the different movements.

Pénétration harmonique [Harmonic Penetration]
Yes, that's it, it's a slow and easy penetration. Penetrating a central note, you travel through it, observe it, get curious about its qualities, its details, the surprises it holds. Then you realise the note isn't that simple, it has affinities or harmonics, and so you end up exploring territories you hadn't planned to explore, because initially, you only had one single note.

But what does "single" mean? Could it be yet another of those ideas to do with purity, or with homogeneity, or with the assumption that something simple cannot be complex? When in fact, penetration reveals the complexity of things. And that's precisely what we're asking for, because otherwise you'd stay on the outside, at the door, and all the philosophical tales, all the stories, all the artworks would collapse all at once, for lack of anyone willing to penetrate them. Of course, the whole of sexuality would be called into question.

This is one of the meanings of the title "Harmonic Penetration". Not to forget the multiple meanings, ambiguities and echoes it can raise in its wake.

Jeu des objets [Playing with Objects]
This is an essentially formal composition linked to a compositional concept I called "tautological" and which has interested me ever since my earliest works. That type of formalism can also be found in a later piece, "Les cloches de Huddersfield" ["The Bells of Huddersfield"].

The idea here is to indicate that silence is a kind of character, just like the object. A cycle is therefore made up of a sound object, plus a silence. The silence is not a prolongation of the object, it plays as much of a part. Dare I say that it plays a soundless role? Or shall we say it's a silent musical object?

The sound objects are present in their own capacity. They are autonomous but they overlap, because of the tautology. They then combine, complement or disrupt each other. They also insinuate themselves into the silences, which act as developing agents, revealing the sound objects.

Thus, through the superimpositions of sounds and silences, a paradoxical and repetitive form emerges, without us necessarily perceiving repetition as such; rather, we perceive a random development in which the objects are sometimes identified, and sometimes not.

Dualité [Duality]

This piece consists of two superimposed monologues. Like two characters talking over each other, but about different things.

The originality of musical discourse, as opposed to speech, resides in the desire to find out whether those two monologues, which are alien to one another, can nonetheless understand each other.

If I'm honest, there is one very fleeting moment where the dualisms appear to combine, but it's so brief that it will probably escape the listener's attention.

Parole déchirée [Torn Speech]

Whereas "Dualité" ["Duality"] might feel uncomfortable, "Parole Déchirée" ["Torn Speech"], on the other hand alludes to feelings, to emotions. And whereas the sound matter in "Duality" was deliberately abstract, here the reference to spoken language is evident, if only because of the recorded voices. Although the spoken words apparently don't mean anything, it is precisely in those moments of inadvertent randomness that speech is at its most meaningful, it acquires a diffuse meaning through the noises produced. In other works, I describe this kind of approach as a search for the "interstice", for what lies in between the words, sounds or gestures, and closely linked to the notion of intimacy. Those "interstices" are deliberately used in loops, the loop itself working as a mechanical cliché, but also as a developing agent, a catalyst.

Jeu de timbres [Playing with Timbres]

Because it is abstract, this piece requires no particular explanation. It has a well-defined form within a pseudo-repetitive system that develops in the pseudo-homogeneity of its tones, making it all a game. It may be one of the more easygoing, or least grimacing, pieces in this suite. Make the most of it. I mean that the suite is based on alternating moments of tension and release, and it is necessary to the overall dramatic balance of the piece.

Jeu des reflets [Playing with Reflections]

Although apparently abstract, this composition is based on an utterly realist idea. As the title indicates, it is about reflections. There are two sequences: one is dislocated and chaotic, the other is undulatory and morbido-harmonic. These are the sun's reflections

f the first sequence, or "reflections on the water", I observed that, seen from above, the water's surface reflects two rays, one on either side of each ripple. As the ripples move, the eye perceives the rays as an aleatory trajectory. So I compiled a stock of notes, silences, nuances, etc. And for each reflection, I chose two (short) notes, a period of silence, a nuance and an instrumentation. Therefore, the duration of the silences is different for each instrument, the reflections can meet, combine or destroy each other through the association of impossible nuances. That's the basic principle. But for me, to play is also to cheat so, when necessary, I reclaimed my freedom.

In the second sequence, or "underwater reflections", I observed that the ripples would trace glimmering and moving undulations onto the seabed. Those lines move at the same speed and in the same direction, but they differ in length. All those lines together formed diamond patterns which constantly shifted in and out of shape. So I wrote different modes, but all diamond-shaped, and I drew up a hell of a plan, with extremely strict rules, which I've now forgotten. But it worked. In fact, what matters to me is the emotion.

The two sequences are separated by a big "sssplassshhhh".

Les cloches de Huddersfield [The Bells of Huddersfield]

After much hesitation, of the kind triggered by a very simple writing project, I was at last overwhelmed by a dubious sense of certainty, a comfortable feeling which appeared following a certain number of simulations.

The composition's premise is the same as for the bells. The memory of bells. The bells at Blandy-les-Tours (I was twelve), probably the first time I was stirred, if not compositionally at least emotionally, when I initially identified what I was later to call "tautology". This is why last year in Huddersfield, when I heard the church bells, they reminded me of my childhood and made me want to write a score… even a simple one would do!

This apparently banal piece would be joyously optimistic if it weren't gradually disrupted by the recorded sound (or "memorised sound") of a terribly dramatic, desperate, tearing noise, gradually increasing until it drowns out the orchestra.

Déchirure [Torn]

This movement is both the end of the symphony and its initial impulse. It is torn, as it were. Indeed, "torn" means split, divided in two, in a violent way perhaps. If I were to define my feelings, I would say that I feel all at once a great appetite for life and some anger in the face of barbarity. Revolt, anger, pleasure, gentleness — what a bitter choice, what a fragile balancing act, and being thrown off balance may result in despair. Here I am, torn.

So how do you translate that into music?

By giving free rein to violence, to anger, at the risk of it having no aesthetic qualities what-soever; and by shattering ideas, by cutting short developments that risk becoming too well established, or by taking them a step too far. Then the anger subsides. And by indulging in extreme gentleness, even to the point of mawkishness, a gentleness that can only turn to grimaces. And lastly, by leaving behind this great endless symphony...

That really is perverse.

Presque rien n°4. "La remontée du village"

Almost Nothing n°4. "The Path up to the Village"

I always hesitated before circulating a *Presque rien*. For example, it took two years for the first one to come out of its hiding place, and things never changed. For the fourth, I hesitated for nine years, maybe because it's a fake *Presque rien* in which reality and lies merge. It's the path that leads up to the old village of Ventimiglia.

Memorised sounds
Produced at Studio Post-Billig
CD Sub Rosa, SRM 252 — 2006

1990–98
— 16 minutes

Les émois d'Aphrodite

Aphrodite's Frisson

From the 1986 version, I kept the feel of the piece, which moves like a sort of disjointed rock music. I added some harmonic 'manipulations', or a progression towards a disjointed harmony, which corresponds to my current interests. Lastly, by introducing the samplers, could convey the live quality of time, and disjoin the timbres.

for clarinet, piano, percussion, two samplers and one CD player
New version 1998
Memorised sounds produced at Atelier Post-Billig
Maison ONA Editions

1986–98
— 25 minutes

Far West News

n this work, autobiography doesn't work as a means to describe a trip. The original idea went something like this: a composer who has led a strange life, full of instrumental and electroacoustic compositions, and who is adept at recording on the move, plans to take an an aleatory trip through the Southwestern United States. Only during the making of the piece did I realise what was going on. This was not reportage, not soundscape, not Hör spiel, not an electronic work, not a portrait, not a presentation of recordings from reality not a transgression of reality, not impressionistic narration: it was a composition.

So I felt that my "radiophonic compositions" were a new way of writing a biographica book. That's why I also called the piece a "sound poem about a real trip", because poetr may well play reality like it would play an accordion — and maybe in certain cases, an particularly in mine, increasingly in my life too, composition is a perverse game with reality

Radiophonic piece in 3 parts commissioned by Piet Hein van de Poel, NPS Hilversum
Episode 1 : From Santa Fe to Monument Valley
Episode 2: From Page to the Grand Canyon
Episode 3: From Prescott to Los Angeles
Produced at Atelier post-billig
Commissioned by NPS Hilversum
WP Amsterdam, 1999
CD Signature, SIG 11014 — 2002 (Episode 1)
CD Blue Chopsticks, BC16 — 2006 (Episodes 2 and 3)

1998–99

— Episode 1: twenty nine minutes thirty seconds, Episode 2: twenty nine
minutes forty five seconds, Episode 3: twenty eight minutes

Jeu du hasard et de la détermination

A Game of Chance and Determination

In a set time of 21 minutes, I selected a number of electroacoustic elements, and instrumental writing with specific characteristics. Then I asked a software programme to fit them, one by one, into those 21 minutes. I produced the tape and wrote the score based on that arbitrary data. Did I cheat? Maybe, but not much.

For piano, percussion and memorised sounds
Produced at Atelier Post-Billig, with the support of the GRM
Special commission from the French Ministry of Culture and Communication
VP Multiphonies, Radio France, Paris, January 2001, by F. Rivalland (percussion), Michel Maurer (piano)
CD L'Empreinte Digitale, ED13171 — 2004
Score published by Association PRESQUE RIEN

1998–89
— 21 minutes 40 seconds

Les Archives sauvées des eaux, Exploitation des concepts n°1

Archives Saved from the Waters, Exploitation of the Concepts n°1

2000

were quite old. I had to take down a pile of boxes from the shelves. Opening them, the cardboard and tapes all looked soaked, I spread them out across the floor as if putting together a giant puzzle.

The idea of using my archives was born from the necessity to update the medium those memories were inscribed on. In my studio, I have analog tapes containing all the recordings I made since 1960, some I have used, some not. While copying those across to CDs I was seized by the impulse to turn that tedious job into a creative undertaking. And so instead of copying, I started composing. Thus was born a new composition that exploits the 1974 archives (I had to start somewhere).

Exploitation des concepts n°1
For 2CDs and a set of LPs
WP Ghent Vooruit, May 2000, by Luc Ferrari and DJ Olive
Commissioned by Hermes Ensemble
Version for SuperDeluxe, Tokyo, 2003, by Luc Ferrari and Otomo Yoshihide
CD Disc Callithump, CPCD-001 — 2008
Version for Plastic, Milan, 2004, by Luc Ferrari and eRikm
CD Angle, angle cd 008 — 2004
Orchestral version, for the Laborintus Ensemble and eRikm
CD Césaré, 06/03/4 —2006
Grand Prix Charles Cros 2005 In Memoriam
Maison ONA Editions
An open-ended electronic piece for two CD players

Cycle des souvenirs

Cycle of Memories

Using memories is nothing new for me, I am a repeat offender when it comes to autobiography. What is different here is the sound and image installation. Just like I am a composer-cum-sound recordist, here I am also a composer-cum-image recordist. I mean that since I don't record sounds the way a technician would, I acknowledge my status as an amateur image recordist. And so, daily life appears as my main topic. You will find here some images from my childhood, my street, my Métro stop; the places I've been and which have struck me enough for me to record them, some villages in Italy or the sea in Portugal, images from my present too, places where I've worked, my souvenir-objects, my house.

The cycle of memories also means that all the elements are arranged into cycles which while they are superimposed, produce random encounters. That's why everything spirals around. With this spiralling of image and sound, memory is written onto a distorting mirror but in which everything is true. Maybe…

Exploitation des concepts n°2
Audiovisual installation for six CD players and four video-projectors
Production: Post-Billig, with the support of Césaré and the CCMix
WP Paris, 2000, by CCMix
CD Blue Chopsticks, BC8 — 2002 (fixed version of the aleatory, continuous piece
Installation for six CD players and four videoprojectors.

1995–2000
— indeterminate duration

Archives génétiquement modifiées — Exploitation des concepts n°3

Genetically Modified Archives, Exploitation of the Concepts n°3

Exploitation des concepts n°3
Memorised sounds solo
Produced at Studio Post-Billig
WP GRM concert, Radio France, Paris, 18 January 2001
CD Robot Records, RR-39 — 2008

2000
— 25 minutes

his composition is made of the same musical elements as *Exploitation des concepts n°1, titled Archives sauvées des eaux*, for two DJs — one with CDs, the other with LPs. It shows to what extent the notion of "exploitation" enables me to return to previously used sounds, whole sequences even, but always with different ideas and a compositional point of view that is altered beyond recognition.

Going back over my 1970s work made me want to create something new, without nostalgia and without allegiance to the past. Also, with the "exploitations", I feel very free and uninhibited towards the original concepts. I am not trying to impose them as they originally stood, but to revisit them thirty years later, to see how the original concept looses its initial shape to take on a new form as it comes into contact with the other experiences of my life. Or disappears. Using the word "exploitation" as the central concept may be provocative, but it is also light-hearted. Anyway I feel perfectly entitled to exploit my ideas as well as my sounds. I listen, and I make a work today that is laden with memory.

And so these archives are deeply, and maybe genetically, modified.

Impro-Micro-Acoustique

Micro-Acoustic-Improv

In 1989, the music conservatory in Boulogne asked me to prepare a concert with some final year students. I was introduced to Roland Auzet, a percussionist, and I asked him to work with me and a pianist on *Cellule 75 [Cell 75]*, a relatively virtuoso piece for piano and percussion. During rehearsals, I realised that not only was he playing what was written but he did so with very individual and theatrical gestures, he was turning the score into drama. It was a very beautiful concert. Years later I met Roland, he was studying computer sciences applied to his instruments while also forming a circus company specialising in musical acrobatics, with the actors playing music while doing acrobatics. It was very good.

A few years ago, I attended an improvisation concert at the Instants Chavirés, a concert venue in a "rough" area of Montreuil. Noël Akchoté was one of the protagonists. From the way he played the guitar, I recognised he was someone extraordinary. There was nothing normal about the way he played, the sounds he produced, or his musical behaviour. He played the guitar, for sure, but more like we used to play in the early days of musique concrète, except we used the artifice of the studio whereas he was making new and extravagant sounds live and without the help of electronics. I took the liberty of calling this "the new concretes of real time". Soon after, through the vagaries of chance, I met Noël and we became friends.

That's when I decided to really take up improvisation in earnest. I had prepared improvisation sessions in the past, and I'd even written scores which leaned that way. But I had never included myself in the players, because I knew I was useless. Still, I decided to forget about my reservations and I contacted Noël Akchoté and Roland Auzet to suggest an experimental meeting at the Muse en Circuit studios. And so I placed myself in an unfamiliar position, working with two virtuosi who specialised in spontaneity, whereas I did my thinking on the score, that was my specialty... I was petrified: "It's a fine mess I've got myself into!" I thought.

And then we got down to it, my friends were very kind with me.

Tautologies et environs

Tautologies and Environs

For fifteen amplified instruments and memorised sounds (flute, oboe, clarinet, bass clarinet, bassoon, trumpet, trombone, piano, percussion, two violins, viola, cello, double bass)
WP Extension du Domaine de la Note IV, Théâtre Silvia Monfort, Paris, 6 April 2004, by the Ars Nova ensemble, dir. Philippe Nahon
Score: Ars Nova
Maison ONA Editions

2000–01
— 25 minutes

This composition uses the same memorised sounds as *Exploitation des concepts n°1 and n°3*. But each time, they are transformed, beyond recognition.

Using the same elements in different works was typical of that year (2000), and those works were composed concurrently; the "exploitations" were also characteristic of a new way of working, taking the same material into different directions. This is when I started working on my archives.

As for the instrumental composition, it stems from the exploitation of certain ideas and concepts I have been digging into, you might say ploughing, since the 1960s, on-and-off. I should say cyclically rather than on-and-off, since tautologies are based on cycles.

"And Environs" indicates a desire to penetrate further into the mechanics of cycles, but also to look around and to examine their natural habitat.

Tautologies et environs is a suite of sequences, each presented and organised differently from the cycles and their superimpositions. This for me illustrates the concept of tautology.

I was tempted to analyse how tautology operates in each sequence, but I won't, that would take us too far.

Because I've been using technology for a long time, I consider that the PA system is as much a part of the exploitation of the concepts as the recorded composition itself (memorised sounds: we used to say "on tape" but that's a little passé). The mics used for the instruments are not meant to make the instruments louder — although… — but to alter their sound through various processes. At least, that's the hope.

Presque rien avec instruments — Exploitation des concepts n°5

Almost Nothing with Instruments – Exploitation of the Concepts n°5

For fifteen amplified instruments and memorised sounds (flute, oboe, clarinet, bass clarinet, bassoon, trumpet, trombone, piano, percussion, two violins, viola, cello, double bass)
WP Extension du Domaine de la Note IV, Théâtre Silvia Monfort, Paris, 6 April 2004, by the Ars Nova ensemble, dir. Philippe Nahon
Score: Ars Nova
Maison ONA Editions

2001
— 25 minutes

In the fall of 1999, I started composing a new series of works whose collective title was *Exploitation des concepts*. The idea was precisely to use the concepts I had experimented with throughout my life as a composer, and to take them into all possible directions. This included instrumental writing, electroacoustic pieces, video, multimedia installations, new and old technologies, "concert-based" compositions (that is to say works compatible with the duration of a concert), or "non concert-based" works (so-called "permanent" works).

The Exploitations were eclectic: tautology, superimposed cycles, the minimalism of the *Presque Rien* pieces, the architectures of chance, anecdotal works, narration, daily life, arte povera, memories, etc — all the concepts that had crossed my work but which I had never exploited fully until then.

Paris-Tokyo-Paris

This sextet may well be the first score in which I used the concept of improvisation applied to writing. In the works that followed, I would use improvisation as a means to plunge into the unconscious, and writing as a reflexive process.

Sextet for oboe, clarinet, bassoon, violin, cello, piano and memorised sounds
Commissioned by New Generation, Tokyo
WP at CM Tokyo, 25 October 2003, by the NOMAD Ensemble, dir. Norio Sato
Maison ONA Editions

2002
— 27 minutes

Portrait of Luc Ferrari in Paris by Brunhild Ferrari

Les Anecdotiques — Exploitation des concepts n°6

Anecdotals – Exploitation of the Concepts n°6

Radiophonic piece
Produced for DeutschlandRadio Berlin
Grand Prix Charles Cros In Memoriam 2005
CD Sub Rosa, SR207 — 2004
Maison ONA Editions

2001–02 — 54 minutes

Having already explored a number of concepts, I'm now at number six, with *Les Anecdo-tiques* I explored an idea I had broached in *Hétérozygote* (1963), a composition I had dubbed without a trace of derision, "anecdotal music". This concern thus runs through much of my work.

For this project, I took the opportunity of several foreign trips, mostly professional, to record whatever sounded interesting to me. With those recordings, or at least those that were successful, I composed short sequences, each dedicated to a location. That is, each was made with the sounds of only one place, so they were more or less representative of reality — in any case, they used that reality. Those sequences are like portraits, akin to a type of audio riddles, since the locations are rarely named, except when I'd thought to mention their name there and then. Sequences, that was one of the main ideas. There were three.

For the second, rummaging through my archive, I found by chance some electronic sounds had never used before, go figure why, but which I thought would make interesting links between the sequences. So there is a constant balancing act between "concrete" and "abstract".

For number three, I remembered a set of interviews of young women I had done a long time ago but had never used either. I'd called them "Women's words". Spontaneous and intimate words. They fitted in that composition, thus generating a parallel discourse that had nothing to do with the sequences or with the electronic sounds, but which created a new oscillation within the discourse.

Those three elements form a continuity, and it doesn't matter if you can't tell who or what you're hearing. What interested me was to produce an ambiguous composition where meaning and lack of meaning alternated and gripped the listener's attention.

All three play on the perception of time, renewing the way time feels and looks, from the most stable to the most active. Also, from the start, an apparently systematic structure seems to establish itself, though it will eventually go awry.

Lastly, although I have repeatedly worked with notions like "anecdotal" or "narration" which are also related to time, I always manipulated them in an intuitive way. The exploitation of concepts is a way for me to be more… "conceptual". I thus demonstrated that *Les Anecdotiques* have nothing to do with narration and this composition thereby clarifies the difference between narrative and anecdotal.

So goes time, and renewed each time.

Overleaf: Luc Ferrari 'playing' the radio and counting money recieved by the radio station

Saliceburry Cocktail

It is the idea of the cocktail. I rearranged elements hiding parts I no longer wished to hear since certain sounds held memories. It is as though I hid the images the sounds suggested to me. I was forced to hide them under synthetic sounds. I was forced to dissimulate by drastic transformations, and I hid the shape in a non-shape or vice versa...

Electroacoustic music
WP Théâtre ABC, La Chaux-de-Fonds, Switzerland, 25 May 2003
CD Sub Rosa, SR252 — 2006
Maison ONA Editions

2002
— 30 minutes

Rencontres fortuites
Chance Encounters

For viola, piano and memorised sounds
WP Dijon, 22 November 2003, by Jean-Philippe Collard-Neven (piano), Vincent Royer (viola)
CD Sub Rosa, SR261 — 2007
Maison ONA Editions

2003
— 21 minutes 25 seconds

Quattro morceaux en forme de promenade

Four Pieces in the Shape of a Promenade

Let's say that out of four brass instruments, two should be saxophones. It's a question of colour, or of timbre if you like. These four pieces correspond to a very specific situation where instrumental writing enters into a dialectic relationship with what I like to call "S & M" [i.e. Sons Memorisés, or Memorised Sounds].

For four brass instruments, two percussions and memorised sounds
Commissioned by GMEA Tarn, Music Centre, Albi, with the support of the French State
VP Toulouse, 5 November 2004, by the Pythagore Ensemble
Maison ONA Editions

2003
— 21 minutes

Les Arythmiques

Arrhythmics

On the morning of May 29, 2003, I woke up and I couldn't breathe. They rushed me t
he emergency room and there, I was told I suffered from cardiac arrhythmia. They did a
ECG and showed it to me. I thought this arrhythmia wasn't very interesting at all, and tha
could do better than that.

This composition, strangely, should be listened to the right way round, but I tried to hav
people remember it back to front. I tried to go back in time…

Electro-acoustic music
WP Théâtre ABC, La Chaux-de-Fond, Switzerland, 17 June 2005
CD Blue Chopsticks, BC19 — 2008
Maison ONA Editions

2003
—40 minutes 20 seconds

Didascalies

Stage Directions

Stage directions help performers and directors perform a score or a libretto. Stage directions are intimate words meant for the participants. They are therefore a secret kept from the listeners or viewers. And yet, without them, the piece couldn't exist or would be totally unintelligible for the audience.

In this piece, the stage directions are particularly important (hence the title), they are an integral part of the score and they have a specific status within the score.
And yet, as I was just saying, they remain out of reach – still, we can take comfort in their presence which somehow, informs the performance. So we can say that what is entrusted to the performers – or should we call them re-creators – is secret in the sense of intimate.

The piece is for Alto and Piano, with a suite of memorised sounds.
It is a great crescendo that starts with ppp and reaches ffffffffff
It is played as a unison, or what I call a unison, which is necessarily something that runs and even skids until it becomes a gigantic and mostly harmonic unison, while respecting the initial monotone, that is to say it doesn't become a chord, but a substance.
The beginning should be considered as a philosophical preamble to the score, whereas the second part of the score will be more programmatic, and it will explain in detail how it can be played.

That's it, thank you for your attention.

For viola, piano and memorised sounds
WP Chapelle de Bloondael, Brussels, 16 May 2004, by Vincent Royer (viola), Jean-Philippe Collard-Neven (piano)
Maison ONA Editions
CD Sub Rosa, SR261 — 2007

2004
— 25 minutes

Après Presque rien

After Almost Nothing

About three years had elapsed between the composition of *Presque rien avec instruments* and its première, so the score was more like a vague memory to me. During the concert, I was very perturbed, not because I found the piece good or bad, but the score really seemed to mark the end of the Presque rien series. And at one point I even felt that it marked the end, full stop. Something like: after this, there's nothing left for me to do. Stuck! So, I thought: "I'm going to call this "après presque rien". And voilà! In fact, because the Presque rien pieces are based on a very strong concept, I needed to free myself from any concept whatsoever. Free and without any preconceived ideas, I decided to let myself be led by time and by chance encounters. So I started composing with no specific project in mind. I let my whims guide me, like: I feel like doing this now, and now I feel like doing that, I've had enough of this now, I feel like trying that, etc. It might be difficult to imagine, because usually, people have a plan. But I don't, I escape, I don't know what I'll feel like tomorrow.

I think that's what it's like to leave time be, to seize it more or less firmly, tighten your grip and then let go, let it flow leisurely, get hold of it again, voluptuously, grab it tenderly, grab it violently, grab it nonchalantly, grab it in bad taste and wrench out its vulgarity and its aesthetics, drown its ethics (I had to fit that one in somewhere), and also rebelliously endure its brutality, its inhumanity.
Here and there, I catch my breath, that's an achievement in itself, you ask the questions you can.

WP Palais des Beaux-Arts, Brussels, 20 April 2006, by Musiques Nouvelles Ensemble, dir. Jean-Paul Dessy
Edition Pierre Neurey, Valenciennes
Maison ONA Editions
For fourteen instruments and two samplers (flute, oboe, clarinet, bass clarinet, trumpet, tenor saxophone, barytone saxophone, trombone, piano, percussion, two violins, viola, cello, double bass, two samplers)

2004
— 25 minutes

Femme descendant l'escalier

Woman Descending a Staircase

What triggered the process was that one day, in the Métro, a woman descended the escalator, her stilettos click-clacking. I thought: there she is, it's her, and I had a friendly thought for Marcel Duchamp.

Sound installation for a bus shelter
Commissioned by Itinerario del Sonido
WP Itinerario del Sonido, Madrid, 21 May 2005
Maison ONA Editions

2004–05
— 40 minutes

Didascalies 2 ou Trois personnages en quête de notes

Stage Directions 2, or Three Characters in Search of Notes

The other day, in a folder dated 1993, I found a score for two pianos, titled *Revenir à la note de départ*. And so I decided to turn this into a new composition without changing a note. There were very few notes anyway, which suited me fine.

For two pianos and a very powerful instrument capable of holding a very loud note
WP German temple, La Chaux-de-Fonds, 26 October 2008, by Jean-Philippe Collard-Neven, Vincent Royer, Claude Berset
Score by Association PRESQUE RIEN
LP Sub Rosa, SRV305 — 2010

2005
— approximately 20 minutes

Les Proto-Rythmiques

ProtoRhythmics

After playing *Archives sauvées des eaux* with eRikm, I suggested we work on this new piece together. That first experience had taken me into a field where I had never before been an active participant; the statement I now made with *Les ProtoRythmiques* took me to more adventurous, and democratic, territories (if one can still use the word democratic after the way the Bush administration abused it).

For two DJs
WP Les Instants Chavirés, Montreuil, 12 February 2005 by Luc Ferrari and eRikm
CD ROOM40, RM417 — 2007

2004–05
— approximately 60 minutes

Luc Ferrari and eRikm photographed by Brunhild Ferrari

Morbido Symphonie

Morbido Symphony

This piece is as morbid as it is morbido (which in Italian means "soft" or "tender") and it's going to be very funny.

For fifteen instruments and memorised sounds (flute, oboe, clarinet, bass clarinet, bassoon, horn, trumpet, piano, two violins, two celli, double bass)
Unfinished composition: only two movements were composed, the third remained at an embryonic stage
WP Paris, 11 May 2007, by Ars Nova Ensemble, dir. Philippe Nahon
Maison ONA Editions

2005
— 25 minutes

Dérivatif

Derivative

"*Derivative* is the title Luc Ferrari gave to what was to be his next piece, but the projec didn't get beyond the very beginnings. That was on April 12, 2005. He was looking t explore his archive in a new and different way. His intention was to go through those cup boards full of magnetic tapes, finished works as well as pre-mixes or recordings, and t pull out every thirteenth tape. He would play it, copy "just any" extract from it, and incluc t in the composition. Because that task was a little too tiring for him, he asked me to hel, We only got through a small section of the sounds or fragments of sequences.

Before undertaking to complete the piece, I hesitated for three years – after his death, was unthinkable, and even the year after I couldn't consider it, convinced as I was th shouldn't interfere in Luc's creation and above all risk betraying his spirit. Many times attempted to consult him but didn't receive an audible answer, and I was sorry not to se hat project come to fruition, so, in early July 2008, I took the cheerful decision to follow h race across so many creative years. I thus carried on the task, copying those fragment each time remembering so very intensely the circumstances, the times, the ambiance he seasons, and I couldn't confine myself to just compiling a private catalogue of sound So I borrowed for my own use all those elements and produced, without cheating at all, 'Derivative", in my own way, without adding any sounds that weren't Luc's, and with mir nal technological artifice.

Hanna Schygulla closes the piece with a short sentence, in German: "In one night, everythir changed" (from *Labyrinthe Portrait,* a radio composition with a text by Colette Fellous – Brunhild Ferrari

Memorised sound archives
Intended for Seven Things, Edinburgh
Begun in July 2005 and left unfinished; completed by Brunhild Ferrari in 2008
CD box-set INA-GRM — 2009

2005–08
— 27 minutes 7 seconds

Autobiographie n°11
Autobiography n°11

… Because I think it's quite a good idea to try and explain the different periods of my life or work, not with the kind of earnestness of those who tilt at windmills, but in the light-hearted way you can apply to yourself, and which makes it easier to bear yourself, and just talk freely about all sorts of things.

… because I have written quite a few contradictory autobiographies, but not for years. My autobiographies have gone stiff.

When talking about my works, I used to classify them by genre. But now, I prefer to speak of periods, even though they merge slightly, but that doesn't matter, it's probably natural, and if I stick to three periods, it's not too bad… All the same, to avoid getting them mixed up, I colour-coded them.

So, the first period of my life, roughly, I called black. It corresponds to a serial, or post-serial (whatever you want to call it) tendency — black, but not in the sense of dark and gloomy, for here, the colour black is not tainted with any "pejorativism", instead it refers to anarchy, since I've always used series in an anarchic way. I don't know why I mention this at all, or maybe just to place *Interrupteur* in its context, as it marks precisely the end of that cycle.

Let's say the black period was a time of experimentation with compositional methods, since I was concurrently experimenting in the fields of musique concrète and electroacoustic music, not meaning any harm by it, it's just that formalism was first and foremost in my mind. But then, the second stage was rather "unformal", in the sense that the form, to be alive, had to carry within it its own "unforming", its own excavation, its explosion and its self-negation through contempt. Or maybe not so much contempt as a sort of gateway that made it possible to desecrate form and to transform it by associating it with eccentric ideas. In pieces like *Visages* or in the *Société* series for example…

That was the end of the black period, without wanting to disown it, there were some good things about it… And it cheerfully overlapped with the red period, since the black period ended in 1967 and the red period started in 1963 — a bit confusing, but it's always confusing, having to explain oneself…

The so-called red period is one of all-out subversion, but it carries within itself its own refutation, just like the black period carried its own de-construction and contradiction. As a matter of fact, at about that time, I wrote a score titled *Subversion-Dérision*, which also implied deriding subversion. Either through the texts themselves, for example in scores like *Le Dispositif et son disnégatif*, or through the musical element reduced to its minimum, in pieces like *Music Promenade* or in *Presque Rien*. So that was a time when the social and the political mingled with musical intentions.

But above all, it was a time for demystification — of the work, of art, of the artist, of both the cult and the manipulation of power in all its forms; a time also for observing society, listening to the landscape, challenging other people's words. And a time for derision, when that devilish curiosity of mine drove me to explore things outside of my domain, much to the exasperation of the music establishment. Which by the way I fully understand, I too would have been exasperated if I were the music establishment, since I also find myself exasperating…

But the current period is a blue period, blue like the Mediterranean, and, let me add, a miscreant and feminine period. Difficult to explain. For example, *Cellule 75* partakes both of the red and the blue. Regarding the term "miscreant", I am aware I should say "atheist", but miscreant is "nicer". It means that I am against any decrepit idea of a god, especially that one-and-only god whom man has made in his image. Obviously, man didn't invent a god in woman's image, that would not be appropriate. This is why when I say that I am Mediterranean, miscreant and feminine, it means that I acknowledge those components in me. Of course, I am not a woman, but it's a way of saying that I am very close to women, in that I see no trace of that god created by man and for whom women never existed. So there, that's my blue period.

Chance with Determination
An Interview with Pierre-Yves Macé and David Sanson
Photograph by Brunhild Ferrari

If today you were to make up an autobiography for yourself, as is your wont, what would it say?

LF: My autobiographies were born out of a desire to debunk the language of musicians in the 1960s, an exceedingly technical and tedious language. So, when asked to write bios for concert programme notes, I would write these caricatures of serious music talk, which — by saying things that were wrong, and therefore true in some way, by playing with fabrication and invention — aimed to show that music could hold a political and even "philosophical" discourse. I put an end to the Autobiographies when I reached number 18, because it included real dates. Since I was now telling the truth, it was time to move on to something new. In fact, nowadays, my writings are to be found in my scores. Which doesn't mean that my music no longer needs to be commented on. Just that I no longer feel the need to deride others. I am content to explain what I think of the score at hand, which is another kind of autobiographical writing. For *Cahier du Soir [Evening Notebook]*, there's a ten-page text, referring to the music world. *For Symphonie déchirée [Torn Symphony]*, I also wrote ten pages, explaining what I'm like, what makes me tick, why I feel torn, torn by society, by war… These are my views, yet they're as funny as they're gloomy.

Where do you fit in, regarding tradition?

LF: I'm interested in tradition, because that's what we're made of. Our memory, our brain, they weren't built in one fell swoop. The first time I went to Greece or to Italy, I identified with the place, I was looking at my origins. All of that is my culture, I own it, it's in my brain, it's everywhere, and I draw from it, or not as the case may be. I draw from it because it enables me to invent new things, and above all to shatter traditions. So I incorporate all of that: culture, psychology, sexuality too…

How come you've felt the need to carry on composing instrumental music even though you initiated "anecdotal music" which, in the 1960s, marked a radical break with tradition, even more so than musique concrete?

LF: Because I am a writer. I need instruments, and not just sounds manufactured in a studio. I need to express myself through instrumental writing as much as through what I call "memorized sounds"… I like to have a dialogue with the orchestra, to discuss what they find possible or impossible, for example. Besides, I can't confine myself to doing the same thing all the time, that's just not me. I made several *Presque rien,* but always ten years apart — because every now and then I come across a very interesting situation that makes me want to get down to it. It's the same thing with the orchestra. When something needs doing, I do it, and if I feel like doing something else, I do that too. It's a more immediate way of interacting with others.

What are your affinities with the world of improvised music? You've been improvising for a while now, or at least, performing on stage — what is the link with your compositional work?

LF: That's an old story!... At the beginning of the 1960s, I was working with a conductor, Konstantin Simonovic, who directed a small instrumental ensemble. We decided to hold improvisation sessions with the musicians, to see how one could articulate an idea without using notes. That was considered outrageous back then because, although all the heavyweights of serial and post-serial music were in favour of open works that allowed for a certain freedom in the configuration of a piece, all the same, for them, anything that resembled improvisation was dirty, unacceptable — or else, it erred on the side of jazz, which was even worse, because those guys weren't even white... [smile] Anyway, I got into improvisation very early on, and I did a lot of it with that orchestra, which didn't prevent me from writing all the notes down when composing one of my scores. I went back to improvisation in the 1970s when I started doing text-scores: scores that included no technical indications, but just a general idea, handed out to musicians or actors, or participants on stage. There, I was organising other people's improvisations. I started doing text-scores in 1965. I wasn't the only one: Stockhausen, among others, also wrote some, and even John Cage's work included all sorts of ingredients that left plenty of room for freedom, chance... However, improvisation is not something I do myself: I'm useless at it. Sometimes I try to improvise at home, and it's always awful, I'm just not an improvisor.

When you performed with eRikm or DJ Olive, wasn't that improvisation?

LF: Yes, but that was a little different, because I wasn't playing a real instrument: for me, machines are machines. I've worked with machines since 1958, when I entered the GRM alongside Pierre Schaeffer and Pierre Henry. For me, machines are a bit like horses: they scare me but at the same time, you can't resist hopping on, just to see what happens. DJ Olive was the first one I worked with, I met him at a concert at the Pompidou Centre, with eRikm and Christian Marclay. I was later invited to do something with him for a festival of improvised music, in Ghent: we met at my studio, we talked, I brought along a few pieces that were typical of my work, I burnt a few CDs, and then we started collaborating at a distance, via email, he would send me things, I would send him things, and then one fine day we met up at the festival.

You mean that for you, that isn't really instrumental work?

LF: At the beginning, I must say I was very self-conscious and I expected him to come up with things that would destroy the over-fabricated, over-composed pieces I had put on the CDs. As for him, he was very shy: in his eyes, I was a great contemporary music figure, so he expected me to put him through his paces; I had a lot of trouble getting him to loosen up [smile]. We did a rehearsal, and eventually I started improvising with the machines — in the way Schaeffer and I had once imagined was possible, when he'd suggested I should do a concert and play with objects the way we did in the studio, which at the time was technically inconceivable. DJs invented something amazing when they started treating sounds that didn't belong to them, using samplers to build a database from other people's material. Having said that, that's what Beethoven was doing: when he composed a fugue or appropriated a tune from popular music, he was sampling… As for me, I don't like the sampler, I never use it to reproduce real sounds, I find the quality of the sound is never good enough. But I must say it's very convenient, and some people are sampler virtuosi.

Do you still work with tapes?

LF: I work on the computer. I have absolutely nothing against computers, on the contrary, I think they brought about a very precious revolution. Having said that, I'm increasingly in favour of arte povera. If my studio today is called "Post-Billig", it's only because of the Pro Tools software. And even then, I never use the Pro Tools effects, I can't bring myself to find them interesting. I like to move about, to touch the dials, to always push things to their limits, do things you're not supposed to do. My music always entails physical gestures.

You have worked on several visual shows. What is your relationship to images, and to what extent is that relationship linked to the visual dimension in "anecdotal music"?

LF: I don't produce images, but I'm fascinated by the skills that go into that: like on stage, when you start working on the lighting for example, I go crazy. That's one of the reasons I like improvisation concerts, you can really splatter the light

around. And also, I've always been passionate about the movies. So that's one type of image. Another type would be as you suggested, when you no longer need images because they are contained in the sound. Sound is even more subtle than images because it's not sharp, there's something out of focus about it, sometimes you feel you recognise it but you might be recognising ten other things at the same time. And so I parachute images in, I play with them, like with an accordion, or a fan, you spread it open, you close it. If I insert sounds from reality, for example, all of a sudden the musicians take on a different dimension and what they do doesn't have the same resonance, it all becomes incredible, it enables you to take off — that's what I aspire to. It still gets me fired up, even though I've been doing it for over forty years…

The Ars Nova Ensemble recently premiered two of your pieces: *Tautologies et environs*, which follows on from the *Tautologos* series, and *Presque rien avec instruments*, a return to the *Presque rien* idea…

LF: Tautology and repetition — or should I say cycles, I'm a little uncomfortable with the term "repetition" — are two pillars of my work. We all have our own cycles, I myself have a work pattern, and I'm very unhappy when I'm not working because I feel as though I've run out of ideas, so I look for another pattern, another rhythm, and I just keep at it until I come up with an idea, good or bad. I wondered how I might translate that into sound, and that's how I came up with the scores for *Société I, II, III*, etc. They're not all "text-scores". For example, *So-*

cte 1, subtitled *Et si le piano était un corps de femme* [What if the Piano Were a Woman's Body], is a concerto for piano, percussion and orchestra; it is completely written, but some theatrical things happen in the piece, they stand for society (what better than an orchestra to represent society, with its hierarchies and activities, its way of being both obedient and absent-minded?). That's what tautology is, and I always come back to that idea because it enables you to see how things combine of their own accord. *Tautologies et environs* is environmental, i.e. it examines what happens to the surroundings of the tautology if I modify and distort the cycles, if I send them spinning round like bent bicycle wheels. Almost the same thing goes for *Presque* rien, since an "almost nothing" is a recorded social or poetic situation, conveyed only through memorised sounds via loudspeakers. I came up with the idea of doing a *Presque rien avec instruments* [Almost Nothing with Instruments]. One of the improvisations we did with Noël Akchoté and Roland Auzet happened to be a *Presque rien* all of one piece, thirty minutes long. I asked them for permission to add instruments on top of those sounds: they were delighted, as was I.

In what ways is this piece related to a *Presque rien*?

LF: Through its minimalism. The title *Presque rien* suggests that nothing, not one sound, allows you to hold on to the idea of musicality, and therefore you can

feel at a loss — just like you can lose your bearings in society, because if you don't take a good look at it, you feel as though nothing much is happening... By the way, the score for *Presque rien* has no bar lines, no measures: it's just people meeting, gesturing to each other, giving signs independently of the conductor (who flags up the most important encounters), conferring and deciding to do this or that. The score therefore exists outside of any normal temporality, there is no "beat" as they say. The only thing that is determined is the duration of the piece, which is the duration of the tape.

Are there other avenues you now feel like exploring?

LF: Many! I have just finished a thing called the *Arythmiques (Arrhythmics)*. I happen to really like the notion of "exploitation". When this place was flooded, all the tapes you see around you were affected, I had to make copies, and that's how I came to compose the *Archives sauvées des eaux* [Archives Saved from the Waters]: for other people, it's like poetry, but for me it's reality, it's exploitation. *The Arrhythmics* came about because I had a heart attack in May 2003, and they found I suffered from arrhythmia, so they gave me an electric shock. I was looking at the cardiologist's notes, and I thought: "this arrhythmia thing, it's not very interesting, surely, as a musician, I can do better than that." So I started a long forty-minute piece — comprising only memorised sound, no instrument, it's very microscopic — completely arrhythmic, and catastrophic: I stuffed all the arrhythmias in the world into that piece, and the result is very very strange. So anyway, that's what I do, I exploit things that happen to me, and it's very entertaining. This heart failure taught me something, it triggered ideas, it inspired me… You know, on the whole, I'm a jolly fellow. I attach great importance to joy, to joie de vivre, it's very important, you create it constantly, at every moment. Life is a conquest, a way of acknowledging that time exists. I live in joy and in fear: barbarity, what is happening in Iraq horrifies me, the way America wants to use the country to make money is tragic and revolting. So I'm caught between that joy and that revulsion: that's what I say constantly, in every one of my scores — it starts off very well and then…

Artworks
Collages + Painting

UNTITLED COLLAGE, 1951
31 cm x 24 cm

UNTITLED COLLAGE, 1951
28 cm x 39 cm

UNTITLED COLLAGE, 1954
31 cm x 24 cm

UNTITLED COLLAGE
31 cm x 24 cm

UNTITLED COLLAGE
24 cm x 38 cm

UNTITLED COLLAGE
24 cm x 38 cm

UNTITLED COLLAGE
26 cm x 29 cm

UNTITLED COLLAGE
19 cm x 36 cm

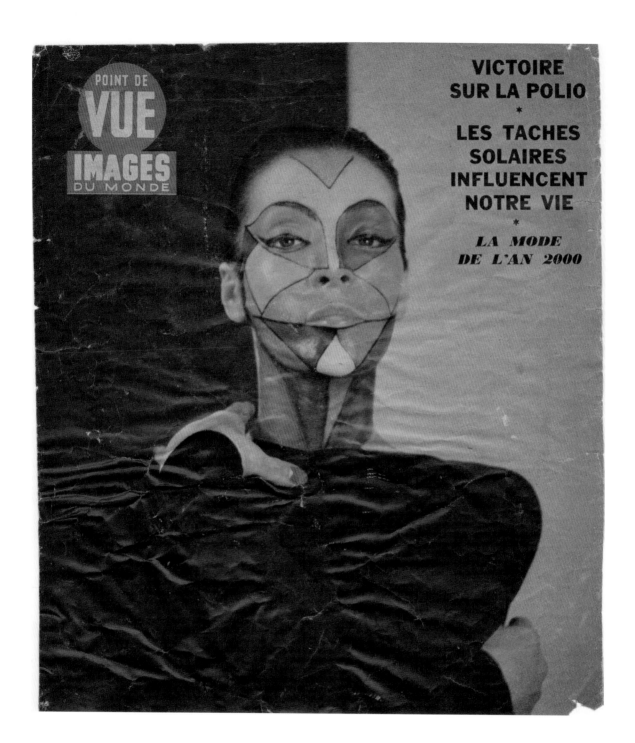

Text on the magazine cover:

POINT DE
VUE
IMAGES
DU MONDE

VICTOIRE
SUR LA POLIO
*
LES TACHES
SOLAIRES
INFLUENCENT
NOTRE VIE
*
LA MODE
DE L'AN 2000

UNTITLED COLLAGE
26 cm x 29 cm

UNTITLED COLLAGE
36.5 cm x 26 cm

UNTITLED COLLAGE
22 cm x 29 cm

UNTITLED COLLAGE

36 cm x 19 cm

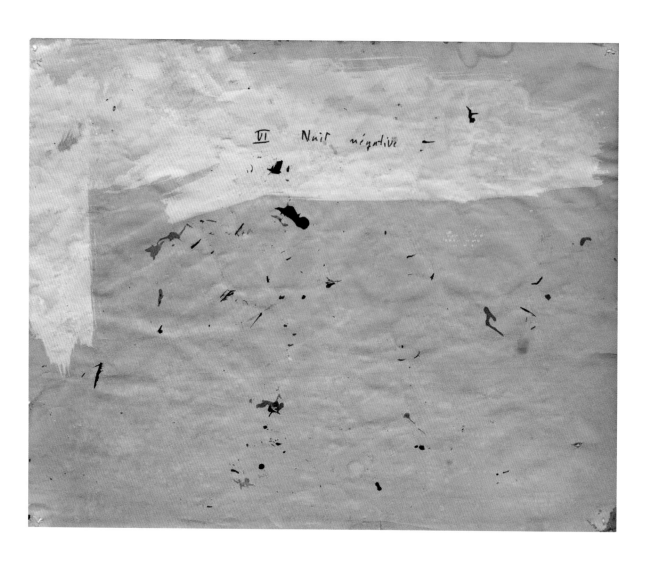

VI NUIT NEGATIVE

29 cm x 21 cm

back

VI NUIT NEGATIVE

29 cm x 21 cm

front

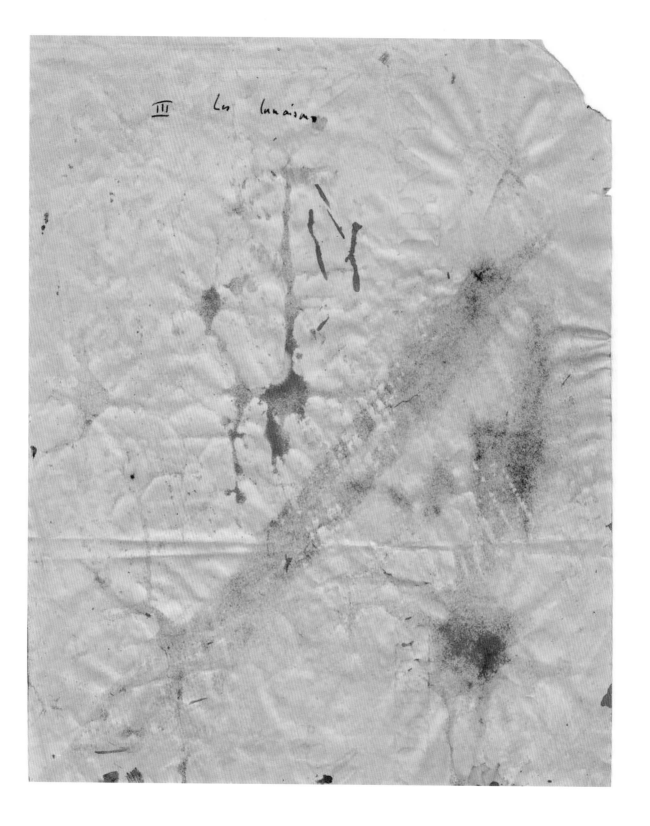

III LES LUNAISONS

21 cm x 29 cm

back

III LES LUNAISONS

21 cm x 29 cm

front

Photoengravings

UNTITLED, 1984
20.5 cm x 29 cm

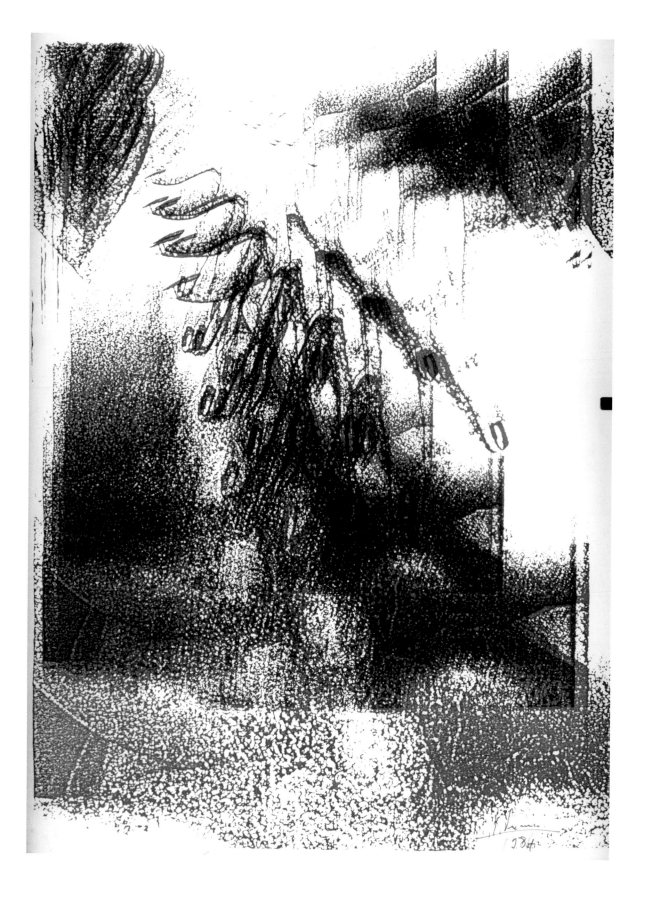

UNTITLED, 1984
23 cm x 30 cm

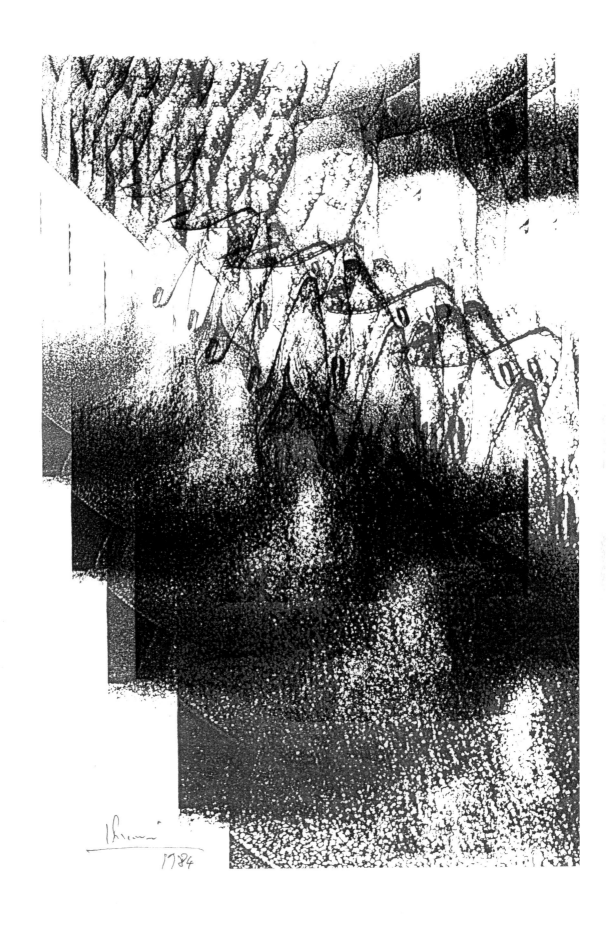

UNTITLED, 1984
24 cm x 30 cm

UNTITLED, 1984
21 cm x 29.5 cm

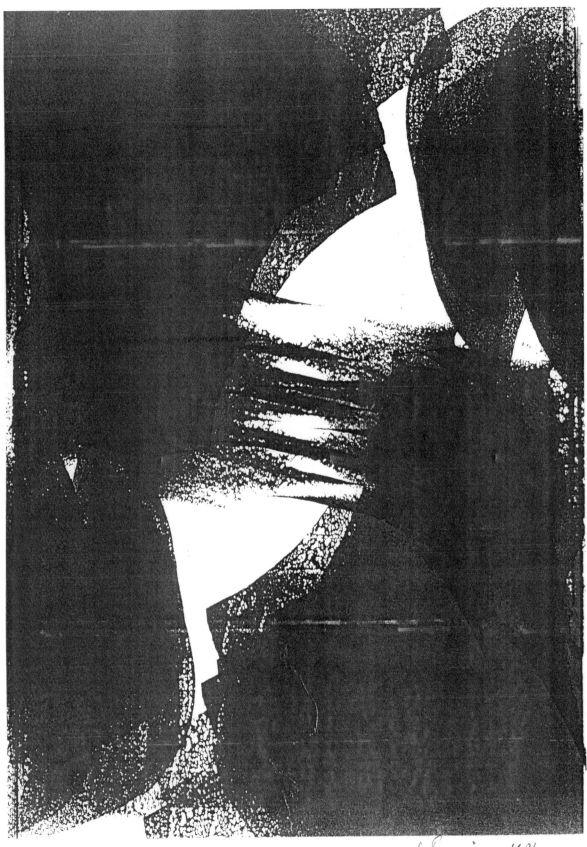

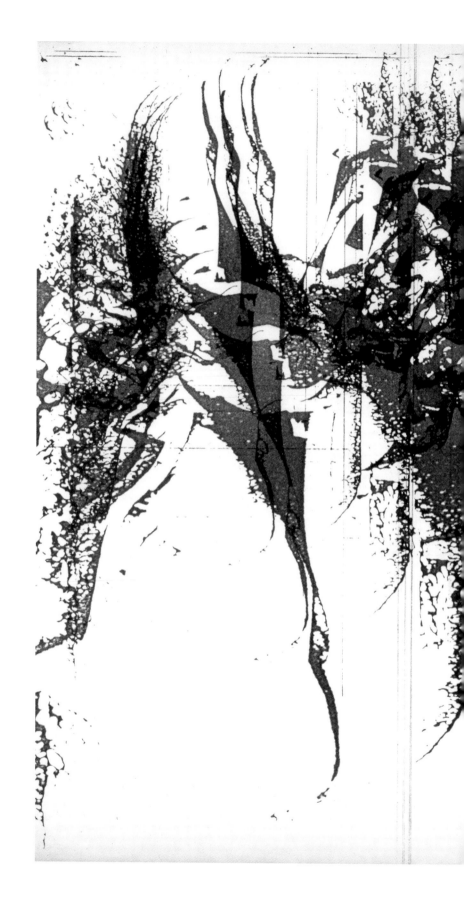

UNTITLED, 1984
29 cm x 20.5 cm

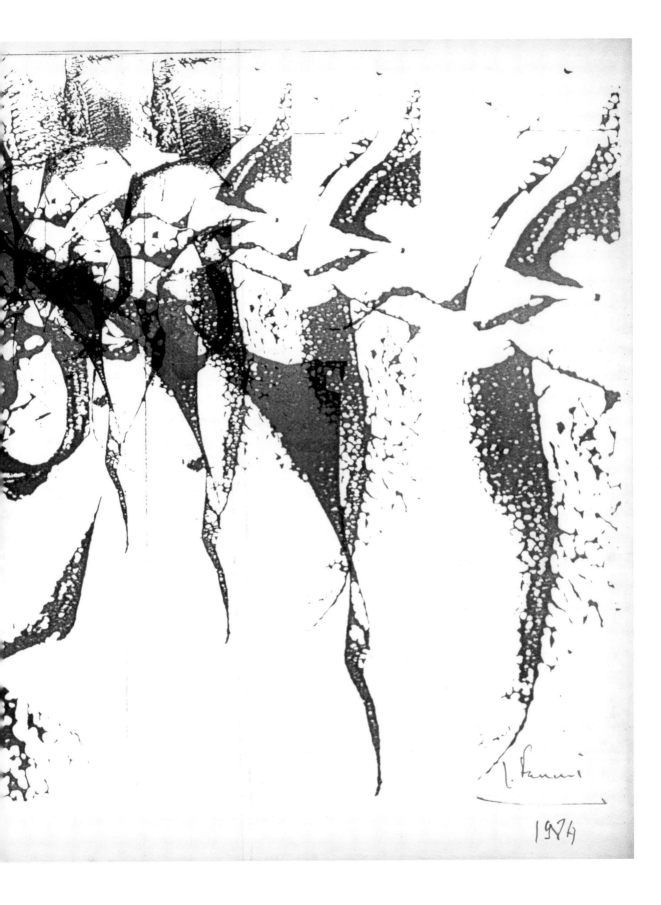

1974

UNTITLED
21 cm x 30 cm

Biographical notes

1929   Born in Paris, February 5.

1946-48   Studies music at the Versailles Conservatory.

1948-50   Studies in Olivier Messiaen's class

1958   Enters the Groupe de Musique Concrète (until 1966)

1958-59   Collaborates with Pierre Schaeffer to establish the Groupe de Recherche Musicale (GRM)

1959-60   Chair of the GRM; pedagogical activities;
            series of radio programmes on musique concrète

1960-61   Research projects on new instruments; study of instruments and of resonant bodies.

1961-62   Artistic director of an instrumental ensemble conducted by Konstantin Simonovic. Schema-based improvisation exercises.

1962-63   Conducts a group composition for tape and orchestra by all the composers of the GRM.

1964-65   Records, provides musical soundtrack and co-directs a series of television programmes: *Chaque pays fête son grand homme (Every country celebrates its great men)* (Wagner, Shakespeare, Saint Anthony, Chopin, Joan of Arc, William Tell, Johannes Strauss…). Broadcast on French, German and Canadian television.

1964-65   Guest Professor of Composition at the Rheinische Musik-schule, Cologne.

1965-68   With Gérard Patris, writes and directs a series of programmes on contemporary music for French television: *Les Grandes Répétitions [The Great Rehearsals]* (Olivier Messiaen, Edgar Varèse, Karlheinz Stockhausen, Hermann Scherchen, Cecil Taylor).

1966	Professor of Experimental Music, Stockholm.
1967	One-year residency in Berlin, as a guest of the Ford Foundation and the DAAD.
1968-69	Head of Music at the Maison de la Culture [municipal Cultural Centre], in Amiens.
1972	Founds the Billig studio, a modest electroacoustic studio
1972	Awarded Karl Sczuka Prize for the Hörspiel Portrait-Spiel (Production: Südwestfunk, Baden-Baden).
1978-80	Professor of Composition at the Pantin Conservatory.
1982	Foundation of the organisation LA MUSE EN CIRCUIT, a studio dedicated to electroacoustic composition and radiophonic creation with Maurice Fleuret
1986	With LA MUSE EN CIRCUIT, organises a series of musical shows at the Café de la Danse, Paris, entitled Vue imprenable sur l'acoustique [Stunning Views over Acoustics], including: Sombres machines à sons [Sombre Sound-making Machines], Radio sur scène [Radio on Stage], La leçon d'espagnol [The Spanish Lesson].
1987	Awarded Italia Prize for the symphonic tale Et si tout entière maintenant [What if now, all of it], presented as part of the multi-media event Brise-Glace [Ice-Breaker].
1988	Karl Suzuka Prize, for the Hörspiel Je me suis perdu or Labyrinthe portrait [I got lost or Labyrinth Portrait] (co-produced by Südwestfunk and LA MUSE EN CIRCUIT).
1989	Retrospective at the Manca Festival in Nice; Grand Prix national du Ministère de la Culture [First Prize granted by the French Ministry of Culture].

1990	Olga Koossewitzky International Prize for the symphonic piece *Histoire du plaisir et de la désolation* [*A History of Pleasure and Desolation*].
1991	Italia Prize for the radio piece *L'Escalier des aveugles* [*The Blind Men's Stairs*] (co-produced by Radio Nacional de España and LA MUSE EN CIRCUIT).
1993	Guest of the electronic music studio of the WDR, Cologne.
1994	On 21 April, steps down as president of LA MUSE EN CIRCUIT.
1995	Parcours confus [Confused Journey], retrospective at Groningen and concert tour in Holland.
1996	Leaves LA MUSE EN CIRCUIT
1996	Builds his own home-studio, called Post-billig.
1997	Invited on a three-week lecture and concert tour of California's main universities (with the support of the Ministry of Foreign Affairs)
1998	Sets up a new studio in Paris, near Nation, named Atelier Post-billig.
1999	Embarks on the series of *Exploitation of the Concepts*, which relaunches all-round creative activities: installations, collaborations with experimental DJs, improvisation work, several major instrumental works, radio pieces, works for memorised sounds.
2001	Retrospective-like event organised by the FUTURA Festival at Crest, with performances of the electroacoustic works since 1958.
2002	"Monographic" festival set up by New Generation, Japan.
2003	Multifaceted retrospective at La Chaux-de-Fonds, Switzerland; Concert tour in Japan: Tokyo, Nagoya, Osaka.

2004	One-week Residency and monographic festival in Poitiers, set up by Ars Nova, and co-produced with Le Théâtre-Scène Nationale de Poitiers and LA MUSE EN CIRCUIT; "8 Jours avec les musiques de Luc Ferrari" ["8 Days with Luc Ferrari's Musics"], as part of the AUDIOFRAMES Festival, Lille 2004, co-produced by Ars Nova and LA MUSE EN CIRCUIT; One week of concerts and installation dedicated to Luc Ferrari by the NOVELLUM Festival in Toulouse and the GMEA, Albi.
2005	August 22, Luc Ferrari dies in Arezzo, Tuscany. Awarded the Grand Prix Charles Cros 2005 In Memoriam, on the occasion of the release of his albums: *Les Anecdotiques. Exploitation des concepts n°6 and Archives sauvées des eaux. Exploitation des concepts n°1.*

Afterword by David Grubbs

The many stylistic shifts within Ferrari's work as well as his wily, idiosyncratic aloofness from post-war music ideologies made him an especially appealing figure to younger musicians and composers. His fundamental drive toward an accumulation of means, rather than the episodic renunciation of forms more common to his peers, served to make Ferrari's work increasingly relevant throughout his life, and his was an artistic intelligence whose laughter could be compared to that of John Cage.

It's little surprise that Ferrari's final decades were marked by encounters with musicians who knew him first from recordings but then were amazed, lo and behold, to make the meaningful acquaintance of an ever-vital, generous, hilarious, wonderfully social artist who didn't hesitate to throw himself into friendships and collaborative working relationships with those he recognized as kindred spirits. There he was, in a strikingly patterned gray wool suit with fire-engine red Doc Martens, ready to extend the conversation.

programme

- Initiation au fonctionnement du studio : la chaîne analogique.
- Recherche d'objets sonores, prise de son
- Manipulations et transformations
- Réalisation de séquences (montage et mixage)
- Utilisation du synthétiseur
- Historique et écoute critique d'œuvres contemporaines

horaires du stage
9 h à 12 h 30 - 14 h 30 à 18 h 30 - 21 h à 23 h

SAMEDI 11
RENCONTRE
avec Luc FERRARI

sur le thème
« l'emploi du son réaliste
dans la musique électro-acoustique »

Luc FERRARI compositeur; à l'origine du G.R.M. Depuis 1960, sans cesser de composer pour l'orchestre, mène un travail d'écriture et d'improvisation (partitions textes). Emet l'idée d'une musique sociologique : reportage sonore. Vient, récemment, de réaliser deux disques.

à 21 h CONCERT PUBLIC
- œuvres de **Luc FERRARI**
  et **Henri FOURES**
- œuvres de **T. Besche** et **R. Ossart**

Renseignements et inscriptions :
Atelier Electro-Acoustique
MJC d'Albi
13, rue de la République - 81000 ALBI
Tél. (63) 54.20.67

---

mjc albi-tarn
stage d'initiation
à la musique
électro-acoustique
du 5 au 12 avril 1981

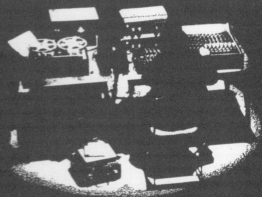

atelier de musique
électro-acoustique d'albi
t. besche, r. ossart

en collaboration avec :
la Maison des Jeunes et de la Culture d'Albi
l'A.D.D.A. du Tarn
- la Délégation Musicale Régionale du Ministère de la Culture et de la Communication

---

THÉÂ

HÈT

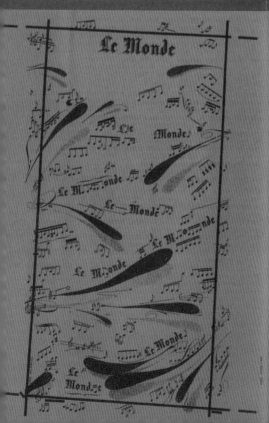

Le Monde

LUC FERRARI

Ensemble MUSIQUE VIVANTE
direction: DIEGO MASSON

Festival
d'Automne
à Paris
Centre Pompidou
14 novembre 1979

programme:
INTERRUPTEUR, pour ensemble de chambre (1967)
CELLULE 75, force du rythme et cadence forcée, pour piano percussion et bande (1975)
entr'acte
PRESQUE RIEN N°2, ainsi continue la nuit dans ma tête multiple, pour bande seule (1978)   création
ENTRÉE, pour quinze instruments (1979)   création
BONJOUR COMMENT CA VA?, pour piano, violoncelle et clarinette basse (1979)   création

UE
SIK

NN

A MUSIQUE - 16 MARS 1970

O-CONCERT

c ferrari

Beethovenhalle Bonn

bonn

Großer Saal   Mittwoch, 3. 5. 1972, 20 Uhr

Tage Neuer Musik

in Verbindung mit dem DAAD
– Berliner Künstlerprogramm –

Uraufführung

Luc Ferrari

Allo, ici la terre...
Hier spricht die Erde

Multi-Media-Show
für Orchester, Tonbänder und Diaprojektore

Orchester der Beethovenhalle Bonn
Leitung Volker Wangenheim

Bildregie **Jean Serge Breton**
Klangregie und Gesamtleitung **Luc Ferrari**

Eintritt frei!

Wiederholung Donnerstag, 4. 5. 1972, 20 Uhr

mit Pop-Gruppe **Amon Düül**

Luc Ferrari   Composé-Composite   (Buntscheckig Zusammengesetztes)

1929 in Paris geboren. Musikalische Studien an der „Ecole Normale de Musique". Gehört seit 1958 der Groupe de Recherche Musicales an.

Im Gegensatz zu Carson geht Ferrari extrem weit in der Ausarbeitung seines
Grundmaterials. Sein Werk gliedert sich in zwei Teile: Composé-kontinuierlich
und Composite-diskontinuierlich. Im ersten Teil unterstreicht er die Art des
Materials durch Überlagerung und Wiederholung in einem weiträumigen
crescendo von drei Minuten, der zweite Teil enthält eine Art Brücke, die aus
einer Vervielfältigung gewisser Töne Parmegianis gebildet wurde.

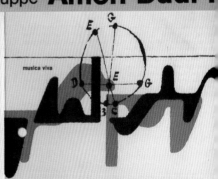

musica viva

Spielzeit 65/66

1. Veranstaltung, 8. November 1965, 20 Uhr
im Theater am Turm

Eintrittspreise: DM 2,–. Vorverkauf: Tages- und Abendkasse Theater am
Turm, Eschersheimer Landstraße 2, Telefon 55 98 64

Veranstalter: Frankfurter Bund für Volksbildung, Oeder Weg 1, Tel. 55 02 31
Künstlerische Leitung und Organisation: Dr. Rudolf Lück

Verantwortlich für den Inhalt: Hermann Schick (Leiter der Volkshochschule)
Grafik: Zollna   Druck: Hugo Haßmüller

Realisation der musique concrete: ORTF Paris, Service de la Recherch
musicale. / Die Angaben zu Werk und Autor wurden der Broschüre „une
expérience collective", herausgegeben von Pierre Schaeffer, entnommen.

Dolmetscherin: Dipl.-Dolm. Brigitte Grossmann

Nächste (vom Oktober 1965 verschobene) musica viva Veranstaltung:
Januar 1966, Theater am Turm.

Witold Lutoslawski (Warschau)   DIE NEUE MUSIK IN POLEN

Vortrag in deutscher Sprache mit Tonbandbeispielen
(in Verbindung mit dem Hessischen Rundfunk)

Concert collectif

mit Werken für Orchester und Tonband vo
F.-B. Mâche, Philippe Carson, Ivo Malec,
François Bayle und Luc Ferrari
(Deutsche Erstaufführung)

Mitwirkende:
Das Radio-Sinfonie-Orchester Strasbourg
Leitung: Charles Bruck

Einführende Worte: Pierre Schaeffer

Teilnehmer des Podiumsgesprächs (nach de
Pause): François Bayle, Charles Bruck, Iv
Malec und Pierre Schaeffer / Ltg.: Rudolf Lüc

Frankfurter Bund für Volksbildung
in Verbindung mit dem Hessischen Rundfun
und dem Service de la Recherce de l'O.R.T.F
Paris.

Theater am Turm, Eschersheimer Landstraße

A note for English readers

Together, Luc & I discovered new places and countries where he was invited for events. Sometimes it was our own desire that inspired us to explore the lives and landscapes and light that we photographed and recorded. Outside of a trip to Yugoslavia through Italy, one of my very first experiences abroad was in London and Stratford-upon-Avon. We collaborated in 1964 on a film about Shakespeare's 400th anniversary that was part of the television series *Chaque pays fête son grand homme*. We had so much fun in Stratford while art students prepared a big exhibition, and whilst visiting and filming actors backstage at the Royal Shakespeare Theatre, and just shooting footage of people in the streets yelling out 'To be or not to be!' In London I loved to watch how friendly people could be on the tube and all the noisy teenagers laughing and singing. (I had never noticed this relaxed behaviour in the Paris metro.)

Discovering San Francisco and Los Angeles in 1997 and then Santa Barbara in 2002 and Santa Cruz in 2003 was also a great experience. We came for concerts, lectures and radio shows. This country introduced us to so many good friends. Of course, to discover New York in 2003 was a wonderful experience for me. I was touched by those historic places such as Grand Central Station and the Chelsea Hotel, and moved by the contrast that came with Brooklyn and its huge sky that we never caught sight of in Manhattan. The most surprising and exciting travel in the USA was our trip from Santa Fé to Los Angeles. That was Luc's 'sound hunting' trip to New Mexico, Colorado, Utah and Arizona through the country's most incredible natural architecture. Discovering the native country out west became our *Far-West News*, a radio piece in three parts, which is also included in this book, the first in any language to catalogue all of Luc's creations and compositions. It is my hope this book finds a warm home in some of these places.
– Brunhild Ferrari

My heartfelt thanks go to Fielding Hope who introduced me to my publishers Eva Prinz and Thurston Moore. I also wish to thank Andrea Zarza for her beautiful exhibition in Madrid about the composition *l'escalier des aveugles*.

I am grateful to David Jisse who took over direction of La Muse en Circuit and continues to oversee the PRESQUE RIEN Prize that I initiated for emerging artists. Maxime Barthélemy who published a crucial part of Luc's scores, some excerpted herein. Thank you to Jim O'Rourke, our friend who wrote his beautiful thoughts about Luc in his Introduction; and especially, of course from the bottom of my heart, my sincere thanks to Catherine Marcangeli for the translation from French, which was not an easy task, and Eva and Thurston for their help in researching documents together with Catherine, and to Christian Corless for his design of this book.

Grateful acknowledgment is made to the following individuals for their encouragement of this English catalogue raisonné of Luc Ferrari: Junya Murakami, Baz Barraclough, David Stock, Raphaël Brobst, Patricia Bobillier-Monnot, Pierre-Yves Macé, David Sanson, Steve Shepherd, Debra Geddes, Steve Beresford, David Toop and to the following individuals, publications and institutions for sources of the composer's statements, liner notes, programmes, remarks, notes and other biographical information regarding his works. The publishers wish to thank the following organisations for access to research in their archives and printed ephemera: BNF, Paris; INA, INA-GRM, Service de la Recherche de l'ORTF/Pléiade, C.N.R.S., Atelier de Création Radiophonique; Radio France; Paris; FR3; The Cirque Productions; Coquelicot Film; Südwestfunk; TV Hamburg, NDR; S.W.F., Baden-Baden; WDR 3 TV, Cologne; Darmstadt Institut; Radio Nacional de España; Alustische Kunst WDR, Cologne; NCRV, Den Haag; Philips, Deutsche Grammophon, Wergo, EMI, Blue Chopsticks, SON SYNOPSYS, Metamkine; BVHAAST; Sub Rosa; Tzadik; Elica; Mode; Maison des Lettres, Paris; Musee d'art moderne, Paris; Théâtre de la Musique, Paris; Maison de la Culture, Théâtre Récamier, Paris; Centre Pompidou; Maison de Radio, Paris; Théâtre du Lierre, Paris; Théâtre du Renard, Paris; Rennes; Maison de la Culture, Bourges; Les Bernardines, Marseilles; Musée Galiera; Nuit de la Fondation Maeght; Musica, Strasbourg; Semana Nueva Musica, Madrid; Neue Musik München Ari-Filmtheatre; Kundstorf Kulturwoche Wuppertal; Bayerishe Staatsoper, Munich; Beethovensaal, Bonn; WDR Department of New Music, Cologne; Cinémathèque, Algiers; Fylkingen Modena Museet; Groningen Fine Arts Centre; Festival Les Musiques, Marseilles; Festival des Manca, Nice; Ranelagh Festival, Paris; Venice Biennale, Zagreb Biennale.

443

Endnotes

1. p. 17   Autobiographie 1, written 1979
2. p. 20   Ferrari's journey to visit Varèse, See also P. 34, Endnote 8
3. p. 25   Ferrari began cataloging his work and wrote this short preface 'Elements for a Confused Journey' in December 1995.
4. p. 27   These notes on *Suite pour piano* written 6 December 1995
5. p. 28   These notes on *Antisonate pour piano* written 7 December 1995
6. p. 30   These notes on *Sonatine Elyb pour piano* written 14 December 1995
7. p. 32   To meet Varèse
8. p. 34   [In an excerpted answer from Interview with an Intimate Iconoclast with Brigitte Robindore in *Computer Music Journal* Volume 22, PP 8-16, published by MIT Press, 1998, Ferrari elaborates: "I heard [Varèse, in] the radio broadcast of the Paris world premiere of *Déserts* for orchestra and electronic tape in 1954, and it absolutely overwhelmed me. Unfortunately due to an extreme fever, I was unable to attend the concert and had to listen on the radio. I had never heard anything like it. I had previously heard a few rare broadcast performances of his pieces, and now I simply had to meet this man...I earned a little money and immediately bought a ticket for the United States. The year was 1955. My sister was living in Miami at the time... I took a train to New York City to meet Varèse. What struck me with Varèse was his use of sound as a thing in and of itself. In *Déserts* it was not so much the tape part that affected me, but the new conception of instrumental writing. The sounds of the instruments had a vitality that made them live from within....I felt that the sounds composed in his scores found just the right way to place themselves in time and space, in the listener's ears and psychological perceptions."
9. p. 35   These notes on *Lapidarium pour piano* collected from writings in 1960 and 1995
10. p. 36   "Sometimes Luc would have a word in mind, not because it was significant or meaningful, but just because of the way it sounded or because it was provocative. So Water Closet sounded to him like an absurd phrase to write on the cover of the score. He didn't explain why." – Brunhild Ferrari
11 p. 40   These notes on *Visage I*, written September 1994
12. p. 42   These notes on *Visage II*, written February 2005
13. p. 52   Notes (possibly provided by LF) on *Etude aux accidents* appear in an excerpt from the programme of the first concert of the Festival de la Recherche in 1960: ...Unexpected sound elements that burst in are produced by rhythmic agitations of rods intervening in the body of a note from a prepared piano...
14. p. 66   *Tete et queue du dragon* written 22 April 1960

Tautologos I

by

LUC FERRARI

A tautology is the useless repetition of the same idea in different terms.

But Nature worries very little about usefulness, nor about logical progress from one proposition to the next. Relentlessly, it harps upon the same cycle of days and nights, of seasons, and the apparent variety of events is only the result of the multiplicity of possible interferences among a few permanent laws. The work of art falls back on the same relationship of repetition and variation. But contrary to nature, it is ignorant of the incompleteness necessary to any evolution. With its whole development already included in the initial instant, this creation of a human spirit ever in love with premature perfection, shuts itself into a tautology more rigorously still.

Life consists of repetitions, but each of these repetitions is marked by subtle differences. Even though we may have to bring about the same event, it is never the same event we find again. Day, night, and Tuesday may return, but this morning is cloudy, that evening the sun sets later; I may get up at the same time every morning, but the butchers are closed on Mondays (if I live in France).

Taking this line of thought to its absurd extreme, one might say no repetition of a sound is ever the same again, simply because it occurs at a different time, when many accompanying circumstances will also be different, even if ever so slightly.

On the other hand, the rock is chiselled by the rhythm of what happens to it, so that it becomes the visual reservoir of time in the form of matter and space.

Thus we have two kinds of tautology: to the repetitions perceptible in time, which are more familiar to us and which we might term "horizontal", are added the "vertical" repetitions relative to the sound medium, or matter.

Taken by themselves, the sounds used do in fact present analogies with respect to the medium. But after a certain number of superpositions the perception of this amorphous medium is replaced by that of sound density which is seen to erect a form in time, and it is this form which is repeated in each of the two sequences of *Tautologos I* or in each of the seven sequences of *Tautologos II* (recorded on BAM LD 071).

Music is an object that cannot be touched by the hands: thus this law looks for inspiration in the organisation of the reality around us.

Tautologos I was made at the Gravesano studios in August 1961 and is dedicated to Hermann Scherchen.

I love women	*(brass)*	*I love women*
I love seeing them	*I love women*	*but what's going on*
I love listening to them	*I love mingling them*	*(so much) jealousy*
I love stroking them	*I love wanting them*	*it's not my fault*
I love guessing them	*I love avoiding them*	*(brass)*
I love smelling them	*I love humping them*	*I love women*
I love opening them	*I love bonking them*	*they get jealous*
I love seeing them come	*CHA CHA CHA*	*they shred each other apart*
(brass)	*I love women*	*(brass)*
I love women	*and yet*	*And yet*
I love feeling them	*they hurt me*	*They knock me out*
I love kissing them	*they scare me*	*They go crazy*
I love understanding them	*I get it in the neck*	*They drive me mad*
(brass)	*they bully me*	*And I'm in pain*
I love women	*they mishandle me*	*Cha Cha Cha*
I love hearing them	*they tear each other apart*	
I love learning them	*(brass)*	

Notes on compositions

The illustrations including excerpted annotated score pages, manuscripts, sketches, programmes and ephemera herein were photographed and scanned from Luc Ferrari's original documents, courtesy Brunhild Ferrari and Association PRESQUE RIEN. For complete musical scores please contact the music publishers:

Editions Salabert

Editions Durand-Salabert-Eschig, Paris

Editions Transatlantiques, Paris

Ars Viva-Verlag, Germany

Allemagne

Moeck-Verlag Lückenweg, Celle

Editions Pierre Neuray

Editions Alphonse Leduc, Paris

Editions Maison ONA, Paris

Association PRESQUE RIEN

Index

NUTIDA MUSIK

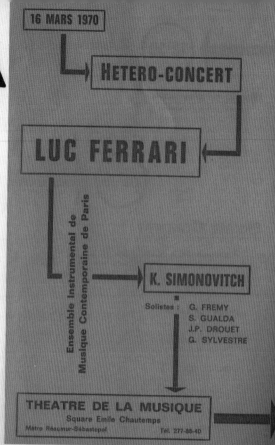

16 MARS 1970

HETERO-CONCERT

LUC FERRARI

Ensemble Instrumental de Musique Contemporaine de Paris

K. SIMONOVITCH

Solistes : G. FREMY
S. GUALDA
J.P. DROUET
G. SYLVESTRE

THEATRE DE LA MUSIQUE
Square Emile Chautemps
Métro Réaumur-Sébastopol   Tél. 277-88-40

25/10 Radiohuset
Life-in – Tape-in – Mix-in – Sleep-in
Ett kompositionsprojekt av Luc Ferrari
Medverkande: Luc Ferrari, Olof Franzén, en ensemble från Musikhögskolan, popgruppen Mecki Mark Men m fl

27/2 Radiohuset
Nutida musiksalong
La Salle-kvartetten samt en instrumentalensemble från Edsbergs musikskola
Verk av Brown, Evangelisti, Ligeti och Schoenberg

18/4 Musikaliska akademin
Ensembler i olika format
Medverkande: Sveriges Radios symfoniorkester samt Ensemblen för Nutida musik
Verk av Berio, Grandert, Scelsi och Hambræus

15/11 Musikhögskolan
Helafton med unga tonsättare och musiker
Medverkande:
En jazzensemble, Opposite Corner, Alfred Janson och Grynet Molvig m fl

14/3 Radiohuset
Elektroniska klanger
Uruppföranden av Lars-Gunnar Bodin, Gunnar Bucht, Bengt Emil Johnson, Arne Mellnäs och Jan W Morthenson

9/5 och 10/5 Radiohuset
Gästspel av Stockhausen
Medverkande: En vokal- och instrumentalensemble samt elektronik
Två kompositionsaftnar med verk av Karlheinz Stockhausen

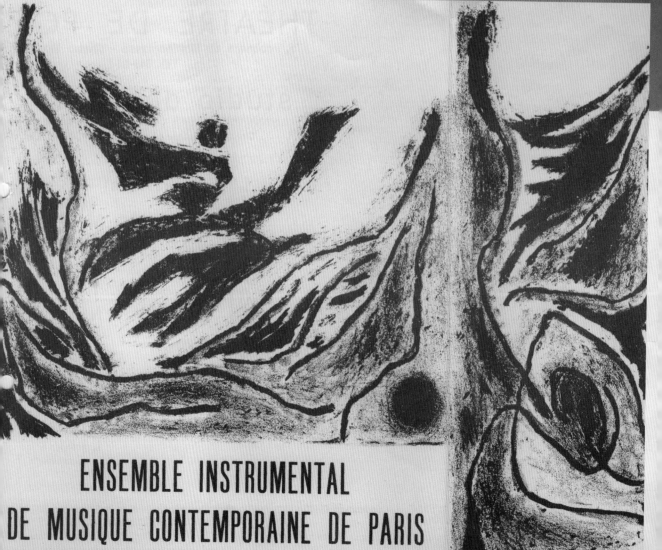

ENSEMBLE INSTRUMENTAL
DE MUSIQUE CONTEMPORAINE DE PARIS

...unk
...es öffentlichen Rechts
...den-Baden
...Abteilung
...Hermann Naber
...gie: Mechthild Zschau
      Maria Elisabeth Petri
      Peter Zwetkoff
...+K Offsetdruck

Hörspiele

SÜDWESTFUNK
Winterhalbjahr 78/7...

A MUSIQUE
LECTRO-ACOUSTIQUE

POSE-CONFERENCE
Luc FERRARI
COMPOSITEUR

JEUDI 26 OCTOBRE
à 18 h 30

AU
ERCLE DU TRAVAIL
ORTE St GEORGES 1bis Rue DROUIN
— NANCY —

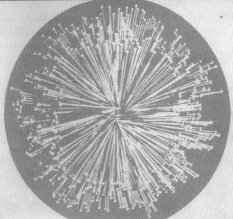

S.M.I.P. - T.N.P. - O.R.T.F.
présentent

35 MANIFESTATIONS
30 PREMIERES AUDITIONS
9 CREATIONS MONDIALES
4 ORCHESTRES SYMPHONIQUES
14 ENSEMBLES ET CHORALES
10 CHEFS-D'ORCHESTRE
32 SOLISTES

5 PREMIERES DISCOGRAPHIQUES

JOURNEES RADIOPHONIQUES
(sur France-Musique et France-Culture)

EMISSIONS TELEVISEES

Les 22 et 23 octobre Colloque du
CONSEIL INTERNATIONAL
DE LA MUSIQUE
(UNESCO)

S.M.I.P - T.N.P.
JOURNEES DE MUSIQUE CONTEMPORAINE 1969
AVEC LE CONCOURS DE L'O.R.T.F.

MESSIAEN Lundi 20
LIGETI Mardi 21
L'ORGUE AUJOURD'HU...
Mercredi 22

GRM
GROUPE DE
RECHERCHES MUSICAL...
DE L'O.R.T.F.
Jeudi 23
Vendredi 24

MUSICIENS
FRANCAIS
Samedi 25
Dimanche 26

LE DANSEUR Lun...
BALLET DU 20e SIECLE MAURICE BEJART
LUTOSLAWSKI

Photography credits